Welcome...

KNOW THYSELF

TO AWAKEN SELF-REALIZATION

Lateef Terrell Warnick

Authored by Lateef Terrell Warnick
Copyright © 2015. All rights reserved. No part of this book may be reproduced or transmitted in any form or by any means, electronic or mechanical, including photocopying, recording, or by any information storage and retrieval system, without the written permission of the publisher **1 S.O.U.L. Publishing, LLC** except where permitted by law.

ISBN: 193919914X
Paperback: 978-1-939199-14-0
eBook: 978-1-939199-09-6
Library of Congress Number: 2015906529

Know Thyself | To Awaken Self-Realization

1. Religion/ Spirituality 2. Mind, Body & Spirit 3. Mysticism 4. Metaphysics 5. New Age 6. Self-Help 7. Warnick, Lateef Terrell I. Title

Printed in the United States of America

Dedicated to all of our prodigal brothers and sisters lost, caught up in the stampede of life, who have forgotten their way home.

"Neither shall they say, Lo here! or, lo there! for, behold, the kingdom of God is within you."
Luke 17:21

Onassis Krown LLC
"Building Kings & Queens!"
www.onassiskrown.com

Your reviews are very important to the work we do. Our goals are to help inspire and educate the masses on holistic living in body, mind and spirit as well as encourage unity, love and transformation. If you share our sentiment, then please take a moment to leave a positive review on Amazon and/or share on your social media outlets. Blessings!

Copyright © 1 S.O.U.L. Publishing 2015
All Rights Reserved.

CONTENTS

Know Thyself: To Awaken Self-Realization

Preface..*i*

PART ONE: GENESIS
Chapter I: In the Beginning..1
Chapter II: The Fabric of Creation...............................19
Chapter III: Veils of Delusion..37
Chapter IV: A Day of God..53
Chapter V: Adam and Eve...67
Chapter VI: The Origins of Religion.............................79
Chapter VII: Reconciling Science and Religion............97

PART TWO: LIFE
Chapter VIII: Who am I?...109
Chapter IX: The Purpose of Life.................................119
Chapter X: The Power of Thought.............................127
Chapter XI: Free Will and the Law of Karma............139
Chapter XII: What is Sin?..151
Chapter XIII: Reincarnation..163
Chapter XIV: Level 1 Consciousness..........................185

PART THREE: REVELATION
Chapter XV: Armageddon or Apocalypse?..............195
Chapter XVI: Keys of the Kingdom of Heaven..........205
Chapter XVII: The Holy Spirit: Kundalini....................215
Chapter XVIII: The Seven Churches: Muladhara........225
Chapter XIX: The Seven Seals: Bhuloka....................235
Chapter XX: The Lamb: Savior or Guru?...................247
Chapter XXI: Beginning Your Journey.......................265

Index..275

PREFACE

γνῶθι σεαυτόν

These are the words inscribed at the entryway of the Temple of Apollo at Delphia. The words translated into English mean **"Know Thyself."** They are considered one of the Delphic maxims and have been interpreted widely different by many people. I use it here in this reading in the similar sense of Socrates, Plato and Ralph Waldo Emerson that no knowledge is greater than self-knowledge. For when one comes to truly know their self... they shall know God.

My passion has always been to help people. As I strive to always be my best, I hope to inspire others to reach their greatest potential. I also believe we are three-part beings and so true transformation requires change in body, mind and spirit. Therefore, all of my work, businesses and service is meant to be holistic in nature. If one aspect of your being is out of balance, then your entire being will be in disharmony. What good is money without health, friends without love or work without passion? Nothing! Life without balance is an unfulfilling life.

To help others, I leverage my extensive experience in varied career fields coupled with having worked with diverse people of all backgrounds from around the world. In the military, I had the honor of serving with professionals from all walks of life. I served 10 years in the U.S. Navy and learned how to not just follow but to observe great and not-so-great leaders. I was fortunate to be able to learn from both types. I was blessed to be able to rise through the ranks quickly serving as an enlisted sailor as well as a Naval Officer to lead others. I matriculated through a great engineering curriculum in the Nuclear Power field, flight training as a a student pilot and some business management skills in the Navy Supply Corp awakening my entrepreneurial spirit.

As a civilian, I enjoyed working in staffing, education, music production as well as a sales professional in telecommunications, real estate, insurance, financial services and business consultation. I've had the pleasure of consulting with entrepreneurs like contractors and photographers, small business startups in insurance and IT as well as large Fortune 100 corporations like Bank of America, Merrill Lynch, Prudential, Principal, USAA, Allstate and others. In my writings and speaking engagements, I tailor my message for the audience as well as the intention of the event. While books can be great for pointing us in the right direction, they are no substitute for personal effort and inner experience. True awakening money, power or living a perfect life. It is always about being fulfilled and content. It is about not succumbing to fear. It is about knowing that your needs come from a Source within you and within you is the ability to overcome or transcend any situation.

Furthermore, no one religion has a monopoly on spirituality and yet almost all of them contain some element of "Know Thyself" within them. This dates back to the ancient Greek civilization, the Romans and even further back to the ancient African cultures, Egyptians and Vedic Hindu cultures. In **Matthew 13:9** Jesus says **"Who hath ears to hear, let him hear."** Within the following chapters of this book I will attempt to convey ideas that may be familiar to you and others which may cause you to cringe. My job is not necessarily to unravel everything you've ever learned but rather to cause you to at least delve a little more deeply into your own beliefs. Regardless of whether at the end of this reading you agree with me, I hope it will inspire you to seek a clearer understanding of your relationship with the Creator in a more earnest way. So, let's see who has "ears to hear."

After countless generations of mankind on the face of the Earth, it is puzzling that we have not yet grown to support the whole of life. As with any examination of a subject there are always two sides to every story. On one hand we can look at the state of human life from the "half full" perspective and say that man has come a long way. We have had much advancement in science, technology and medicine. Man has walked on the moon, created computers to communicate with people on the other side of the globe and has harnessed energy in numerous ways. We travel in flight to foreign lands in a matter of hours and with a hand-held device can receive phone calls from family members, check the weather, news and enjoy many luxuries of life.

On the other hand, from the "half empty" perspective man still seems to glorify violence. We will take another person's life after a simple disagreement. We live off a principle of "might makes right!" We have individuals and entire nations that suffer from homelessness, starvation and lack of education. We still discriminate against others based upon their skin color, cultural appearance, socio-economic background, religious practices and other foolish reasons. No doubt, we've come a long way from some of the more horrific historical stories of past. Yet surprisingly, one issue that has plagued mankind perhaps like no other is our simple belief in a Higher Power!

While most religions believe in a loving God, we seem to justify our biases and dislike of others for not worshiping the "right god." Sure, there are many who may not pick up a brick to hit another person of a different religious faith but inwardly they accept the notion that the "non-believer" will suffer an eternity in Hell for their wrong faith. Yet others call people of the wrong faith infidels and think they deserve whatever punishment they can dish out to them as if the world would be better off without them. Although the average person may not be this extreme, the lack of ability to try to recognize the commonality of our humanity is the breeding ground that leads to hate. The typical person is not a follower of a particular faith because they've studied all of the options and made the best-informed decision. They belong to a religious faith because their parents chose that for them, or they were born in an area where the majority of the people adhere to that faith. Most of us spend more time investigating career paths or choosing mates than we do exploring the reasons why we worship a particular god. We do the bare minimum in understanding the principles of our own faith much less attempt to understand the tenets of another's faith. If we are unable to accept every man, even our enemies, as being equals then none of us are fit for a life in heaven!

The purpose of this book is to stimulate and provoke thought. "Thought about what?" you may ask. Thought about the most important topic – life itself! If you've ever experienced a quiet moment, then surely, you've asked yourself some of these questions. "Who am I"? "How did I get here"? "What is my purpose"? Some of us may have already answered these questions. Yet some of us may not have asked them. For those of us who have then this book is for you. For those that may have already answered these questions then this book may help you to ask new ones. And for those who have not yet asked these questions then you're probably not reading this book. But obviously since you are... welcome! ☺

This book is not necessarily intended to answer these questions but perhaps just suggest possibilities. I invite you all to scrutinize this book. Accept the ideas you choose and discard the ones you may not agree with. Nevertheless, the important thing is that you begin to ask your own questions and to hopefully seek your own answers from your Highest Truth. This is the soul's journey to Self-Realization.

    I have written this book in 3 parts. I believe that the Bible is written in 3 parts as well, so I figured why not emulate one of the greatest literary works of all time. The first part is Genesis. Genesis is like the prelude to the Bible. It contains a theme and a story that embodies the rest of the story. It includes foreshadowing, establishes the characters, lays the backdrop and peaks your interest. The beginning builds the foundation and more in-depth, formulates the components needed for creating anything whether it's a story, movie, recipe, piece of art or any other dream we can imagine.

    The last part is Revelation. Revelation is the conclusion to the story. It summarizes and tells you what happened. In any good story, in the beginning you're told what the story's going to tell you, it then tells you the story and then it tells you what it told you. In a great story, you're revealed something of truth, significance or importance. It completes the package and puts an exclamation point at the end. If you've missed the revelation, then sometimes you have to re-read the whole story in order to capture what was meant for you to see. The truth is both books taken at face value are not a very good read. Genesis has so many details that you get lost in what it is supposed to convey. Revelation is so "far out there" that it is difficult to make proper sense of it. I believe the reason for this obscurity is because there are many layers in these writings that tell several stories in one. Oftentimes, jewels of truth are hidden right under our noses in order to protect their sanctity. When man's understanding has grown to a point of comprehension better able to embrace deeper truths, then the breadcrumbs of spiritual treasure left behind by spiritual masters will lead the masses to a new plateau of Divine Experience.

    Those are the two obvious parts to any story. The "beginning" and the "end." Everything else is what comes in the middle. That essentially is the transitioning. It gets us from point A to point B. The transitioning can be a very short path or a very long and winding journey. That transitioning can be very direct or very scenic with many stops along the way. Like a car that helps us to travel to a destination, the ride can be just a necessary trip you make routinely, or it can be an extravagant experience of many unforeseen detours. That transitioning I call here – Life! Life is the journey in between the beginning and the end. It is what we make it. It takes us from "not knowing" to a place of "knowing." The crossing over generally takes place in an instant. But there will most likely be many pivotal moments that will lead up to the ultimate "leap."

Within these three parts the beginning, middle and end will be chapters with subplots that will help to serve as those pivotal points along the way. I have written this work as a representation of who I am. It may be thought provoking at times. It may be deep at others. It will be humorous as well. It may be poetic or mathematical at certain points, formal and yet informal. It may be a great piece of literary work in moments and in others seem like something you'd get in an email or text page like "duh!" But in all I hope it entertains you and, in some way, inspires you to seek your True Self in life and ultimately God! So, I hope you will join me on this journey to… "KNOW THYSELF!"

GENESIS: PART I

CHAPTER I

In the Beginning...

As the old cliché goes, "Money can't buy you love." However, money can attract a whole lot of people who may claim they love you; especially if they know you possess significant amounts of money. Even when it comes to love, what is it we are truly seeking? The answer is happiness! When it comes to love, money, careers, knowledge, travel, friends, family or otherwise, we are all truthfully seeking happiness. Regardless of your age, race, gender, nationality, religion, beliefs and so forth, we all simply want happiness. Now obviously what makes one person happy will not necessarily make another person happy. Of course, what good is money, love, fame, status or any attainment if we're not happy? The other peculiarity about happiness is that not only does it vary from one person to another, but it even varies from day to day within us. What used to make us happy as children, no longer does so as adults. Likewise, what made us happy yesterday may not make us happy today. So, what exactly is this ever-elusive happiness that we all seek? The answer, in fact, is *completeness*.

We all unconsciously feel a certain sense of lack. We search outside of ourselves for something to make us feel whole. Love just happens to be one of those experiences that comes the closest to making us feel content and complete. As Jerry Maguire stated in the same titled movie... **"You complete me!"** Of course, in this world that we live in, money comes in a very close second or perhaps even first place to making us feel complete. However, as evidenced by essentially everyone with massive amounts of wealth – they still seek love. But for those people who have found love they may not necessarily be concerned with the pursuit of money. It is my assertion that even those who may be madly in love still feel a sense of incompleteness and must continuously put forth effort to feel happiness.

The problem with the way most of us seek happiness is we utilize the wrong means. We are attempting to satisfy the desires of the fickle senses, which often have perverted ways of stimulation, hence even alcoholics, drug abusers, gluttons and sex addicts are merely seeking happiness. Those who reject these pleasures and walk the "straight and narrow" do so normally to gain Heaven as a just reward in the afterlife to deliver ever-lasting happiness. Happiness of course is a state of mind for most of us. It is intangible and cannot be described. If you were able to describe your happiness to another, they still would not get the same sense of satisfaction from your happiness as you might. If we were to attempt to materialize happiness as a substance it would be closest to the element of fire. Fire has no true definition or form. It merely consumes one substance and transforms it into another. Fire possesses no definite borders or outline. If you ever stared at a campfire, it never stands still. It shifts in appearance every moment. You can't grasp it with your hands and yet you can perceive it. Happiness, as experienced by most of us, is similarly ever-changing. We can't really grasp it and hold on to it. It seems to be forever fleeting, coming and going.

However, there is a lasting happiness that exists that can be grasped although not literally. It is permanent and changeless although it is always replenishing and new. This happiness is something that is inside of us that we all, whether or not we know it, are truly seeking. This inner happiness is the only satisfying attainment we can find that is ours forever once

Chapter I: In the Beginning

captured. This ever burning, eternal happiness within is our connection to a Universal Spirit. We, as souls, know ourselves to be an inherent part of this Oneness, this connection that has no beginning or end. It is this inner presence we wrongly seek in the form of desires and worldly objects. However, worldly attainments can only produce temporary happiness while the inner happiness of awareness can be permanently fixed. Until we learn how to enjoy this treasure within, we will go about life being continuously disappointed. In fact, many people will go from cradle to the grave never finding this lasting happiness or the reason why they were here in the first place.

This lasting inner happiness Jesus referred to as "the kingdom of God within you" while Buddha called it Nirvana, mystics and yogis call it Samadhi, some as Gnosis while Shamans and Medicine Men call it "Great Spirit." New Age thinkers and quantum physicists attempt to analyze it. Law of Attraction enthusiasts and alternative health seekers attempt to harness it. But It comes from an inner awakening realization that you are not what you appear to be. In truth, your consciousness consists of no-thing other than the awareness of self. Many call it the "I Am." Through this non-attached state of being we become inherently part of all things, one with everything while still existing beyond these infinite number of "things." This state of consciousness for man is known as Self-Realization. It is not an imagined state of being or a mental construct of the mind. In fact, it resides beyond the mind and can only be reached through conscious stillness. However, once you find It, you find Completeness and Eternal Bliss. Those who have attained It, gain the powers to manipulate all of creation to do their bidding such as witnessed by the miracles of Jesus among others and yet there is an irony that these awakened beings have no desire to manipulate their environments because their inner joy is independent of all outer experiences or circumstances.

If they do perform a "miracle" for others to witness, it is generally done to inspire others to seek this shared state of consciousness. This is the Source of all true contentment!

This leads us to the fact that there are two kinds of people in this world – those who are made of the essence of God and **KNOW** that they are one with this Essence and those who are made of the essence of God but do **not** know it. Whether you are consciously aware of it or not is irrelevant because it is who you are, nonetheless. It is this underlying presence that gives you your sense of self, consciousness and the ability to observe, witness and choose. This experience of existence, we call life, is what allows one to come to KNOW his or her true relationship with the Source, creator of all Consciousness. Now when I use the word "know" I am not simply referring to a person who has heard of God or believes in God or goes to church frequently. I'm characterizing the soul that comes to **know** that there is no distinction between the Father and the son or any other aspect of life. This is the goal of every soul to **realize** his or her true Essence.

This series is not meant to be a line-for-line interpretation of the Books of Genesis and Revelation; that would be far too boring of a book. It is meant, however, to be a symbolic comparison of the esoteric truths hidden in these two important books. Genesis represents the beginning of man and his purpose in creation. Revelation, so to speak, represents the "coming of age" of the soul. It is the culminating completion of the soul's journey. We will attempt to highlight the important aspects of these points metaphorically representing the "starting and finishing lines" for man. We will explore the spiritual truths that man need apply in his every day life, step by step, in order to progress along the path God has set us on. In fact, since God is completeness, all It could do was to "distort" Its completeness by becoming consciously

Chapter I: In the Beginning

"incomplete" through placing Its attention on limiting aspects of Itself. This is what leads us to the relative world – one aspect or idea relative to another. Man's sense of separation is a result of our limited ability to only focus on our bodies or material objects. We must learn to expand our consciousness by going within the "space" of ourselves, un-identify with all limiting ideas of self and reunite with this all-pervasive consciousness that holds all things as One within its Being.

There is a lot more to the books of Genesis and Revelation than meets the eye. Although we will primarily focus on the story of Genesis as portrayed by the Jewish Torah as well as the Christian Old Testament, we will also touch upon many other religious approaches to the story of man's beginning. All faiths including Islam, Hinduism, Taoism, Shamanism, Mayans, Egyptians and so forth have their legends and tales of our birth. Hidden within these stories are not only symbolic messages but scientific truths that explain how man was "put together." Within Revelation are also deeper meanings to explain how man will symbolically be "taken apart" not through annihilation but through revealing man's True Self. We will also touch upon other historical writings such as the Book of Enoch, which is authentic and mentioned in the Bible but was unfortunately not included in most versions. The Beta Israel canon, however, does include this book as part of their Canon of Scripture. The Ethiopian Orthodox Church also includes this book as a current day Christian teaching.

Throughout this series, we will attempt to show how the all-pervading formless Spirit descends Its Consciousness into all matter, how these "matter identified" variations of consciousness have not only the opportunity but the ultimate destiny to return to the Absolute Formless Spirit. As long as man feels "disconnected" from our awareness of Oneness with all, we will never find lasting happiness. As a side note, it is challenging that we must begin with Genesis because it may prove to be a difficult read for some but if you can make it through the first few chapters then it'll become a much simpler read later, so bear with me. ☺ Now let us begin with... "The Beginning."

1 In the beginning God created the heaven and the earth.
2 And the earth was without form, and void; and darkness was upon the face of the deep. And the Spirit of God moved upon the face of the waters.
3 And God said, Let there be light: and there was light.
4 And God saw the light, that it was good: and God divided the light from the darkness.
5 And God called the light Day, and the darkness he called Night. And the evening and the morning were the first day.

The Book of Genesis opens with the line "In the beginning God created the heaven and the earth." The phrase "in the beginning" represents the opening of a story. The story obviously hasn't been told yet, but the storyteller is setting the scene. In this case, the storyteller is none other than God! The story about to be told is this thing we call life. As with most books of interest, readers want to know a little something about the author. So, the next question is who is this storyteller "God"?

Well, the first thing we can gather from the opening of this story is that the author, God, clearly existed prior to the opening "in the beginning." Any curious mind will naturally question, "How did God exist before the beginning"? "Who made God"? "How did he become all powerful enough to create everything"? Or "Was there anything else that existed with God"? These and all the other possible questions we can conjure up cannot be answered or grasped with the human mind. Since the human mind is part of this creation it cannot fathom a concept that exists outside

Chapter I: In the Beginning

or beyond this creation. While it is impossible with the limiting ability of words to define a concept that is incomprehensible, infinite and indefinable, there are some words or ideas that more closely relate to the Creator than others. These ideas don't encompass the Creator, but they can point us in a direction that can lead to greater understanding.

First, we must understand that God exists in an Absolute state where nothing in Creation resides other than God. The Bible perhaps gives the best description of the Creator simply as **"I am that I am!" Exodus 3:14** The minute we try to define "I am" is the instant we cross over from His Absolute state to this state of creation that is based upon relativity. Saying "I am Joy" is great but only describes an aspect of Him. Saying "I am Powerful" may be profound but still only has meaning in relation to that which is not powerful. Saying "I am this or that" is still limiting because God is this, that, all of the above and none of the above. When something is Absolute then by definition there is nothing "relative" to it other than Itself!

Hence, this may lead us to the best explanation of why God began telling this story in the first place. It has been said that God being the Alpha and the Omega, the Beginning and the End, the Question and the Answer simply wanted to experience Himself as such. Note I didn't say that God wanted to *know* Himself; I said "experience" Himself. God already knows Himself as all things. But to experience Himself as such is another matter. Get it... "another matter"? The universe is made of a substance we call **matter**... another *matter*... ☺ Oh, never mind, but anyways I digress; the definition of **experience** is the process of direct observation or participation in events as a basis of knowledge. I guess you can say that God is directly observing as well as participating in the events that we call life.

Again, since God is Absolute and the only True Substance there is, it in essence would be impossible for Him to experience Himself unless there was something to contrast Himself with. But where would God get the building blocks necessary to contrast Himself other than from Himself? The moment He tries to create something that exists outside of Himself or is separate from Himself, He would instantly falsify the truth of Him being Absolute. To be Absolute means there are no equals or other truths than His own. To be Omnipresent means there is no place that exists where He isn't totally and completely present. See the dilemma? Here in lies a great mystery of Creation... HE CAN'T!

I think this point deserves elaboration. Most of us who believe in a God accept the fact that He is Absolute, Omnipotent, Omnipresent and Omniscient. If this is true then you must acknowledge that He is totally conscious of every space, place, idea and action that takes place. Yes, He's even aware of you reading this book. Yet He, for some reason, remains quietly subtle, unobservable for most. This also means that it is a mathematical and computational **impossibility** that any thing can exist that He/She/It is not completely and totally intrinsically intertwined within. If there were such a person, place or thing that exists then it would falsify His Absolute Presence. So why does God remain hidden? We'll explore this question in much greater depth incrementally throughout.

Now some people may have difficulty with the idea that there's something that God "can't do." But if we think about it, it's really not that hard to accept. For example, God cannot stop being God! To do so would negate His Truth of being all there is. Since everything comes from His Being, He is the Alpha and the Omega and there is nothing before Him or shall come after Him. Because He is all-powerful and all-knowing, anything He creates must fall in line with these Absolute Truths. Anything that makes His Absoluteness "not absolute"

Chapter I: In the Beginning

would negate this first truth. Perhaps "limitation" may not be the right word but there are some things that have to coincide with being the Lord that cannot be changed otherwise He couldn't be the Source of all things.

If you haven't seen the movie "Dogma" I suggest you rent it. It is a pretty humorous movie with a nice cast of stars in it including Ben Affleck, Matt Damon and Chris Rock. In the movie these fallen angels have found a loophole created by the church in order to get back into heaven that would ultimately make the Lord fallible. Of course, if this is to transpire then what would it say for heaven, much less God, if His universal laws could be so easily manipulated by His own creation? If such a thing were even feasible, I guess the entire universe would just implode or something. Of course, undermining God's will is an impossibility, which the end of the movie supports as well, but it is enjoyable to explore as an entertaining story. Nothing in God's creation can violate, negate or override His Truth.

So, the next best thing the Creator could do was to create the "idea" of something other than Himself in which to contrast and experience Himself. There you have it – the entire creation of the universe is nothing more than a collection of God's ideas. Now the next thing to understand is that any idea of God instantaneously becomes one with God and therefore immediately dissolves back into its Source – being God. In order for God to hold a thought or idea long enough to observe and experience it, He had to create an opposing thought. The act of these two thoughts acting or pushing against each other is what leads to this "world" of duality. It's the reason why we have polarities.

These dueling ideas or "forces" is the foundation of this creation of relativity. Remember in God's Absolute state there is nothing "relative" to Him. Only in the physical cosmos is there a sense of relation. Now let us also remember these original two, "opposing thoughts," both originate from the same Creator. From **Isaiah 45:7** we have **"I form the light, and create darkness: I make peace, and create evil: I the LORD do all these things."** As long as God holds these "ideas" in play we have what appears as the physical world. The instant God withdraws his ideas is the instant everything dissolves back into His Absolute state!

According to Newton's Laws of Motion:

1. A body continues to maintain its state of rest or of uniform motion unless acted upon by an external unbalanced force! And secondly...

2. To every action there is an equal and opposite reaction.

It can be said that God in His Absolute state is in a "state of rest." In this state of being there is no motion just Pure Consciousness. The moment we explore God's thought we transition from His Absolute state into a state of motion or creation. This state of motion or creation can also be called energy. Even science confirms that bodies at "rest" still contain potential energy and when this energy is set in motion is becomes kinetic. Energy in its finer form simply represents a "mass-less" idea or motion of God coming into creation or dissolving back into the Absolute.

In physics, the law of conservation of energy states that the total amount of energy in an isolated system remains constant. God is that isolated system and God is that constant! A consequence of this law is that energy cannot be created or destroyed only altered in form. This altering in form is simply changing thought. So, to work backwards, the universe is made up of matter, matter is an appearance of mass, mass is

Chapter I: In the Beginning

a conglomerate of energy, energy is a result of God's thought in motion, thought comes from Pure Consciousness – God! Yet God exists even beyond thought. In fact, God in His purest state is without the ripples of restless, changing thought. God is Absolute!

It has been said that God is "center everywhere; circumference nowhere." If you've ever thrown a pebble or watched a raindrop fall into a still body of water, you would see the outwardly expanding ripples of water in a perfect circle in all directions. Of course, in this physical creation we have friction; therefore, that expanding ripple gradually fades the further out it expands. Likewise, in God's Absolute state His idea would continue to expand infinitely outward unless some external, unbalanced force acted upon it. Again, if we look at Newton's second law of motion it states that every action has an equal and opposite reaction. It is these "equal and opposite" reactions (or ideas) which hold creation together; otherwise, these ideas, forces or reactions (whatever you would like to call them) would just instantaneously expand and dissolve back into where they came from – God! These "equal and opposite" forces also represents a universal law that is known as karma, which is another discussion we will explore.

Again, I would like to reiterate that it is impossible to describe the Infinite and Absolute concept of God, but I do think it deserves a little further penetration to understand our Creator, at least on an intellectual level, more personally. It doesn't take a stretch of imagination to conclude that God being Absolute coincides with the descriptions in the Bible of Him also being omnipresent – "being everywhere at once;" omniscient – "knowing everything there is to know;" and omnipotent – "being all powerful." Since everything in creation is a result of His thought and will, it is impossible for there to be a place that exists that He wouldn't be present. It would be impossible for there to be an idea that is secret to

Him or to even be thought of since everything comes from His Original Thought. Although the universe exists based upon a system of laws, since He is the creator of those laws, He is not confined or restricted by them in any manner. Hence no law, idea or experience can be greater than the Creator Himself.

Another important aspect of God is that He is always in a perfect state of Bliss. Some may question, "How do we know He is in a perfect state of Bliss"? In truth, the only one capable of testifying to the validity of God's state of Bliss is one who knows God! Again, when I say, "knows" God I don't mean a person who has read about, prayed to or simply believes in God. I'm referring to those very unique souls who have directly experienced God and remain in an eternal state of Oneness with the Creator. The simplest answer as to why God is a perfect state of Bliss is because He is unto Himself already Complete. There is nothing for God to achieve, work for or to obtain. He is the sum of all things... and then some!

To try and put this into terms we may better grasp, let's explain it in terms of man. Most of us have had moments of serenity, joy, ecstasy, happiness and fulfillment. For every person those moments will vary. For some, graduating from high school or college may feel like their greatest accomplishment in which for that one instant they could have "died and went to heaven!" For others, giving birth to a child or marrying the love of their life or finding out the person you had a secret crush on for years likes you as well. For some, achieving a long-term goal such as buying their first home or starting their own business or receiving the praise of others for an accomplishment may have been the highlight of their life.

To others, hitting the lottery becoming rich or even having the best sex of your life may have created a moment where you just felt complete and nothing else could have made that point in time any better! For

Chapter I: In the Beginning

the majority of us who may have actually experienced some of these moments, we come to realize the actual event isn't all that grand. Our grandest thought always seems to be the "one thing" we haven't experienced yet. In other words, the "idea" of a previous experience or the expectation of an experience we desire always seems to be greater than the actual achievement.

But nonetheless, the shortcoming for most of us is that these spectacular moments in time are just that – a moment in time! They are always fleeting. We can't capture these intense moments of pleasure or satisfaction and bottle it up to make it last forever. Well guess what – God is that Bottle! Imagine all the greatest moments of your life intensely happening all together at the same time! Then imagine before the height of that moment could subside it was intensified by the addition of even greater joy! Imagine before you could even ask the question of what could make it better – it was already better! Now imagine that state of magnificent happiness and then multiply it by a million! No, better yet, multiply it by Infinity! That still wouldn't compare to God's Bliss! God's Bliss is Completion!

There is nothing else that can make it any better. There is nothing that can be added to it. There is no further longing or possibility that could make it more fulfilling. It is Perfection and it is ever-newly replenished in the Eternal moment of Now. That is the state of being our soul knows! That is the eternal place in time that we crave! That is the center of perfection, the summit of completion, the pinnacle of love that our hearts yearn to feel! That is why nothing on this Earth, this plane of existence will ever satisfy us. Our souls already innately know this Truth. This is why we continuously seek the fulfillment of new desires – because no attainment or fulfillment of a worldly goal brings the lasting satisfaction and joy of being immersed in God! There is only one way to immerse our self in God and that's to look within.

According to the Eastern science of Yoga, creation has three possible qualities. They are sattvic (positive), tamasic (negative) and rajasic (neutral and/or activating). Not only is all of creation made up of these qualities but because man identifies with the matter in creation, he too is made up of these potential characteristics. Man has the challenge of learning to first balance these traits but ultimately to transcend them. In truth, nothing is really good or bad but mostly the interaction, perception, intent and outcome is what determines the nature of an idea. Herein lies the great potential of mankind to realize that all ideas are meant to be tools that can be manipulated by the soul. The soul is the superior master of all ideas, but it is through the ego's interaction with the world of ideas that the soul transcends the ideas and knows the ego itself to simply be the result of an idea.

While I was in college, I underwent a pledging process to become a member of a fraternity. Of course, pledging is now illegal by the fraternity as well as most state laws but originally this pledging process served a purpose. The concept was borrowed from the Masonic pledge process, which was borrowed from the Egyptian mystery systems of ancient times as well as many other civilization's ritualistic practices. There are many objectives of the pledge process but the main idea behind it is the notion that man possesses many unfavorable characteristics. In order to bring out the best in the individual you must first "break him down" to his most basic components so that you can "build him back up." This is accomplished through tests, trials, tribulation and adversity. For whatever reason, man seems to rise to his greatest potential when there is a resistive force that he must overcome.

While on line for this fraternity we were forced to memorize the poem **"If"** by Rudyard Kipling. At the time that was all I did was *memorize* it. It wasn't until years later that I was going through some difficult times that I

Chapter I: In the Beginning

made an effort to truly *understand* what it meant. During this particular juncture in my life, I had just lost the girlfriend I was with for a number of years. I had also lost my job and only source of income. Thus, I was on the verge of losing my apartment through eviction. Most of my luxuries such as cable and some utilities had already been cut off. My car at the time had an electrical problem so when I attempted to go out somewhere for a ride to relieve the stress, I would find myself stranded on the side of the road. Finally, after being tired of the embarrassment I just avoided driving the car as much as possible. I felt helpless because I didn't have the money to fix the car and all I could take care of was the basics to feed myself. Thank God for that little bit. It could have been worse.

    It was at this time that I began dissecting the poem to truly learn to understand each and every line. I would take one line and not just memorize it but analyze it and examine it to see if I embodied the qualities in the verse. I would stare at the ceiling at night partly because I didn't have cable to watch any television and I was also having difficulty sleeping. So, I tried to use my time wisely by making an effort to apply the characteristics suggested in each and every line. Then one day while speaking to my ex-wife, I asked her about how a couple we used to spend time with was doing. She said she hadn't spoken to them in a while but gave me their number.

    I called and spoke to my old friend's wife who informed me that they were no longer together. She informed me that he was now living in Atlanta, the same city I was in. So, I called him just to say hello and see how he was doing. We caught up on old times and I told him what was going on with my life at the time. He didn't have much but happened to have a trailer hitch large enough to get my most important valuables out of the apartment that I had to be out of by the next day. He also offered me the bed in his spare bedroom. It just so happens I hadn't seen this friend in nearly ten years at the time, so it was definitely a Godsend for me! It was the break I needed to find new work and begin to get back on my feet. I don't necessarily think it was the poem that brought about the blessing but more so the attitude it helped to instill. They say life is 10% what happens to us and the other 90% is our attitude.

Some time later I did some research about Kipling's personal life and found out that he himself may have had some character flaws. I don't know for certain if any of the hearsay was true, so I won't bother repeating it. In my mind, the Bible tells us *"he who is without sin can cast the first stone."* I believe we all have our shortcomings but even so we can have moments of impeccable inspiration. I believe his poem "If" to embody this regality. I think the poem captures the reality that life presents us with – positive, negative and neutral opportunities to choose how we define ourselves. But even in the midst of our choices the greatest choice lies in man's potential to choose to rise above the dual nature of the world. I believe the greatest good in speaking on any spiritual matters is not just to show the great things God can do but to show just how great man can be when he's in tune with God. So, I'll share this poem with you and hope it inspires you the way it has inspired me.

The poem signifies how we are presented with many moments in life where we have to make a choice. The greatest choice we will ever have to make is to realize our relationship with the Creator and our potential to live as a Son of God. Thus, we have a glimpse of the Creator and His Being. Each and every soul is born of this Being and is made in His image and His very essence. God is the Supreme Writer of life and we are all his co-writers! In the Hindu religion they refer to God as the Supreme Soul known as Purusha. Not much more can be said about God through words. Some believe you must wait until heaven to get to know

Chapter I: In the Beginning

God any better, but it is possible to not just speak with God but for Him to speak to you as well. You don't have to wait for the afterlife to enjoy true happiness here in the moment. You just have to learn from those who have achieved this relationship and follow their path to nurture the same for yourself. Now we know a little something of the Author of Life. Let's venture a little deeper into His story, in which we all have not only a role, but are the starring actors in our own personal director's cut version.

IF

If you can keep your head when all about you
Are losing theirs and blaming it on you,
If you can trust yourself when all men doubt you
But make allowance for their doubting too,
If you can wait and not be tired by waiting,
Or being lied about, don't deal in lies,
Or being hated, don't give way to hating,
And yet don't look too good, nor talk too wise

If you can dream--and not make dreams your master,
If you can think--and not make thoughts your aim;
If you can meet with Triumph and Disaster
And treat those two impostors just the same;
If you can bear to hear the truth you've spoken

Twisted by knaves to make a trap for fools,
Or watch the things you gave your life to, broken,
And stoop and build 'em up with worn-out tools

If you can make one heap of all your winnings
And risk it all on one turn of pitch-and-toss,
And lose, and start again at your beginnings
And never breath a word about your loss;
If you can force your heart and nerve and sinew
To serve your turn long after they are gone,
And so hold on when there is nothing in you
Except the Will which says to them: "Hold on!"

If you can talk with crowds and keep your virtue,
Or walk with kings--nor lose the common touch,
If neither foes nor loving friends can hurt you;
If all men count with you, but none too much,
If you can fill the unforgiving minute
With sixty seconds' worth of distance run,
Yours is the Earth and everything that's in it,
And--which is more--you'll be a Man, my son!

--Rudyard Kipling

CHAPTER II

The Fabric of Creation

All right, I think we've done the best we can to try and paint a picture of God the storyteller. As I've already stated, it is impossible to convey in words any true description of the Creator. For example, I could describe to you in every possible way every detail of an apple. I could tell you about the variety of colors they come in. I could talk about the many different textures of an apple. I could tell you all the different types of desserts that can be made from apples. I could try to explain to you how it feels on your tongue, the smell of it, how it's grown, where they're best grown and when they're ripe. I could even tell you how the body digests it. But none of that would compare to you actually taking a bite of the apple for yourself! To truly know the apple is to experience the taste of the apple. Likewise, to truly know God is to experience God. This is the key to true happiness!

We will get into deeper discussion on ways to experience Him later but for now let's continue with the opening scene from Genesis. If you will, please allow me to apologize in advance if some of the following explanations become confusing. For those of you who are not "science buffs" this may not make much sense, but I will try to highlight the important points. To avoid getting too technical, I will invite you to do your own research to expand on any of the following ideas. So, let us begin with the line from Genesis that tells us God created **"the heaven and the earth. And the earth was without form, and void; and darkness was upon the face of the deep. And the Spirit of God moved upon the face of the waters."**

In the movie Shrek, Shrek was trying to explain to Donkey what ogres were like. He went on to say that ogres were complicated and gave the analogy of comparing an ogre to an onion. He said that, like onions, ogres have layers. Similarly, God's creation has layers as well. In fact, the many stories we see in the Bible often have layers to them. These layers lead to different meanings based upon the "layer" or context of the story. I think it's important to examine this statement about the heaven and earth and look at its possible meanings from the different layers.

Science has already proven to us that nothing we perceive in this physical creation is actually solid. Every "solid" object we behold can be broken down into the elements in which it is composed. So, whether we're talking about the human body, a tree, a car, a metal, a rock or a liquid they all are made up of the same substance. The smallest unit we can observe as a stand-alone object is the atom. If we move upward from the atom, we find that atoms make up molecules, which form various compounds, which form cells and so on. We also know from science that these atoms on a microscopic level are constantly moving around and "bumping" into other atoms. So, every solid object we perceive is actually not solid or stationary. Rather all objects are swirling masses of atoms in constant motion. Nonetheless, most solids tend to maintain their shape. The bonds of solids hold the atoms together more tightly. Liquids and gases, however, tend to be less tightly held together and will take the shape of whatever container that they're in. Liquids can often times evaporate into the air and then disperse theoretically infinitely outwards. One thing is consistent, no matter what the object, it has been proven that there is actually more space in between the atoms of that object than there is actually substance. In other words, if you removed all the space

Chapter II: The Fabric of Creation

between the atoms of your body for example and just left behind the actual "matter" you would end up with an extremely small object estimated to be about the size of maybe a golf ball! In fact, this isn't even quite accurate for all matter is merely energy, which is as a result of thought power. Quantum physics continues to penetrate more deeply into how thought and will power influences energy which of course influences matter.

In fact, if we penetrate deeper into the atomic make-up of objects, we find that atoms contain a nucleus made up of protons and neutrons along with orbiting electrons and thus nothing is truly solid. Beyond this point science has a difficult time "solidifying" (pun intended) the components of matter on a subatomic level. There are many theories of quarks, photons and string theory. It is very difficult to analyze any of these objects obviously because they're very small and moving very fast! But the overwhelming belief currently is that these particles are for the most part mass-less balls of energy that operate on a level of light or vibration. So, if we break small particles into their even smaller components, we begin to see a pattern where items are so infinitesimal that we consider them immeasurable and thus "mass-less" or actually not really containing any solid substance whatsoever.

In particular, string theory is a primary candidate for the theory of everything! A "theory of everything" is a way to describe all the known natural forces (gravitational, electromagnetic, weak and strong) and matter (quarks and leptons) in a mathematically complete system. According to the string theory, the electrons and quarks of an atom are like little strings or threads. These threads in essence are all the same but what makes them different is how they vibrate. As any musician knows the strings of a guitar can produce various notes based upon tension and frequency. Likewise, these strings can take on negative or positive charges based upon the frequency upon which they vibrate. Now hold on to this idea and I'll see if I can tie it all together for us. Get it? Tie... string... I'm gonna tie the "strings" together... string theory...? Okay, I give up. Hopefully, I'm a better author than comedian.

Now if we study the ancient teachings of Eastern scripture and science, the sages state the universe exists on three different "layers" or planes. The most obvious plane is the physical world we observe through the senses and actually is the third and most gross stage. For all the physical things we observe there is an underlying nature that is referred to as the astral or heavenly realm. This second, heavenly realm, made up of certain elements of consciousness, is perceived as a magnificent universe of light. This astral universe is said to be much larger than our physical universe and expresses many colors beyond the spectrum of the rainbow that our eyes cannot imagine! The astral universe is then composed of even subtler energies that are referred to as the causal universe. The causal universe being the first plane is known as the first cause for creation or the original "thought" universe of God.

So, these three planes being the causal, astral and physical world make up the perception of existence. There are reoccurring themes of things happening in threes in scripture. We have the Father, Son and the Holy Spirit known as the Trinity. There's the past, future and the present. We refer to things as either here, there or the in-between. But if we analyze scripture there are often three meanings or interpretations intertwined in the same truth. A scriptural truth may have a literal, symbolic or a spiritual meaning that may apply to the physical, heavenly or causal realms. All three meanings can stand as truth without negating any of the others. Often times, Jesus spoke in parables that stood for a truth that the masses were able to comprehend while at the same time referencing a deeper spiritual meaning.

Chapter II: The Fabric of Creation

Again, just to keep track here, we have God the Absolute that exists beyond all creation. When God creates, He actually moves His consciousness that descends from thought in the causal world; vibrates further into a finer form observed as light mostly prevalent in the heavenly manifestation; and finally materializes into grosser form in the physical cosmos. If we go back and examine the phrase "heaven and earth" it refers literally to the physical creation we exist in and a heavenly place that we all seek to consciously enter when we die or leave this earth. Symbolically speaking, it also refers to a hierarchy of creation wherein man concerned with physical creation and materialism is considered "earthly" while beings such as advanced souls and angels exist in a more "heavenly" state. In addition, spiritually speaking, "heaven and earth" deals with the fabric of creation which all descend from God.

"In the beginning was the Word, and the Word was with God, and the Word was God. The same was in the beginning with God. All things were made by him; and without him was not any thing made that was made." John 1:1-3 Most of us have probably at least seen a movie that featured Buddhist monks meditating while humming or chanting. The sound that is being hummed is the word Aum. According to these ancient teachings, Aum is the equivalent of "the Word" that is the same as the Holy Ghost in Christian teachings. If you're able to hear the sound of the universe it would sound like "aummmmmmmmmm" in constant resonance. So, the original Word uttered by God was this sound of Aum, which not only set the wheels in motion for the creation of the universe, but it also maintains creation in its current state. This Aum will ultimately be the primal force in the dissolution of creation as well.

Some believe if God has a name that this would be His name. Aum, (sometimes written as Om) although it is only one syllable, contains within it three sounds that represent creation, preservation and dissolution. The letter "A," also known as akara, represents creation and usually starts the alphabet of all languages but also is significant because it starts at the root or base of the tongue at the back of the throat. The "U" known as ukara, representative of preservation, makes the "uuu" sound that is formed at the middle of the tongue and mouth. The "M" known as makara represents dissolution and completes the word or mantra (chant) with the meeting of the lips at the front of the mouth.

"And the Spirit of God moved upon the face of the waters." Now I would like to further examine this "Spirit of God" also known as the Holy Spirit or Holy Ghost. The East equates it with Aum. The sacred word Aum came originally from the ancient scripture of the Vedas and evolved into the sacred word Hum of the Tibetans, Amin of the Moslems, and Amen of the Jews, Christians, Greeks, Romans and Egyptians. All of the world's great religions believe that creation originated in the cosmic vibratory energy of the Word or Aum also defined as this "Spirit of God."

Now the Holy Trinity is a concept that is not exclusive to Christianity. In Christianity it is known as the Father, the Son and the Holy Ghost. Most Christians believe it to represent God, Jesus Christ and the Spirit of God. In Hinduism it is known as Sat, Tat and Aum or Sat-Chit-Ananda. The Father (Sat) is known as the unmanifested, absolute, pure consciousness, the alpha and the omega, the Silence existing beyond vibratory creation. **"Be still and know that I am God." Psalms 46:10 The** Son (Tat) is known as the sole reflection of God; the "only begotten son" and exists within vibratory creation. This aspect of God is known as the Christ Consciousness, the Intelligence that permeates all of creation. Many people are under the false impression that the body or persona of Jesus is the Christ when rather it is his Oneness in the Christ Consciousness that equates him with the only begotten son of the Creator.

Chapter II: The Fabric of Creation

"No man hath seen God at any time, the only begotten Son, which is in the bosom of the Father, he hath declared him." John 1:18 We will discuss this in further detail in Chapter XX.

Now the Holy Spirit (Aum) is somewhat of an obscure aspect of the Trinity that causes much confusion. The Holy Spirit is known as the Word or the activating force that upholds all of creation through vibration. This aspect of God is His primal energy that at times may be latent but is always with Him from the very beginning. When this Spirit becomes active it leads to creation. ***"In the beginning was the Word, and the Word was with God, and the Word was God."*** What is interesting is that this Holy Spirit was originally known in the feminine sense. The word "Spiritus" is Latin and means "breath." Hence, God in His Absolute state is known as stillness and silence yet when He "breathes" He becomes motion. This signifies His "Spirit of God" moving across the waters and calling all of creation into existence. These two aspects of God are also referred to as the "positive and negative," the "masculine and feminine" or the "reasoning and feeling" qualities of the Creator. (positive and negative should not be taken as "good and bad"). But this paints a very different picture of God and the Holy Spirit giving "birth" to the universe and thus its first "offspring" being the only pure reflection and begotten Son, the intelligence in creation and the Christ Consciousness.

In the Old Testament and Dead Sea Scrolls, the Holy Spirit is known as "Ruach" which also is of feminine gender. In the New Testament, it became the word "Pneuma" which is gender neutral and through time, editing and translations became the masculine aspect. It is important to keep in mind that God has no gender and is ultimately neither male nor female. However, in creation His aspects are reflected due to the types of energy as more positive or negative and thus the male and female sense. This is reflected even in the first family unit of Adam, Eve and their offspring. This perhaps explains why we always refer to "Mother Nature" and heavenly bodies in the feminine aspect. This same Holy Ghost is also referred to as the "comforter" and if we examine our own family, who is normally the backbone and comforter for everyone? The father may traditionally provide but it is the mother who **supports**. She is the one who comforts the children... not to mention the husband as well! ☺ **"But the Comforter, which is the Holy Ghost, whom the Father will send in my name, (s)he shall teach you all things, and bring all things to your remembrance, whatsoever I have said unto you." John 14:26**

Some argue that the editors of the more popularized versions of the Bible today remolded this aspect of God to be masculine to make it coincide with the Father and Son. Since most of the priests of the day were men, perhaps they had a cultural problem with identifying God in any manner as feminine or maybe it was just blatant discrimination to keep women subservient. While ultimately order is not important, I like to think of the "first family" as Sat, Aum, Tat. In which, if we take the first letter of each "personification" we still end up with S.A.T. – Sat, which is still God and thus the Holy Trinity is nonetheless one and the same, just variations of the One Creator.

Now it is important to understand that while it may be helpful for man to conceptualize God by personifying Him, we must realize that Spirit has no sex or gender. We often try to make God in our image. Since man thinks of himself as a body we try to impose or imagine God to have one as well. While we may say symbolically that the universe is God's body, in actuality, He has no form. Something infinite like the Creator cannot have a body. You cannot have an infinitely sized body. It just isn't mathematically possible. He is not a person and doesn't function as a human might. The truth is the reverse – man was made in God's image.

Chapter II: The Fabric of Creation

Since God is Absolute Consciousness, the soul likewise is merely consciousness.

The only difference is that our individual conscious has become identified with the body. In order to live in our Father's likeness, we must eventually realize that we are not flesh and bones. For example, when we sleep at night, we become less aware of our bodies. We simply become consciousness (or Subconsciousness that is). If we dream, we may visualize ourselves as having bodies but in truth that dream body is just a manifestation of our consciousness. Even if we don't dream when we awake, we know if we slept well or not because our consciousness remains aware of our bodies even if only to a small degree.

As always, man is limited in trying to elaborate spiritual matters with words. If we were to use the analogy of trying to describe a star or other form of light each person would express differently what he or she saw. Some will describe the brightness or brilliance. Some will explain its luminosity, opacity, magnitude, color, temperature, intensity etc. While they would all technically be accurate, from each other's perspective they would be describing something different which may lead one to believe the other was wrong and yet none of their descriptions would perfectly capture the true essence of the light. Now this is assuming the light remained perfectly constant. Imagine if that light were continuously changing in form. Now you get an idea of how challenging it is to describe the constantly changing vibration of the Holy Spirit, which sustains all of creation!

Genesis continues further to say that the earth was without form and void. In an instant God multiplied His consciousness within the bosom of Himself and from His stillness He sent forth His "Holy Spirit" sending His/Her vibrational breath amongst the "waters" multiplying His/Her Consciousness into many particles of forces. Science has called this beginning of the universe the Big

Bang. This is also the beginning of polarity and duality. Some Theosophists might disagree but again it's relative. This big bang was the result of numerous positive and negative forces (thoughts) of God interacting with each other pushing and shoving with rapid momentum. For every action there was an equal and opposite reaction which caused an exponential multiplication in energy. I've always visualized the birth of the universe as similar to what happens when the sperm and the egg unite. These two cells combine and then rapidly multiply forming the human body.

In the early stages of the universe, these positive and negative forces were very chaotic and unorganized. The entire universe was just a giant sphere ever expanding without any apparent direction or purpose. So, when we refer to the earth in this sense, we're not just talking literally about our planet Earth, we are talking about all matter. Early on, all the matter of the universe didn't have any true structure or form. Yet keep in mind that all of these atoms are simply the result of God's thought and energy. Inherent within each and every particle of matter is God's consciousness. Over time, which amounts to billions of years based upon our point of reference, God's Intelligence, inseparably present within all of creation, began to mold and shape the universe into living expressions of His/Her consciousness.

This Intelligence is the aspect of God as the Creator manifest in the entire cosmos. The same way in which through the original one cell of the embryo, certain cells become blood cells, skeletal, muscle and ultimately all the organs of the body, the universe likewise by some seemingly mysterious hand formed all the galaxies, solar systems and planets. God the One, through His/Her Holy Spirit, breathe life into creation and molded it into form through His/Her only begotten son – the Intelligent Christ. These three aspects are still nothing more than the One thus it is difficult to tell where one begins and ends, and the next aspect begins. At what point does water become ice? It doesn't happen instantaneously. Rather the bonds gradually one by one solidify until all the water present changes state. The highest state of God is found in the stillness and yet His intelligent and loving "Spirit in action" is inseparable from His Being. It is this universal intelligent consciousness which Jesus was one with which allowed him to undoubtedly declare *"I and my Father are one!"* **John 10:30** So God in His Absolute state, God in His "only begotten son" state as Creator, and God as Her Word or Holy Ghost make up the Holy Trinity!

"And darkness was upon the face of the deep." Once again, we have God's original thought which makes up the causal sphere that descends downward into the astral sphere which then descends further downward into this grosser physical sphere. Each atom that exists as a structured thought of God is "coated" to separate it from other atoms. This "coating" in Eastern teachings is known as individual avidya or ignorance. This "ignorance" is simply a result of the perception atoms have of an individual existence. In Truth, there is only One Existence, which is Changeless Spirit. But in essence this avidya or ignorance serves a purpose in allowing every atom to experience itself as its own identity and thus God to witness it all. It has been said that we are God's muse. The collective avidya becomes known as Maya, the "darkness" or cosmic delusion. This collective darkness does have consciousness and although it has a purpose by God, it of its "own power" from a certain perspective can be said to work adversely against His Divine Plan, which is for all of His creation to experience Itself but then to ultimately return to Him! This collective darkness has come to be known in Christian teachings as Satan or the devil. Jesus spoke of Satan as *"He was a murderer from the beginning, and abode not in the truth, because there is no truth in him. When he speaketh a lie, he*

speaketh of his own: for he is a liar, and the father of it." John 8:44

This concept of the devil, Satan or maya is a very puzzling concept. Remember without some level of avidya, it is impossible for mankind to experience itself apart from everyone else as individual beings. Yet it is this collective avidya, which becomes conscious in mass form and becomes man's greatest obstacle to overcome! It can be said that it is our greatest gift and curse. Satan has no true power over man to command us since God endowed us all with free will. Satan's true power is to tempt man from recognizing our oneness in order to keep us separate, divided and "earthbound." Satan tries to keep us fixated by looking outside of ourselves through the senses to identify with our separateness. As long as we seek completeness outside of ourselves, we remain under the spell of ignorance that prevents us from returning to our complete Self, which is the soul unified in Spirit. We will go further into depth on these concepts but for now let's try to stay focused on how the universe that was void became orderly and organized.

Within every atom there is God's consciousness. Since the atom became the building block for the universe, as an independent structure, it was still necessary to direct groups of these atoms to form higher forms of being. Therefore, God's intelligence had to be within every atom in order to guide them. This intelligence is what causes the gases of various molecules to form stars with revolving planets. It's God's intelligence, which holds the heavenly bodies in their orbits. It's God's intelligence, which forms the various elements of creation. Its God's intelligence, which causes a seed placed in the ground to grow into a flower with the proper watering and sunlight. It's God's intelligence, which takes a sperm and ovum and multiplies those cells to form the complex human body. I don't think any rational minded person can dispute the

Chapter II: The Fabric of Creation

evidence that the universe is a highly organized system that is clearly built upon some sort of blueprint and intelligent design!

"And the Spirit of God moved upon the face of the waters." Through the conglomeration of atoms, we form the five different elements found in creation. Those elements are earth, water, fire, air and ether. Merriam-Webster defines the word ether as the rarefied element formerly believed to fill the upper regions of space; heavens. The ether is the bridge between the earthly physical realm and the astral heavenly realm. Ether can be thought of as the backdrop or blackboard upon which creation is painted. This ether acts like a fluid out in space, which is why light, sound, stars, planets, and galaxies tend to move in wave-like motions. This ether in accordance with gravitational forces affects the movement of objects in space and can even cause the bending of light. Remember all matter is composed of moving atoms and collectively it appears in the universe like a fluid moving like "waters." Again the "Spirit of God" is His intelligence present in creation and His Holy Ghost.

People have often thought of space as a vacuum and soundless. This isn't quite accurate. You may be able to say that space is a "relative" vacuum because the particles of mass are extremely sparse. Nonetheless, the ether and God's consciousness is always present. The assumption has also been that because of this vacuum, sound in space cannot be made or heard. The truth is there is sound in space; we're just learning how to listen to it. I already mentioned how every atom that makes up matter is vibrating in harmony with the universal Aum sound – the Holy Ghost. Recent scientific studies have shown that the Earth and all heavenly bodies emit a whining sound that is picked up as radiation.

So now to recap, we have God the Absolute. God, with the power of His conscious will, creates through the power of thought. That thought appears from "no where" and begins to take form through the interaction of positive and negative forces, which interplay like a tuning fork producing the peculiar sound of the universe known as Aum or the Word. These vibrating energies can take on numerous forms due to varying frequencies. The first evidence of this vibrating energy appears as light on the astral level. Through God's intelligent consciousness, this energy of light vibrates even further becoming all the objects of the universe like a unique and perfectly played note. We can now imagine the entire universe like a brilliant light show and fluid symphony orchestrated by the Intelligent Grand Conductor – God!

    Now if we deal solely with the physical universe, as we know it, we are aware of essentially three levels of awareness. The distinction here again is – awareness. We have the first level or that of the microcosmic level of matter, which is the atomic level of all things. We know that the atom consists of a nucleus of protons and neutrons orbited by electrons. Science has experimented with trying to split atoms known as fission and even to combine nucleuses in a process called fusion. Einstein, one of the chief engineers in helping to create the atomic bomb recognized the immense amounts of energy that are released when you split atoms. The second level of awareness is that in which we interact with our environment – mankind or the world. We inhabit a planet and manipulate our environment to serve us. Man's body is also made up of these atoms and is said to contain massive amounts of energy that is recognized mostly as thermal energy. The third level of awareness is the macrocosmic level in which holds the planetary bodies. This space is far too massive and distant for man to have much of an impact upon it and yet it contains the same immense energy potential as man and the atom.

Chapter II: The Fabric of Creation

As we've already discussed, science has already proven that no object is truly solid. Our physical bodies, as well as the planetary bodies, are all made of atoms. Spirituality tells us that all objects have consciousness and are therefore "alive." Now some objects may not appear to reflect "life" as we know it but there are many ways of expressing life. In addition, some heavenly bodies may be in a sleeping or dormant state. If we look on the macrocosmic level, we see a "coincidental" similarity between the atom and a solar system. The sun looks strangely like a nucleus and the planets mirror electrons. It's also been shown that the Sun along with its planets move through space. Science, through experimentation, also tells us that the universe is moving. The common term most accepted currently is that it is "expanding." But if for a moment we call our solar system a large "atom" and observe its movement through our galaxy, it appears to move in another orbital motion around a grander center of our Milky Way galaxy. Isn't that what all electrons do – revolve around the center nucleus? If we zoom out even further, notice that our galaxy moves through space similar to numerous other galaxies. It's almost as if the galaxy itself is nothing more than an electron moving around an even more enormous "nucleus."

My suspicion is that if we were able to zoom out to the outer edges of our known universe, we may find that our entire universe is nothing more than another "electron" moving around an even greater system. In fact, it is my belief that our physical plane of existence extends upwards infinitely and downwards infinitesimally! Most of us who believe in a Creator don't have a difficult time accepting that He is infinite, but we truly have no idea what that really means or how large infinity can really be. However, it is also my belief that how massive or minute the universe may extend in both directions is ultimately irrelevant. What is important is that man raises his consciousness above identification with the world of matter and reunites his being with Spirit. In order to help accomplish this man must learn to love all unconditionally as one's self. This also happens to be one of the first requirements towards lasting happiness and that is to treat all others as your self. By doing so, you become a "giver" and in order to give you must receive from the universe or rather Spirit all that you have to give. So, by giving happiness to others you naturally feel happy. Studies of the brain have shown that we are actually "wired" to experience elevated levels of happiness when we give to others. If we try to stop thinking of man as a human form but rather as the hidden consciousness that gives the body life, then we're on the right track. As formless consciousness, there are specific techniques to help man redirect his attention inward and thus begin to separate the attachment to the senses, desires and gross form. The true fabric of creation is merely an idea and that idea originates from a formless Spirit, which is united by the Holiest of Loves.

Love Is...

Someone once asked me exactly what love is...
I pondered for a moment before I said this:
Love is complicated and somewhat tricky to spot
Perhaps it would be easier to say what it is not –

It's not selfish or controlling, conditional or greedy
It's unselfish and free, unconditionally given to the needy
It's the nurturing of a mother as it's given to a child
While its quickly reciprocated with just a gentle smile

It's butterflies of anticipation on your first blind date
And the stillness of time when you combine with your soul

mate
Love is honor and valor, the courage to face fear
Yet the soft, sweet whisper of fondness in your ear

It's the beautiful words of your favorite love song
It flourishes when it's right and corrects you when it's wrong
Love is cold... *passionately* hot! But never lukewarm
When life's a hurricane it's your eye of the storm

It's the long, hard journey, the pain in your feet
Also a job well done, it's the mission complete
Love sometimes waits before its springs into action
To transform all hate with magnetic attraction

It changes colors every moment yet its Essence is changeless
You recognize it when you see it although It remains nameless
It's center is everywhere and circumference is none
Without it we are nothing but with it – we are One!

Once you find it within you'll come to understand
That Love's never complicated; it simply says... "I AM!"

Lateef Warnick

CHAPTER III

Veils of Delusion

3 And God said, let there be light: and there was light.
4 And God saw the light, that it was good: and God divided the light from the darkness.
5 And God called the light Day, and the darkness he called Night. And the evening and the morning were the first day.

    Great job! So far, we've examined some ideas of God and His absolute state beyond the creative world of relativity. We've looked at how, through the action of His will, He structures the universe based upon the building blocks of the atom. From these atoms, He forms more complex expressions of life and beings capable of interacting with their environment. From here we begin to get into a hierarchy of creation. The atoms that were all "created equal" now begin to evolve into higher forms. There becomes greater separation and division. This separation and division allow for experience and growth. Thus, there becomes a purpose for all of creation.
    If we could use the analogy of a painting, the artist first makes the decision to want to express herself through the piece of artwork. The artist chooses her painting tools such as brushes, sponges etc. She chooses the type of canvas upon which to place her design. She chooses what colors she would like to work with. Now she begins applying the paint in various strokes and applications to bring about the desired picture. Likewise, the Grand Painter has selected Her pieces of equipment in designing the universe and has now begun drawing the outlines for the desired masterpiece!

"And God said, Let there be light: and there was light." Now if we continue with the idea of there being layers in the scriptures of Genesis and if we examine the surface layer then we can interpret that "the light" simply refers to the sun in our solar system. And this would be true. When the sun shines on the side of the Earth facing it then it is "good" in the sense that it warms the planet and provides necessary light to help plants grow and mankind to function. When the Earth rotates on its axis and faces away from the sun then that part of the Earth is in darkness. This leads to our experience of day and night.

If we dig a little deeper to the next "layer" in metaphor we notice that although the light was called "good" the darkness was never actually called "bad" although some people may make that inference. The point of this is the fact that the concepts of good and bad are simply relative terms of creation. In God's absolute state there is no good or bad. There simply IS! Since both ideas originate from the source being God, can we truly call anything "bad"? In absolute terms the answer would be – No. But in relative terms of this world then the answer would obviously be – Yes. But does this mean that since "darkness was upon the face of the deep" comes before "let there be light" that this entire creation is somehow "not good"? (That's actually a rhetorical question but let's examine it a little bit to see if there's some merit to it.)

In order to penetrate the top layer, we must go back and try to understand God in His absolute state. In the beginning there was only God. That means there is only One original substance (if we can call Him that). If we accept this as absolute truth, then anything that suggests other than the "One" would have to be a non-truth. (I refrain from using the world "lie" simply because there's a connotation that would make it a bad thing.)

Similarly, God in his absolute state is eternal. Time is a reflection of change. Since God is eternal, He is also changeless and timeless. Again, if we accept this as absolute truth then anything that is subject to change or time would have to be temporary and thus a non-truth. Likewise, God is omnipresent. Space is a result of division or separation. So again, in accepting God as omnipresent to be absolute truth then anything that would suggest otherwise would have to be a non-truth.

Now if we observe our universe as our environment then we can clearly see that instead of "one" there are "many." Time and change are inevitable circumstances of this creation. There is obviously space and distance between objects. Based upon these variables, we would have to accept that this entire physical universe is based upon "change" and therefore a non-truth. **"And the light shineth in darkness; and the darkness comprehended it not." John 1:5** There are some who would interpret that what we perceive as darkness and space is actually God's light and what we perceive as light in this world is actually "darkness" because it draws our attention outward through the senses. Relatively speaking, what we must understand is that in this creation and beyond, God is the true Light! I think a more befitting way of putting it is that all things that pull or direct us towards the Creator are "good." All things that pull or direct us away from His Light would have to be bad or "not so good" as it denies His Truth.

"and God divided the light from the darkness." So how do we know the difference between "good" and "not so good"? Well, all we have to do is ask ourselves "Does this idea direct or pull me toward oneness" or "is this self-serving and pulling me towards the limited idea of me amongst many"? If it were the former, then it would be good. If it were the latter, then it would have to be not so good. Does this idea direct or pull me towards an eternal truth or does it pull me towards gratification in this moment? Again, the former

– good. The latter – not so good. Lastly, does this idea direct or pull me towards an awareness and consideration of all things everywhere or is it only beneficial to my personal space here and now? Former – good! Latter – not good!

    Now the good news is that this game of life is already rigged! God has coded every idea of His in existence to return to Him! He is like the hottest source of energy in creation and we are all like heat-seeking devices. The same way plants are naturally drawn towards the sunlight; all of God's creations are designed to come back to Him. The biggest challenge for God's most evolved beings is our free will and the only difference between the average person and a Divine Incarnation is that the latter is a person who has reached their Goal. But at some point, even the most advanced soul had to make the committed decision to seek God first and foremost above all other desires. When God knows that we want nothing more than His Presence then through His grace, He will reveal Himself to us. But we all must, through the use of our free will, overcome the "darkness" of this world of non-truths and find the everlasting Truth of God within. Some of us will get there sooner than others but all things evolve towards the Light of God!

    I would briefly like to touch upon a subject of evolution versus involution. Evolution in the metaphysical sense is not quite the same as what Charles Darwin suggested in how man's body evolved from other lower species. Evolution in this sense deals more with the Original Consciousness or some say "Unconsciousness" evolving Itself through the identification of Its parts until It eventually becomes Its "whole" Self again. This same concept some refer to it as actually "involution." In general terms, involution is the process in which man goes from having a consciousness identified with outer gross matter to now going inward to identify with more subtle realms of energy, mind and ultimately pure being. When viewing this concept in macrocosmic terms some say evolution and involution are happening simultaneously.

When referring to man's personal ascent, it is often viewed that man primarily goes through stages of evolution before becoming self-conscious and then upon the raising of the question "who am I?" that the soul begins the process of involution. Of course, it would be hard to determine distinct lines of where one ends and the other begins. Similar to a flame, it is hard to tell where it begins and where its outer edges are. God, the Absolute conscious/non-conscious through thought becomes the ego and through many experiences the ego again becomes the thought, which ultimately melts back into the Absolute Conscious/Non-consciousness. Meher Baba, an author, wrote an interesting book called "God Speaks" that attempts to explain this esoteric phenomenon.

Now in order to understand what separates one soul from another and why some seem to advance along the spiritual path more quickly we need to first understand what separates the different "classes" of creation. Let us recall all things of creation are simply an idea of God. These "ideas" find their expression as a result of the Holy Ghost or the Aum that is the word of God. The expressed word is the vibrating interplay of positive and negative forces. The positive forces are akin to Love or Attraction. The negative forces are akin to Separation or Repulsion. The resulting affects of the idea of separation lead to space. The resulting affects of the idea of change lead to time. These effects produce the particles known as the atom. As mentioned earlier, every individual atom being a result of God's idea has a certain level of consciousness and is under the influence of Avidya or Ignorance. Collectively speaking, multiple atoms under the influence of Ignorance is called Maya or the darkness. The process of each atom birthed from God's Consciousness experiencing and metamorphosing until it returns to His complete Consciousness again is called life!

Every atom, as stated, has a "coating" which separates it from every other atom. This coating again is called ignorance and is actually made up of five different layers that are gradually dissolved until the individual atom evolves from the idea of separation back into the realization of Oneness. From Eastern teachings, these coated layers are known as **koshas**, veils or sheaths. These five veils separate into classes the inanimate kingdom, the plant kingdom, the animal kingdom, the angelic or heavenly kingdom and finally the free, liberated or emancipated kingdom. **"Him that overcometh will I make a pillar in the temple of my God, and he shall go no more out: and I will write upon him the name of my God, and the name of the city of my God, which is new Jerusalem, which cometh down out of heaven from my God: and I will write upon him my new name." Revelation 3:12**

These five koshas are essentially screens, which limit the "consciousness" of all things in creation. Think of the koshas as curtains that must be withdrawn or pulled back in order to reveal another stage of consciousness. The koshas appear as stages of expression of life forms and in descending order are as follows:

1. Anandamaya Kosha – the bliss sheath.
2. Jnanamaya Kosha – the wisdom sheath.
3. Manomaya Kosha – the mental sheath.
4. Pranamaya Kosha – the life energy sheath.
5. Annamaya Kosha – the gross matter sheath.

Let me try to paint a picture of how the formless Spirit beyond creation descends Its Consciousness into the form of matter and creation. The Original Substance we refer to as God is uncreated and unmanifested. The ancients refer to It as Sat. It is Absolute and thus has no relative comparison or counterpart and no beginning or

Chapter III: Veils of Delusion

end thus even terms like omnipresence have no true meaning. If you're all there is then there in essence are no other places and infinity has no meaning because everywhere is right here. In other words, something infinitely large is equally infinitely small since it's all relative. So, the first "distortion" of this Absolute Essence is to actually play the limiting role of the Creator. This Creator is what is known as the "perfect reflection" of Sat in creation also called Tat. Likewise, since this "Creator" has a clear beginning it must therefore have a clear end as well. This is what leads to the concept of the dissolution of universe(s). It is said that the entire experience of creation for God is a finite amount of time and He chooses to experience an equal amount of time in "non-manifestation." We'll explore this further later. However, to continue, this Creator inherently has the powers of Omniscient "knowing" and Omnipotent "force." This Creator because it is "all there is" is therefore Omnipresent as well because space has not yet been defined. The qualities of this "reflection of Spirit" are that it possesses **Intelligence**, giving consciousness to all of creation, and **Energy**, giving life or experience to all of creation.

    The Creator arbitrarily chooses or defines a fixed point from out of "no where" (remember space has no meaning yet) and uses this as a starting point for creation. Scientists may refer to this as the "big bang." This is the macrocosmic beginning of the universe. By simply choosing a fixed point, the Creator indirectly defines every other point that is not the "starting point" as possibilities thus creating the idea of differentiation, infinity (countless other points) as well as rise to the first element – ether! Ether is simply space and serves as the backdrop or canvas for all the created cosmos. From out of this one element all other elements have their beginning. These infinitely numbered "points" exist only from and as part of the One become known as "thoughtrons." These thoughtrons in actuality have no form since they are nothing more than individualized ideas emanating from One Consciousness.

The Creator's first words are **"Let there be Light."** But in order to do so, He had to first have the idea. So, the subtlest form of creation will always be the "thought." The next subtlest expression of creation is "the Word" or rather vibration. So first comes Consciousness, then the thought and then the vibration or word. The vibration of these "thoughtrons" gives rise to radiation, which en masse becomes the Light, which only can be seen with the backdrop element of the ether – the darkness of space (**God divided the light from the darkness**). Following this the Creator makes the first "judgment" of the cosmos and defines it as "it was good" giving rise to the first kosha – the **Anandamaya kosha** or Bliss sheath. This is the inherent quality of being close and aware of the Absolute basking in the glory of the Light of His creation. It is here that the Creator also creates what many religions refer to as co-creators, demi-gods, archangels and/or deities who help to oversee and govern God's creation from the macrocosmic down to the microcosmic. Divine man, as the soul, also is unique in being able to ascend to this state of consciousness to see creation as the Creator sees it! Man's soul is best described as individualized Spirit.

The next "phase" of creation is the possible movement of the thoughtrons. From out of this "movement" across the ether we have the subtle expression of the next element – air! With movement comes the necessary idea of duality. In order to go left there must be a right. To go up there must be a down, in thus out, forward and thus backward. Hence there cannot be any absolutes in creation since it is dependent upon relativity of one thing compared to another. This also gives rise to choose, experience, right or wrong, judgment and thus discrimination. These essentially are the qualities of the second sheath or

Chapter III: Veils of Delusion

curtain known as the **Jnanamaya kosha**. It is the wisdom stage of expression and hence the greatest wisdom becomes that which either leads you closer to the Highest Truth of the Absolute or that which takes you further away from this Truth into greater gross matter.

Also, at this stage, the thoughtrons evolve through "experience" to become what are called lifetrons. Lifetrons become the building blocks for all visible atomic structure scientists can observe – the quarks, photons, electrons, protons, neutrons and ultimately the atom, which is all on the macrocosmic level. Along with time, space, vibration and the atom we give birth to what is called Maya. Maya is the delusive spell of creation which gives rise to the perception of "separate existence" also known as the ego in spiritual terms. This also gives rise to our next sheath or closed curtain, the **Manomaya kosha** known as mind. Just as Jnana is that wisdom that pulls consciousness back towards the Absolute, the mind attempts to draw consciousness "outwards" or away from the Absolute. It becomes the sense-driven mind that pulls the consciousness towards greater gross matter. As a side note, any scientist or atheist who doesn't believe in a creative hand at play in the universe will have an extremely difficult time explaining the symmetry that is apparent in everything. Suggesting that "un-intelligent" pieces of matter somehow formed and grouped themselves into planets, stars, solar systems and galaxies is about as likely as a person throwing buckets of paint on a wall and producing the Mona Lisa!

From a scientific perspective, the movement of the original atoms, hydrogen, through space leads to interaction of these forces and the subsequent subtle quality of transformation, our next vibrational element – fire! This elemental quality leads to all the burning gases of the stars, which become the centerpiece of solar systems, revolving planets and thus the potential suitable qualities for microcosmic life. The subtlest thoughtrons become the lifetrons, which through further combinations become the building blocks for the atoms and of course atoms become molecules. The inherent energy present in all of these particles is what sustains them, and this energy field gives rise to the next sheath known as the **Pranamaya kosha** or the energy life sheath. This is the fourth veil or drawn curtain that hides Absolute Truth.

Through the continued interaction of gas clouds some becoming stars while others becoming planets, we give rise to the next vibrational element – water! The initial "water" is the subtle vibration of gases cooling, condensing and taking on more fluid-type motion. The planets that didn't have the fuel necessary to become burning stars develop cooler cores, which lead to atmospheric conditions through gravitational pulls and (sometimes) water. The closely held atoms of water, its fluid type qualities of slow movement and the interaction with fire leads to heating and cooling effects and ultimately the atoms that become "stationary" and thus the final vibrational element – earth! The earth or gross matter is what is called the fifth sheath known as the **Annamaya kosha** meaning "food." This is the last "curtain" drawn in which all gross matter exists and disguises Absolute Truth. From the Indians Taittiriya Upanishad (2.1) comes a quote: *"The infinite is Brahman. From it, from this SELF, space came to be; from space the wind; from the wind, fire; from fire, water; from water, earth; from earth, the plants; from plants, the food; and from food, the body of man (and animals)."*

Now let us visualize for a moment... the particles that creep up from the core of the Earth are the same particles that came from the original substance of first matter at the beginning of time. These particles through volcanic eruption land on the surface of our planet and become the continents and newly formed islands. This lava, as proven by science, is already thriving with the life of various bacteria and microbes even at these high

Chapter III: Veils of Delusion

temperatures. These once-cosmic particles containing the hidden consciousness of the Absolute become the life we experience here on Earth as minerals, plants, animals and ultimately man thus the macrocosmic now becomes the microcosmic. Everything up to this point was the outward evolution of the Absolute becoming countless expressions encapsulating Itself within five "veils" or put another way hiding Itself behind five curtains. Reaching this last **Annamaya kosha**, microcosmic consciousness begins the inward "involution" back towards Itself to become the Absolute once more!

These curtains or sheaths are nothing more than "veils of delusion" that separate life's awareness of God. I also think of the koshas as veils that separate us from our permanent happiness in Absolute Truth. Starting with the outermost veil, **Annamaya kosha,** life must "unfold" each veil through greater expressions of consciousness to ascend and attain ultimate freedom back in the formless Absolute. All physical gross matter is encased within all five sheaths; however, the "consciousness" within all life spiritually evolves through unfolding. Consciousness in all rocks, minerals, metals, planets, moons and stars make up the inanimate kingdom. Even at this level these objects are capable of receiving stimuli from their outer environments as well as having certain responses to stimuli. Science has already conducted experiments to monitor electrical impulses exhibited from metals and minerals when affected by outer stimuli suggesting a "response." With the dissolution of this outermost "gross sheath" consciousness finds itself residing in the plant kingdom.

The fourth veil, **Pranamaya kosha** is known as the "life sheath." This sheath or veil is said to contain the organs of action. Likewise, within the plant kingdom we have all sorts of trees, herbs, fruits and vegetables. There have been many studies which show that not only are a variety of these plants capable of photosynthesis, they have circulatory systems and react to sunlight as well as heat, cold, music and other stimuli from their environments. At this stage of evolution, the atoms are said to have begun shedding some of the ignorance of Life and begin to embrace each other more closely to the heart in the organic state.

The third sheath or veil, **the Manomaya kosha** contains all of the animal kingdom. At this class of life, animals express a level of mind or thinking ability. The animal kingdom is where the organs of sense come into play. Although animals are capable of being mobile and interacting with their environments, they do not possess the intellect to make decisions between right and wrong. However, because of their instincts and mind they can often perform at levels that seem to express intelligence, but they lack the discrimination, which is a result of self-introspection. As this third sheath is unfolded, we next have the human kingdom.

The second sheath or veil, the **Jnanamaya kosha**, known as the intelligent sheath, encompasses man. Mankind is God's highest expression of life on the physical plane. We are the only ones capable of the abilities of thinking, reasoning, reflecting and utilizing our free will. Mankind actually or technically contains all five sheaths within the body that make up the physical, astral and causal bodies. Many people, by the way, tend to confuse the koshas with "bodies" which isn't quite correct. Some may argue but most yogis agree that man has three bodies – the physical, astral and causal. Amongst these three bodies we find the five sheaths.

Chapter III: Veils of Delusion

Correlation of Koshas, Chakras & Elements
(not literal)

- Sahasrara - Crown
- Ajna - Aum
- Visshudha - Ether
- Anahata - Air
- Manipura - Fire
- Swathisthana - Water
- Muladhara - Earth

Self - Absolute Reality (no koshas)

First kosha: Anandamaya kosha associated with Causal Body, Aum & Christ Consciousness

Next three koshas associated with Astral Body:
Pranamaya kosha
Manomaya kosha
Jnanamaya kosha
& the Four Elements:
Water, Fire, Air & Ether

Last kosha: Annamaya kosha associated with Physical Body & Earth Element

To paint an analogy, as man's consciousness is identified with the physical body, he remains behind all five curtains separating him from Absolute Bliss. As man through meditation is able to go within, he disconnects his consciousness from the physical body and thus "opens" the first curtain, the **Annamaya kosha**. Man's consciousness then becomes identified with his astral body and remains separated from Absolute Bliss by four remaining curtains. Man's consciousness remains identified with the astral body until being able to withdraw the next three koshas. By controlling prana, he is able to pull back the **Pranamaya kosha**. By silencing the mind, he is able to pull back the **Manomaya kosha** and finally by intuitive discrimination man becomes able to pull back the **Jnanamaya kosha** of wisdom. Through deep meditation, man's consciousness now becomes identified his causal body and the last remaining curtain, the **Anandamaya kosha**. Man experiences his consciousness as Bliss known by yogis as Samadhi. This is the last thin veil that allows for the individual experience and distinction between soul and Self. Through the continued deepest practices of meditation, in time, man's consciousness becomes able to withdraw the last curtain Realizing that All is One! Only Self remains with no distinction between the meditator, the act of meditation and that meditated upon. This is Self-Realization.

The physical body correlates to the **Annamaya** kosha since it is made of earth or food. The astral body is comprised of the next three sheaths **Pranamaya**, **Manomaya** and the **Jnanamaya** koshas hence it contains the qualities of energy, mind and intelligence. The third causal body, which is the last thinly remaining sheath, is the **Anandamaya** kosha or bliss state of expression. Man is meant to be the rational beings within creation. Our bodies are composed of electricities and are a microcosmic reflection of the universe. However, the average man has still not consciously unfolded these **last two sheaths** and is therefore subject to ignorance and the ideas of separation. Up to this point all the other classes of life existed primarily on an unconscious level due to the many veils of ignorance. Even a vast portion of man goes through life in almost a "dream like" state not fully conscious of himself in relation to Spirit.

Upon the unfolding of this intelligent sheath, we through discrimination nurture spiritual intelligence, now have just the **one remaining sheath of Bliss.** This last thin veil remains and is the last sense of individuality between man and God. The attainment of this state is only accomplished through the conscious will and effort of man to ascend to this level. Spiritual masters are those that have risen above the intellect and have united the bliss of their souls with the **Source** of that bliss being God. Man is then more in tune with God's will and can serve as advanced souls that help to counter the negative energies of the ignorant man. The Blessed Soul can appear as angels and other higher forms of living expressions of heavenly beings.

When this last bliss sheath is unfolded then there is nothing that separates the soul from God and that soul melts into infinity fully reunited with the Creator. When this last curtain is "opened" the only thing that remains is the Absolute Truth of Oneness! However, it's important to note that the Kaivalyam, liberated soul, always remembers the history of its path and retains its uniqueness. As God's Will determines, those fully liberated souls can descend into whatever form necessary to assist mankind in finding liberation. These *"My father and I are One"* souls are often directed by God to return to Earth to guide and teach man the essential steps necessary to overcome the pains and sufferings of this existence. Of course, ignorant man likes to debate and draw contrasts but these liberated souls such as Krishna, Buddha, Jesus and others, but they all come to remind us of our true identities in Spirit and to inspire us to renounce our ignorant concepts of the separated ego. **"Jesus answered them, Is it not written in your law, I said, Ye are gods"? John 10:34** We crucify the Messengers when they are present on this Earth and then we divide ourselves over who was the "right" messenger after they are no longer here. All of God's Messengers were sent here to share one message. Only when we travel the path of these messengers reaching the destination, they reached are we able to recognize the Universal Source present within them all. Here is where our completeness resides, and the joy found as a result of this Realization.

CHAPTER IV

A Day of God

"And the evening and the morning were the first day."

    It amazes me that to this day we still have debates on whether or not God created the heavens and earth in a day. The fact of the matter is, yes, he did create it in a day. But the real question is "what is a day"? If we're talking about 24 hours then the answer would be, no, he didn't create this planet in that amount of time. There is overwhelmingly too much evidence that proves this planet has been around a lot longer than some thousands of years.

    Once upon a time, man thought the Earth was flat, but we now know that it is not. Similarly, man once believed that we were the center of the universe, which has also been proven false. However, when it comes to trying to understand spiritual matters man still seems to approach it from a "flat, center of the universe" type of thinking. The truth is God could've created this entire universe in seven nanoseconds, milliseconds, minutes, days, centuries or any other measurement of time you would like to use. The reason is that there is no time to God. Every concept dealing with time only has meaning when it comes to this physical universe. God exists beyond this physical creation, which means that "time" is a non-truth or an illusion.

    We have defined one complete rotation of the Earth as one full day. However, if we were on Mars, Venus or any other heavenly body then a day there would be something else based upon that planet's diameter and speed of rotation. The story of the creation of the world in Genesis is simply a symbolic story for man to enjoy. But if we try to seriously examine or determine more exact increments of time then we have to think outside the box and see the larger picture. There are many good books and examinations on astronomy and the movement of the planets within our solar system and beyond. I encourage you to do your own research.

Since a time, immemorial, man has been trying to understand our place in the universe. Astronomers have studied the movements of the Earth, planets and visible stars. And perhaps every one of us has at least had the fleeting thought of "what else is out there"? We've wondered "are we alone"? I like the line from the movie **"Contact"** in which the character played for Jodie Foster answers *"We don't know if there is life out there or not but if there isn't then it sure is a terrible waste of space..."*

Now I don't mean to overwhelm you with scientific data but there is a method to the madness. Bear with me and you'll be able to better understand what all this mathematics may mean for society as a whole. From what we currently understand from science, the universe started from an infinitesimally small point and exploded into what is known as our continuously expanding universe about 13-14 billion years ago. According to current scientific calculations, the universe is approximately 880×10^{24} meters or 93 billion light years in diameter and growing! Within this universe there are billions of galaxies. Each of these galaxies consists of billions of stars with even more planets revolving many of these stars. Some of these galaxies are older than our own galaxy while others are younger. All of these galaxies appear to move in a circular-type of rotation sort of like a whirlpool.

We live in what is called the Milky Way galaxy. Within our galaxy there are likewise billions of stars. The Milky Way is approximately 100,000 light years across or 9.5×10^{17} kilometers – extremely small compared to the

Chapter IV: A Day of God

size of the universe. The Milky Way supposedly has 200-400 billion stars within it that revolve around its center, which is called the Galactic Center. Our sun is just one of these many stars and according to our current best calculations takes about 225-250 million years to complete one orbit! Again, based on current scientific data, our Sun is estimated to be about 5 billion years old. So according to these calculations our Sun has made approximately 20-25 complete orbits since its birth. Our sun is neither the biggest nor the oldest star in our galaxy but if we compare it in volume to our Earth then our planet would fit inside the sun about 1.3 million times! I've chosen to take this "outside looking in" approach for a reason, so we can better put things in perspective. In the grand scheme of things, our planet is nothing more than a mere dot, an almost meaningless speck, in the magnitude of the universe. If it were to disappear today it would barely even register as a ripple in space. And yet our Omnipresent Creator is not only aware of every galaxy, star and planet in the universe – He's completely and totally aware of every grain of sand on the beach! *"But even the very hairs of your head are all numbered. Fear not therefore: ye are of more value than many sparrows." Luke 12:7*

I've presented this grand scale picture to present to you the incomprehensible awe in scope of God's creation. And while everybody of mass exerts a gravitational force of attraction upon one another, it is more important to understand the things that have the greatest affect upon man in proximity. All great ancient civilizations had an understanding of the astral influence of the stars upon man. The Egyptians, Mayans, Greeks and in particular the ancient rishis of India have shown magnificent comprehension of astronomy. The Mayans and their astronomical predictions for the winter solstice of the year 2012 have most recently become popular. Since this is a conversation grand enough to deserve its own book, I will mention it here, but we will explore at another time.

Sri Yukteswar, an Eastern Yogi, wrote a great book called "The Holy Science" which describes with a significant amount of detail how our sun moves through the galaxy. We already know that the Earth rotates on its axis and revolves around the sun in 365 days. According to Oriental astronomy and his determinations the sun with all of its orbiting planets has another star in space known as its dual. There is still ongoing debate to prove whether or not our sun actually has a dual. There are some statistics out there that suggest 90% of stars do in fact have a dual or binary star. Some have suggested that Sirius is our dual. Others suggest perhaps our dual is an astral star, dwarf star, black hole or star we just haven't identified yet because of a lot of intergalactic interference from radiation or otherwise. The Binary Research Institute has done some great work on this subject matter. I recommend you look into their data if you're more interested in this idea.

Now these magnetic pulls on the Earth from the moon, sun, etc cause a wobble-like movement known as the Precession of the Equinoxes. This precession has a movement equivalent to about 1 degree every 72 years and takes approximately 24,000 for the Earth to return to its original point. As most of us know the twelve signs of our zodiac are based upon twelve constellations in space. The sun, along with its dual, orbits the Galactic Center that is also known as the Grand Center, Center of the Milky Way or Vishnunabhi according to the Hindus.

The sun's orbit causes a backward movement of the equinoctial points of the zodiac constellations as the Earth moves through space. As the sun makes its orbit around its dual it comes closest to the galactic center every 24,000 years. This grand center is said to regulate man's *dharma*. Dharma is defined as the mental virtue of mankind at any given point in time. When the sun

Chapter IV: A Day of God

and its dual revolve to a point that is closest to this grand center, the mental virtue of man becomes evolved to a point to understand all scientific matters as well as their relation to Spirit. Equally, when the sun and its dual revolve to a point that is furthest away from the grand center then man's mental virtue, dharma, devolves to a very crude mindset incapable of comprehending even the very basics of science and especially ignorant of Spirit. If we do the math based upon today's accepted numbers, then our 5 billion-year-old planet has completed approximately 208 thousand cyclic periods of this rise and fall in virtue; not necessarily implying that man has been around for them all.

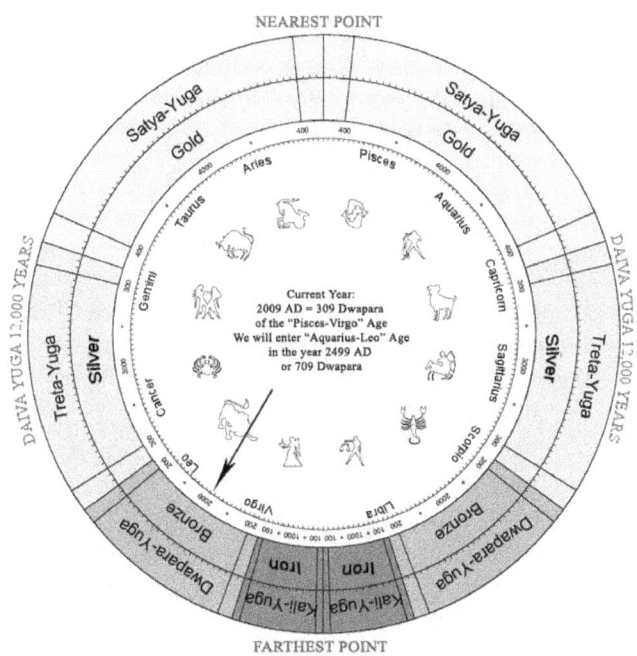

Now this circle of a 24,000-year cycle can be broken up into two 12,000-year arcs. Coincidentally, our watches with hand dials resemble this method of time tracking for periods of day and darkness. The chart helps to give you a visual of what this orbit with its ascending and descending arcs look like. The ascending arc is known as the Autumnal Equinox and the descending arc is known as the Vernal Equinox. Each of these two arcs is divided into four periods known as Yugas. These four yugas are known as Kali, Dwapara, Treta and Satya. They have also been correlated to the Greeks stages known as the Golden, Silver, Bronze and Iron Ages. Respectively, these stages are also defined by man's understanding and are accordingly classified as the Material, Atomic, Mental and Spiritual Ages. It has been said that in the beginning God multiplied Himself into many forms gradually descending into the causal, astral and physical form and ultimately into human beings. In this "original" stage of Satya Yuga or "Golden Age" creation brilliantly manifested His Divinity. Gradually through man's free will of choice we became more greatly distant from His Presence. Eventually God through His loving attraction embedded a magnetic pull to always redirect man back to His Bosom when we stray too far from home. It is during these times when the Earth is farthest from the Grand Center, and man's dharma is totally engrossed in matter or "darkness," that the Lord sends a Savior such as Jesus to redirect man's consciousness back towards Spirit!

Starting from the top half of the arc in the 12 o'clock position down to the 6 o'clock position is the descending arc in which man's dharma or mental virtue gradually declines over the course of those 12,000 years. Likewise, on the ascending arc, as a result of his magnetic pull, man's dharma retraces its lost wisdom back to full understanding. Each Yuga lasts for varying amounts of time in addition to having a transitioning period from one phase to the next, which is shown in the table.

The Kali Yuga is 1000 years with two 100-year transitioning periods to total 1200 years. The Dwapara Yuga is 2000 years long with two 200 transitioning periods for a total of 2400 years. The Treta Yuga lasts 3000 years with two 300-year transitioning periods. Finally, we return to Satya Yuga of 4000 years with two transitioning periods of 400 years. Because we are still learning to grasp many of these concepts there is much controversy concerning the correct amount of time in relation to many of these concepts. While I often trust scientific data to be rather precise, I do acknowledge that it may have its limitations in understanding matters that are more of the Spirit than of matter. Since all things of matter are ultimately spirit in essence, it is not always clear on where that fine line lies. Scientific observation still has its limits of observation conducted through the senses, which by nature are imperfect. I've scrutinized the available information out there as best as possible but have chosen to trust the intuition of a divine personage whom I believe gains his understanding directly from the Source rather than just from the "outside looking in."

Hence, while most western astronomers may use the Vernal Equinox as their defining point of reference in determining the Earth's position, the Eastern metaphysicians go by the Autumnal Equinox due to its more accurate correlation with man's dharma. In the West, we tend to hear that we are in the "Age of Pisces" moving towards the "Age of Aquarius" but that would place us in the Satya Yuga, which is the highest stage of man's spirituality and understanding. I think that the average sensible person would agree just from looking at the state of humanity that we are a far cry from that! So, if we give the Autumnal Equinox the prevalent influence over man's dharma then we see that we are in the Dwapara stage of the "Age of Virgo" moving towards the "Age of Leo." We are only in the Piscean Age, in the complementary sense, of "Virgo-Pisces" and then "Leo-Aquarius." This seems to coincide more closely with our recent past over the last few millennia of "darker ages." Mankind has given rise to great societies, governments and technology. We continue to gain further understanding of the sciences and how to improve the lives of our people from medicine to transportation, communication and quality of life, hence progressing.

Therefore, utilizing 0° Aries marked by the star Revati or Zeta Piscium as a starting point, we are said to be in the current year of 309 Dwapara (2009 AD). We entered the Virgo-Pisces Age around 499 AD. We are likewise growing in our understanding of fine matter and electricity, which is indicative of the Dwapara era. We will enter the Treta Stage around 4099 AD and will then begin to fully understand the essence of divine magnetism, which is the essence of all electricities. Once we fully grasp this relation, we will begin to understand all of matter and its relationship with Spirit in the Satya Yuga starting around 7699 AD!

Now we should examine, historically speaking, why this conclusion seems to make the most sense. You've probably heard legendary stories of Pangaea, Lemuria and Atlantis. You may or not believe that any of these "lost continents" ever existed. Maybe they were just mythical tales. There is some interesting data on these alleged advanced civilizations, but we'll instead explore some other places like Mexico, Egypt and India in which we still have concrete remains that these civilizations existed. The only debate by anthropologists is how old do these civilizations date back and exactly how advanced were they. The Mayans had temples they built that indicate they clearly had an understanding of the equinoctial changes of the Earth and the sun.

The Egyptians not only had temples erected but they had an advanced hieroglyphics system, scientific understanding and fabulous monuments built including the famous Sphinx. There are some interesting examinations on these "Monuments of Light." One reconstruction of a hieroglyphics structure actually was shown to conduct electricity! Most anthropologists

Chapter IV: A Day of God

won't put up much of an argument that the Egyptian civilization can easily date back to 3000 BC. But some studies of water erosion exclusive to the Sphinx and its nearby temple suggest that they were built at a different time from the Pyramids. According to Dr Robert Schoch, a geologist, the weathering effect was due to precipitation that occurred when this area was subject to tremendous rainfalls that would date back conservatively to around 5000-7000 BC!

In the Gulf of Kutch, off the coast of India, there is an underwater city claimed to be one of the original cities of Dwarka. According to legend, Dwarka was the capital city founded by Krishna. According to the Mahabharata, the world's longest epic poem, Krishna foretold the sinking of this prosperous city. The government of India is still attempting to recover remnants from this lost city. Some of the ruins have thus been carbon dated as far back as 9,000 BC. India has left behind great scriptures and writings and many of these ancient epics reveal fascinating descriptions of weapons of war, flying machines and ages of great prosperity!

As stated earlier, there is debate over the time of the Precession of Equinoxes. Most scientists state that it takes 25,920 years based upon 1 degree every 72 years. Therefore, 72 x 360 = 25,920. But they also acknowledge this conclusion is based upon the assumption of a constant rate. According to Laurie Pratt, she and the ancient Hindus assert that the rate is not constant and varies according to the stage and positioning of the planet. There is agreement that the current rate of precession is approximately 1 degree every 72 years. There is some justification that the rate may vary based upon the bulge of the Earth at the equator, the tilt at the axis and its varying distances from other gravitational pulls at different times in its orbit.

Pratt goes even further to state that the precession rate is even connected to man's heart rate, breathing and concentration. According to her assessment, the average adult with a healthy heart has a heart rate of about 72 beats per minute in accordance with this precession of 1 degree every 72 years. She also states that the normal respiration of a healthy person is about 72 breaths every four minutes. There have been studies to show that a person's breathing is in direct relation to their state of mind. In other words, if a person is agitated or restless their breathing and heart rate go up. Their breathing is short and shallow. Likewise, a person who consciously slows and deepens their breathing will calm their mind, nerves and heart rate. Animals such as elephants and tortoises, which have very slow breathing patterns, tend to live very long lives. Pratt claims that as man evolves through the four yugas, the precession rate will slow down to 1 degree every 60 years in the Satya Yuga in which man's heart rate and breathing patterns will slow accordingly affording man greater clarity and concentration of mind along with longer, healthier lives!

Now the Hindus call God by the name of Brahman. Brahman, as described through Wikipedia, is defined as the unchanging, infinite, immanent, and transcendent reality which is the Divine Ground of all matter, energy, time, space, being, and everything beyond in this universe. The nature of Brahman is described as transpersonal, personal and impersonal by different philosophical schools. This absolute aspect of God is not to be confused with Brahma, which the Hindus think of as a personified expression of God as the Creator. Similar to other religious teachings, they believe God in relation to the physical world exists as a trinity of Creator, Preserver and Destroyer.

G. E. Sutcliffe a renowned astronomer has calculated a very precise cycle of 23,892 (24,000 rounded) years for one equinoctial cycle. What is most staggering is the fact that Venus, Earth and Mars are all in line with the first degree of the fixed zodiac indicating

Chapter IV: A Day of God

the beginning of a new cycle at that point in time! After 180 equinoctial cycles the planets are again in alignment, which amounts to 4,300,560,000 years also designated as a Day of Creation. When we multiply this number by two it gives us 8,601,120,000 years known as a Day and Night of Brahma. This period is stated to represent a period of creation and dissolution of a solar system.

Now we can get to a very interesting observation. Remember I said that many things from the Bible and scripture are often hid in layers. The surface layer reveals a physical truth that man can generally understand and comprehend. However, there are still deeper correlations that will often reveal a deeper truth. If we look closely at these numbers and do a little math, we will see some astounding "coincidences." A day as we know it on Earth is defined as 24 hours. One revolution of the Earth around the sun takes 365.256 days to be exact. The relation of the diameter of a circle to its circumference is an intriguing number. For any size circle it gives you a mathematical constant named by the Greeks as π (pronounced Pi) calculated as 3.1416. This number is the result of an equation that is the only one known to man that continues indefinitely without ever repeating. Now there are significant meanings about a circle in most religions as being symbolic of completion, birth, femininity, infinity, having no beginning or end, etc.

If we take the number of 8,601,120,000 (Day and Night of God) and multiply it by 365.256 (days in a year) we get 3.1416×10^{12} years! This has been defined as the Age of Brahma or the life span of a universe. As I discussed earlier in Chapter 2, man is capable of observing physical creation on three levels, our plane of existence, the microcosmic plane of the atoms of matter and the macrocosmic plane of outer space. It has been suggested that the cause of the Precession of the Equinoxes is not only due to gravitational/magnetic forces but also due to a contraction and expansion of the Earth's orbit. I'll admit I haven't been able to find a sufficient explanation as to the cause of this phenomenon, although scientific evidence concludes it is true, but if we play with the idea for a moment, we see some highly "coincidental" math.

For example, it is known that the Earth's day and hence years are not exact. In fact, there are some who believe during precession or contraction that each day of the Earth is 3.1416 seconds shorter (or longer depending on expansion versus contraction) than the previous day. This contraction and expansion have been said to be the cause of global warming and the ice ages because the Earth would be closer to the Sun at certain periods and further away at other times. But more importantly, the assumed math suggests that the longest year of Earth's orbit is 366.7518535 days and the shortest year is 365.1810572 days. The distance between these two circles or "orbital extremes" is 3,141,593 miles and takes 86,400 years to go from one extreme called the Aphelion (Earth farthest from the Sun) to the Perihelion (Earth closest to the Sun). By the way, there also happens to be 86,400 seconds in a day.

The assumptive conclusion is that a minute of our time would be equivalent to a day on the microscopic level (imagine looking through a microscope) and yet only a second on the macroscopic level (think galatically). Similarly, one day would be one year on the microscopic level and a minute on the macroscopic level. Likewise, one year of our time would only feel like a minute to the cosmos.

Hopefully, you see the connection between man's day, the value of π (circle, completion), God's day and the Age of a universe. One analogy I came across that I really liked was stated as such: If circumference equals Pi times diameter ($C = \pi D$) and diameter equals one (One Universe) then the circumference is equivalent to infinity since Pi is an

Chapter IV: A Day of God

infinitely long number that never repeats. Therefore, if the universe were truly infinite then each and every spot would be the center of the universe! So, the next time someone says the world doesn't revolve around you, you may have some grounds to dispute that! LOL, but seriously, what this reveals is that man's world and man, himself, is truly a microcosmic version of the macrocosmic Creator!

"And God said; Let us make man in our image, after our likeness." Genesis 1:26

TABLE OF THE YUGAS

Yuga	Transitioning In-Sandhis	Cycle	Transitioning Out-Sandhis	Total (Human Years)
Kali	100	1000	100	1200
Dwapara	200	2000	200	2400
Treta	300	3000	300	3600
Satya	400	4000	400	4800
One Arc – Daiva Yuga Electric			– Divine Age Age of the Gods	**12,000 (or 11,946)**

Term				Value
Couple				
Electric Cycle				**24,000 (or 23,892)**
Day of Brahma	(1000 Divine Ages or 1000 Yugas)			**4,300,560**
Day of Creation			Period of Existence of a Solar System	**4,300,560,000**
Day and Night of Creation			(x 2)	**8,601,120,000**
Age of Brahma	(100 years of Brahma)		Lifespan of an entire universe	**314.159 trillion years**
Π (Pi)	(mathematical constant of circle's diameter to circumference)		(endless number that never repeats)	**3.1415926**

CHAPTER V

Adam and Eve

Thus far we've examined the first day of God's creation dealing with light and darkness, spirit and matter, evolution and involution, consciousness and experience and concepts of time. This information is to set the stage for understanding the dynamics of our world. The most important thing is how it all pertains to man and how we utilize these ideas. I think it's appropriate to begin to talk about the beginnings of man. Since this can be a very intricate and

Chapter V: Adam and Eve

controversial discussion, we need to explore these concepts in small increments.

If you haven't noticed the pattern yet, this "Know Thyself" examination will take place within seven books as a 'journey of the soul' series. Each book is meant to examine one day of the seven days of creation, one level of the seven levels of man's consciousness and one of the seven stages of man's ultimate upliftment or revelation. As you may already know, God doesn't create man until the sixth day. We will consequentially discuss in great detail the making of man in day six "Know Thyself" according to God's sixth day of creation. But it is important to get a basic understanding of man's uniqueness and role in creation starting with the first human beings created as Adam and Eve.

Every religion has its own version of the makings of the first man and woman. Staying in concert with the current theme, we will elaborate on the Christian tale of Adam and Eve. But bear in mind that every religion's story of first man and woman varies simply according to language, culture and perspective. The Christian Bible focuses more on the "fall" of man while others may sing the praises of the divinity of the first beings. Either way, I think we all agree that man has been endowed with free will; and depending on how we choose to utilize this gift determines how divine or sinful we may be. Man has the choice to be good or evil which makes us different from any of God's other creations. However, it's important to recognize that in this relative world good and evil, like hot and cold, vary in degrees in comparison to one another. In other words, a hot 98° day outside isn't very hot compared to a 2,500° furnace nor is a furnace considered even tepid compared to the millions of degrees Fahrenheit reached on the sun's surface! Similarly, an evil deed committed by a child against a defenseless animal doesn't compare to a career criminal who takes another person's life during a robbery nor does his actions compare to a serial killer responsible for murdering dozens of innocent people. Yet in spite of our sins there is hope for all of us and Jesus said: *"He that is without sin among you, let him first cast a stone at her." John 8:7*

To better understand how Adam and Eve came into being I think it's worthwhile to recap on how God brings His ideas into physical form. From God's Absolute state, He consciously vibrates His Being through the interplay of positive and negative forces, which become the subatomic particles that make up the atom. All of these particles descend from the "first cause-all" plane of existence into the heavenly astral realm of light and finally into grosser form which we perceive as physical. Therefore, man was first created in "thought" in causal form, that "thought body" intensifies in energy and becomes reflected as a heavenly "body of light" and finally condenses into what we perceive as "solid human flesh;" metaphorically similar to the fashion in which water vapor condenses into ice.

Again, every atom is encased within five sheaths, which form the inanimate, vegetable, animal, human and divine expressions of Life. What this means is God's universe is constantly changing in form. Everything we perceive is continuously being created, preserved, dissolved and ultimately re-created. This is the cycle of life. In fact, the human body is said to completely regenerate every cell in the body roughly every 7 to 8 years. Only the DNA's memory is passed down through the generations, which is what lends to the familiar appearance of the same person. So, in essence "physically speaking" you truly are a completely different person "reborn" multiple times within one lifespan! ☺

Now let's examine how "man" is introduced in the Book of Genesis. The first mention of man is from **Genesis 1:26** in which says **"And God said, Let us make man in our image, after our likeness..."** Up to this point everything God created was from the singular point of

Chapter V: Adam and Eve

view. Now all of a sudden it says "us" and "our." It begs the question of who this *plurality* is that is now making man in **"OUR"** likeness. Hold that thought for a moment and let's look at the next mention of man from **Genesis 1:27** which states **"So God created man in his own image, in the image of God created he him; male and female created he them."** It says here that He created "male and female" but Adam isn't created until Chapter II of Genesis verses 7 – 8 and Eve isn't actually created until verses 20 – 23. The answer to this apparently confusing dilemma is simple. It may be difficult for some to swallow but once you understand the metaphysics of God's creation then it makes total sense.

Here's the explanation for the mechanics of the creation of man. God created man from two opposite ends of the spectrum similar to the pull of two oppositely charged magnets coming together. Again, let's understand that everything in creation comes from Spirit. Nothing in actuality is truly "solid" but only the perception of such. Divine beings are capable of overcoming the limitations of the physical world because they've become one with Spirit. This is why Jesus could say **"If ye have faith as a grain of mustard seed, ye shall say unto this mountain, Remove hence to yonder place; and it shall remove; and nothing shall be impossible unto you."** Matthew 17:20 We must remember that everything in existence is ultimately just another expression of the one God. God manifests His Absolute Self into innumerable forms as Creator, Preserver and Destroyer of the cosmos. Also, as other evolved celestial beings, angels, planets, animals and so on, God multiplies his Infinite Being. The One becoming many is simply the illusion of creation. Ultimately the many must again become the One... this is the purpose of life! Thus, when a soul becomes able to not only see God in everything but to feel his soul expand into everything from a flower, to the beasts of the land, to the mountain tops, to the stars in the sky then he is able to know everything to be an illusion of the One true substance – God!

There are a lot of ignorant misunderstandings about the Native Americans, Aztecs, Egyptians and others worshipping "sun gods" or the Hindus having polytheistic beliefs. Granted there are individuals within various beliefs who have themselves misunderstood advanced teachings of their spiritual predecessors, but this is no different from ignorant individuals who either misinterpret teachings of Christianity and Islam or who intentionally manipulate scripture for their own selfish purposes. God manifests Itself in all things hence the truth of His omnipresence. There is no thing "more perfect" than another. There is no "savior" more Divine than the next.

All things in creation are inherently perfect; the only difference is the degree of expression. The best metaphor I've ever come across to relate this truth is that God shines His light everywhere on all things. All the forms of creation are like lakes that reflect the rays of the moonlight. If the waters are ruffled, then the moon's reflection is distorted. This, however, doesn't change or alter the perfect rays of the moon's shine in any way. But the stiller and more placid the lake, then the "more perfect" its reflection becomes. When the lake becomes perfectly still then its reflection essentially becomes one with the moon and indistinguishable!

But I digress, back to this two-fold process of creating man. God created man from His own Spirit of Divinity. Again, He first created man in thought form and then into astral form. These heavenly beings vary in expression but are known to many as angels, celestial beings, "gods" etc. So, when God says to **"let us make man in our image, after our likeness"** He is not only referring to Himself as the Holy Trinity, He is talking about Himself as the "man" that had already been created causally and astrally. Secondly, as science has already

Chapter V: Adam and Eve

proven, although there are "creationists" who disagree, God created man's physical body through a process of billions of years of evolution. I won't bother arguing about whether man came from a "monkey" or not; to me it is an irrelevant point and a foolish discussion. The Book of Genesis already clearly states that every animal, beast of the land, bird of the air and even man were made the clearest intent. However, what it doesn't do is specify as to how.

Irrespectively, we have too many skeletal remains of ancient humans and fossils that prove man didn't always physically appear as he does today. Since evolution is an ongoing process, there's no guarantee that the man of the future will appear as we do today. The important idea to recognize and appreciate is the fact that man in a physical body is the "marriage" of Spirit with flesh. God brought together man's untouchable soul with a physical body molded through the ages of evolution specially designed to assist man in reuniting his soul with eternal Spirit. **"And the LORD God formed man of the dust of the ground, and breathed into his nostrils the breath of life; and man became a living soul." Genesis 2:7**

Man is the only creation of Gods that has the ability to express immaculately His Divinity. Adam and Eve are simply "symbolic" first beings to inhabit physical form. If we take Genesis to literally mean that Adam was the only man and Eve was the only woman then somewhere in their children's procreation, they would have had to engage in incest to produce further offspring. If man believes incest to be immoral today, why would it be any different for then? The Bible mentions three sons by name, Cain, Abel and Seth but nonetheless if there were others born afterwards then they still would have been brothers and sisters. The truth is Adam simply represents first man and Eve first woman. These first beings descended from heavenly form into physical form for a purpose to enjoy this creation, to "till the ground" by establishing a hierarchy throughout the Earth led by God-endowed wisdom and to be God's divine link between physical creation and the "non-physical" Spirit. **Genesis 2:5** tells us **"for the LORD God had not caused it to rain upon the earth, and there was not a man to till the ground."**

Again, as consistent throughout this discussion I've stated that there are often several layers from scripture hidden in metaphor or parables. In **Genesis 2:8** it states, **"And the LORD God planted a garden eastward in Eden; and there he put the man whom he had formed."** On the surface layer the Earth is being referred to as the Garden of Eden. But ancient yogis believe that this "Garden of Eden" is also referring to man's physical body. In this sense, man was placed inside the body. Therefore, he is not the body but rather a living soul who inhabits a body. "Eastward" also has a metaphysical meaning related to man's necessary "spiritual gaze" to focus his attention and consciousness at his spiritual center but we will penetrate that concept later in this discussion.

"...the tree of life also in the midst of the garden..." Genesis 2:9 As children, and for many as adults, we have always imagined some sort of "apple" tree in the middle of a botanical garden in which Adam and Eve both took a bite. This taste of the forbidden fruit led to the fall of all generations to come. The Eastern yogis believe the tree of life is actually the brain, spinal cord and nervous system. If you were to take an x-ray of this energy system and turn it upside down it would look like a tree. The brain being the roots, the spinal cord serving as the trunk of the tree and the nerve endings are the branches.

"And the LORD God took the man and put him into the garden of Eden to dress it and to keep it." Genesis 2:15 Again, if we accept for a moment that the garden is actually the physical body then man was put in it to dress it and keep it. It doesn't say that man

Chapter V: Adam and Eve

was to "become" it. The important distinction is to understand that man is a soul or spiritual being having a "physical" worldly experience. We are to care for our bodies but not to become overly consumed with them or attached to them for everyone that is born into a body must eventually depart from it. The soul's true home is in infinite eternity and not confined to a limiting physical form.

"And out of the ground made the LORD God to grow every tree that is pleasant to the sight, and good for food; the tree of life also in the midst of the garden, and the tree of knowledge of good and evil." Genesis 2:9

"And the LORD God commanded the man, saying, Of every tree of the garden thou mayest freely eat: But of the tree of the knowledge of good and evil, thou shalt not eat of it: for in the day that thou eatest thereof thou shalt surely die." Genesis 2:16-17

This "tree of life" and the "tree of the knowledge of good and evil" are essentially one and the same tree! When man lives in accordance with God's instructions and guidance then man's consciousness ascends to become a "tree of life" that brings us closer to God. When man's attention becomes fixated with outward attainments and sensory pleasures then his tree becomes a "tree of the knowledge of good and evil" being mostly evil due to man's inability to practice self-control and feel God's presence. So, to put this in terms of Adam and Eve, God instructed our symbolic ancestors to enjoy the playground of this Earth but not to eat of the tree of the knowledge of good and evil. The sexual organs happen to be this "tree in the midst of the garden" which are not the only culprit but perhaps the main culprit in drawing man's attention downward or "sense-ward" and away from the ability to experience higher spiritual perceptions. Let me clarify this point. I do not concur, along with a lot of religions, that sex is somehow a bad thing. I do not feel there are a bunch of rules or laws necessary to abide by for a healthy sex life. The consequences of our sexual decisions are more than enough to speak for themselves. However, it is the lust, desire, attachment, lack of self control etc associated with any overindulgence in sex or other sense-stimulating phenomena through repeated abuse that limit man's ability in time to experience higher states of spiritual ecstasy.

Man was originally placed into the body through the Divine act of God "breathing life into the nostrils of the body." However, man's body having been evolved through the process of evolution was still susceptible to temptations of procreation practiced by the lower form of animals. It is important to understand that all sensory engagements tend to pull man's attention away from the spiritual connection with our Creator. However, when the attention becomes absorbed in the physical "playground" of the world then the ego becomes king and man's consciousness becomes lost in the labyrinth of worldly desires. In order for the soul to regain its regal stature, man first grows tired of the temporary pleasures of life and desires more. Man then undertakes a proven process to find God within, while learning to simultaneously renounce the temptations for worldly objects, which only limit man's contentment short of the Supreme Bliss of Spirit.

Prior to the eating of the forbidden fruit, Adam and Eve saw themselves as spiritual beings in a physical form. Our physical bodies are reflections of our astral bodies of light. For every action we perform there is a karmic "equal and opposite" reaction. Once they indulged in the sexual act of gratification from the tree in the midst of the garden, their consciousness began to descend from the spiritual centers in the brain down to the lower centers of the flesh. It was then that they began to see themselves as physical bodies, hence "they were naked," and no longer could see themselves as spiritual beings. Adam and Eve, in spite of their

Chapter V: Adam and Eve

indiscretion, were still able to communicate with the Lord. However, as they gave physical birth to children "of the flesh" all the future generations would become more distant from the Source from which they came.

"In the sweat of thy face shalt thou eat bread, till thou return unto the ground; for out of it wast thou taken: for dust thou art, and unto dust shalt thou return." Genesis 3:19 As spiritual beings our souls, made in the image of God, are therefore eternal as well. After man's "fall," the consciousness, now identified with its gross physical form, is subject to all the limitations that come with being "earthbound." Since the physical body comes from the ground then it must return to the ground along with our limited awareness. Previously, spiritual beings could descend their consciousness into physical form and likewise ascend out of it at will. Now with man's consciousness attached to the flesh, he is born and "dies" along with his physical form. **"And he humbled thee, and suffered thee to hunger, and fed thee with manna, which thou knewest not, neither did thy fathers know; that he might make thee know that man doth not live by bread only, but by every word that proceedeth out of the mouth of the LORD doth man live." Deuteronomy 8:3**

Many religions have a concept of a "life force" that courses equally all throughout creation. Some call it the Holy Ghost, the Word, Chi, prana and others. Our physical bodies are supplied through the Word (Aum) of God with universal nourishment. No longer could man's soul consciously feed off the energy within the ether. The man of today and our ancestors are ignorant of the true substance, which sustains the body. It is this "manna" which allows all of the involuntary internal organs to function and operate. Without this spiritual energy the physical body would not be able to intelligently digest food, eliminate toxins, enliven the cells or serve as a suitable housing for the soul. The physical body would be no more than a lump of decaying cells that would eventually turn to dust.

So, there you have it – every human walking the face of this Earth is a descendent of the first symbolic beings of Adam and Eve. Until we learn to overcome the sensory attachments of the flesh, we will continue to be born of "the dust" and return to "the dust!" The only exceptions are the liberated souls that have already overcome the flesh and return to this physical plane of existence by the direction of the Creator to help man realize the shortcomings of our ways and ignorance. Even our spiritual cousins who serve as angels or "free" beings will only find complete liberation in an incarnation as a human being. The same way there is an entire race of billions of human beings walking the face of this Earth searching for happiness, there are innumerable other planes of existence which are inhabited by more highly evolved souls. By God's will, these souls come to teach man and redirect his attention to Spirit. Depending upon God's desire, these souls may come to Earth to play a variety of roles such as saviors, avatars, angels, spiritual leaders, messengers, subtle guides or "chance encounters."

"And the LORD God said, Behold, the man is become as one of us, to know good and evil: and now, lest he put forth his hand, and take also of the tree of life, and eat, and live for ever:" Genesis 3:22 Here are the instructions provided by God for man to follow to regain his rightful place in heaven. Man lost his "tree of life" and command over the physical world when he allowed his consciousness to fall to the lesser state of sensory attachment. Man's tree now battles between "good and evil" – the good spiritual truths that keep us near the Creator and able to walk with God and the evil actions born of ignorance that bind man to physical pleasures that become a hellish reoccurring nightmare of insatiable desires. In order for man to once again "live for ever" in heavenly Bliss, he must "put forth his hand" by consciously using his will to choose God. When man learns to master the weaknesses of the flesh and begins to "eat" of the spiritual sustenance within then he becomes fit to grow his true spiritual nature into a "tree of life!"

CHAPTER VI

The Origins of Religion

The United States Declaration of Independence states: **We hold these Truths to be self-evident, that all Men are created equal, that they are endowed by their Creator with certain unalienable Rights, that among these are Life, Liberty and the pursuit of Happiness.** These founders obviously had an understanding that there are certain laws natural to man endowed by God. God is Life and is the Source which allows all expressions of Spirit to experience such. Liberty essentially is the concept that every person has the freedom of choice and expression – another God-given gift. But it's this "pursuit of happiness" that seems to have the most intrigue. It is this pursuit that seems to motivate man to wake up in the morning, to explore, to try to become more than what he believes himself to be and it's this chase that seems to keep man equally discontent!

Why did they not say that every man has a right to be happy? What is happiness? Is it something concrete or just a state of mind? Obviously, happiness has no true definition other than what the individual defines it as. It is this pursuit of happiness that every being on the face of the Earth has in common regardless of your religion, race, nationality, gender or age. Everyone simply seeks to be happy! But what makes one person happy may not make another person happy. In addition, when a person does find happiness it never seems to permanently satisfy. We all seem to be like the greyhound chasing the ever-elusive rabbit. We may relish in the moment of seizing a particular rabbit but inevitably there always appears another "rabbit" and the chase begins anew!

Subconsciously, every individual knows that we are somehow incomplete. This feeling of incompleteness is what leads to the constant flurry of new desires for us to pursue in order to capture the ever-elusive happiness. The truth is the only thing that will provide permanent happiness is God. Our souls are incomplete until they are reunited with Spirit. The bliss of the Creator's Love is what will eternally quench the thirst of the soul. Anything outside of Completion Itself will only wet the palate of the soul but can never truly satisfy our longing for happiness and end the pursuit.

    Ever since the fall of Adam and Eve, man has been wandering aimlessly about the Earth in pursuit of his divine birthright. To assist man in finding his way home, God will often send His divine emissaries to spread His message and shine the beacon of His eternal lighthouse to guide man homeward. Keep in mind that throughout the ages of time the sections of the planet have all reflected different expressions of humanity. During less-technologically advanced eras, God has sent messengers to assume the culture and dialects of an area best suited to impart His message. There was no network of computers with internet access, no cable television or satellites and no planes or modes of rapid transportation for these messengers to spread their doctrine.

    Although, any liberated soul who has overcome the limitations of the physical world could materialize himself at any point on the planet they desired, God seems to prefer subtlety over flamboyance. God wants to attract sincere followers through His simple message of love and not as a result of a fascination with miracles. Each Divine Emissary is sent to specific areas of the globe appearing in contrasting forms, with different languages, styles of presentation and roles to play. Nonetheless, to those willing to listen most importantly to the message without becoming fixated on the messenger's form, their words of truth are universally the same.

Essentially all true religions have come about as a result of the spiritual teachings of these divine messengers. These divine beings are like spiritual Suns with numerous souls orbiting their bright centers. Those closest to these divine teachers who were ready to accept their messages benefited the most. These spiritually ready individuals themselves would be assisted in overcoming their last tests of the flesh to find permanent freedom in Spirit. Others not quite yet ready to achieve final liberation may have served lesser roles befitting their spiritual state. These spiritually advanced souls often became the scribes and disseminators of the teachings of the divine masters to the masses abroad. However, no true spiritual messenger of God has ever come to start a new religion. They have simply come to deliver a message, less by their words but more importantly with their lives as the example, to lead the masses to a truer understanding.

A religion is defined by Merriam-Webster's as a cause, principle or system of beliefs held with ardor and faith. A religion in its early stages is normally a sincere attempt of certain followers to record a master's truths and provide longevity of his teachings. It is often in sincerity that this mission is begun but it is also here where the message often becomes lost in translation. The message becomes diluted, distorted and misinterpreted. Those who have not fully perfected their understanding feebly attempt to capture the Savior's story to the best of their ability.

Unfortunately, over time the story gets handed down to generations who twist or add their spin on it. The egos of the ignorant also inject their foolish pride into the stories to separate themselves to feel superior to other's beliefs. Some would even go to the point where they are willing to go against their own Savior's teachings in order to "defend" their personal dogma by killing all non-believers who may believe a different story... and even claim it's done in the name of God! Of course, no true liberated soul of any religion who has become one with the Creator would ever approve of such tactics to defend their teachings.

The major religions of the world today all essentially fall into three major categories. The **Abrahamic Religions** all trace their historical roots to the biblical figure Abraham. These religions are considered Christianity, Islam, Judaism and sometimes the Baha'i' Faith. The second major category is called the **Indian or Dharmic Religions**, which consist of Hinduism, Buddhism, Sikhism and Jainism. The third major category is called the **East Asian Religions** and consists of Chinese folk religion, Confucianism, Taoism and Shinto. Each of these religions can then be broken down even further in various sects or churches. Most of these religions, but not all, are based upon some central spiritual figure's teachings. Those who truly listen and study the actual teachings of those individuals will often see strikingly similar concepts. They often can be boiled down to the principles of Love or the Golden Rule. The semantics may differ but if their quotes were jumbled into a basket and read aloud there would be many who wouldn't know exactly which teacher was responsible for which saying.

Hinduism is known as the oldest religion and is based on Santana Dharma – the eternal law. Hinduism unlike most other religions isn't based on any one particular spiritual figure. The writings of the Vedas form the basis of Hinduistic thought. The Vedas are perhaps some of the most ancient texts. The word Veda "knowledge, wisdom" comes from the word vid, which means, "to know." Before they were ever written down, they were passed verbally amongst the rishis, divine scribes or seers, of India. They don't credit any man with authorship of the Vedas and say the teachings were "revealed" to these spiritually advanced individuals from

Chapter VI: The Origins of Religion

the Creator Himself before the beginnings of time. A sage named Vyasa is most commonly credited with being the author of the written Vedas. There are four parts to the Vedas and as spiritual scripture they are unique in that they are perhaps the only texts that encompass mathematics, astronomy, techniques for realizing God inwardly, prophecies, poetry, philosophical thought, historical references, chants and more.

The Vedas were first spoken and then written in Sanskrit. Sanskrit is an ancient language that means "put together, well or completely formed, refined, and highly elaborated." The English language has 26 sounds consisting of vowels and consonants and Sanskrit is said to have almost twice as many approximated between 50 – 52. The Vedas have stories within them, part of which are the Upanishads which in turn contain the Bhagavad-Gita. In this well-known story the spiritual figure known as Krishna, the manifestation of Godhead, gives guidance to Arjuna who represents every human being faced with the task of spiritual battle against the evils of ignorance. Like other religions, Hinduism has many sects or denominations within it. Because of some ignorance and misunderstandings, Hinduism has many variations from atheism, monotheism, panentheism to polytheism due to the various interpretations of the Vedas.

Buddhism is an Eastern religion predominantly found in Asia. The religion is based on Siddhartha Gautama's teachings that lived around 500 BC. He became known as "the Buddha," which means – the awakened one. Buddha was born as a prince, son of the king Suddodhana. It was prophesized that he would grow to become either a great king or a holy man. In order to ensure that his son would become king, his father attempted to confine him within the palace walls and create an artificial "heaven" for his son.

However, Gautama eventually ventured outside the palace against his father's wishes and became exposed for the first time to the real world and those suffering within it. He determined that he would meditate incessantly, seeking answers to his questions about life and suffering until God responded. Along this path of renunciation, he overcame all the tests of man and ultimately found his eternal emancipation as an awakened soul free from the sufferings of man. Taoism, Confucianism, and Buddhism have been ideological and political rivals for centuries but at the same time have deeply influenced one another. They all share some similar values and all three embrace a humanist philosophy emphasizing moral behavior and human perfection.

Of the Abrahamic religions, Judaism is the oldest. Judaism is based on a set of beliefs, as well as practices, that originate from the saga of the ancient Israelites, embodied in the Hebrew Bible known as the Tanakh and also later further expanded in the Talmud along with other texts. Judaism originates itself as a covenantal relationship between the Children of Israel, known as the Jewish nation, and God. Many historians consider it the first monotheistic religion. The followers of Judaism are called Jews, and while Judaism is open to converts, the Jewish collective is regarded as an ethno-religious group. This belief is a result of the interpretations from their sacred texts that define them as a nation, rather than as the followers of a faith. According to Jewish tradition, the God who created the heavens and earth established a covenant with the Israelites and their descendants, and revealed his laws and commandments to Moses, who "lifted up the serpent in the wilderness," on Mount Sinai in the form of both the Written and Oral Torah.

Abraham is a key figure from the Book of Genesis and a common ancestor in several monotheistic religions. Jewish, Christian and Muslim traditions regard him as the founding patriarch of the Israelites, Ishmaelites and the Edomite peoples. The name

Chapter VI: The Origins of Religion

Abraham means "Father of Nations" – "Av" is Hebrew for "Father," and "Raham" is Arabic for "Nations or Multitude." It is also considered to mean "High Father," coming from the Aramaic words "Aba Rama." According to the book of Genesis, Abraham was brought by God from Mesopotamia to the land of Canaan. It is here that Abraham entered into a covenant with the Creator. In exchange for sole recognition of YHWH as the Supreme Universal Deity and Authority, Abraham would be blessed with innumerable progeny.

In the Jewish faith, he is called *Avraham Avinu* or "Abraham, our Father." God then promised Abraham that through his offspring, all the nations of the world would also come to be blessed. The Christians interpret this reference particularly to the coming of Jesus Christ. Jews, Christians, and Muslims consider him father of the people of Israel through his son Isaac. For Muslims, he is considered a prophet of Islam and the ancestor of Muhammad through his other son Ishmael whom was born to him by his wife's servant, Hagar.

Islam is a monotheistic, Abrahamic religion originating with the teachings of the Islamic prophet Muhammad, a 7th century Arab religious and political figure. The word *Islam* means "submission" or the total surrender of oneself to God. An adherent of Islam is known as a Muslim, meaning "one who submits to God." Muslims believe that God revealed the Qur'an to Muhammad, God's final prophet, through the angel Gabriel, and regard the Qur'an and the Sunnah, the words and deeds of Muhammad, as the fundamental sources of Islam. They do not regard Muhammad as the founder of a new religion, but as the restorer of the original monotheistic faith of Adam, Abraham, Moses, Jesus, and other prophets. Islam includes many religious practices. Adherents are generally required to observe the Five Pillars of Islam, which are five duties that unite Muslims into a community.

In addition to the Five Pillars, Islamic law has developed a tradition of rulings that touch on virtually all aspects of life and society. This tradition encompasses everything from practical matters like dietary laws, banking, warfare and welfare. Almost all Muslims belong to one of two major denominations, the Sunni (85%) and Shi'a (15%). The schism developed in the late 7th century following disagreements over some religious differences in practice and who was the next rightful heir to Muslim leadership. Sufism is not considered a denomination but is a mystical-ascetic form of Islam. It focuses more on the spiritual aspects of the religion. The Sufi strives to obtain direct experience of God by making use of "intuitive and emotional faculties" that one must be trained in to utilize.

The word Islam is given a number of meanings in the Qur'an. In some verses, the quality of Islam as an internal conviction is stressed as: **"Whomsoever God desires to guide, He expands his breast to Islam."** Other verses connect *islam* and *dīn* (usually translated as "religion") as: **"Today, I have perfected your religion for you; I have completed My blessing upon you; I have approved Islam for your religion."** Still others describe Islam as an **"action of spiritually returning to God"** — more than just a verbal affirmation of faith.

Muslims consider the Qur'an to be the literal word of God; it is the central religious text of Islam. Muslims believe that the verses of the Qur'an were revealed to Muhammad by God through the angel Gabriel. The Qur'an was reportedly written down by Muhammad's companions while he was alive, although the prime method of transmission was orally. In Muslim tradition, Muhammad is viewed as not only the last but the greatest in a series of prophets — as the man closest to perfection, the possessor of all virtues. During this time, Muhammad preached to the people of Mecca, imploring them to abandon polytheism. Although some converted to Islam, Muhammad and his followers were persecuted by the leading Meccan authorities. After 13 years of preaching, Muhammad and the Muslims performed the *Hijra* (emigration) to the city of Medina (formerly known as *Yathrib*) in 622.

There, with the Medinan converts and the Meccan migrants, Muhammad established his political and religious authority. Over the years, two significant battles were fought against Meccan forces: the Battle of Badr in 624, a Muslim victory, and the Battle of Uhud in 625, without a declared victor. Conflict with Medinan Jewish clans who opposed the Muslims led to their exile, enslavement or death, and the Jewish enclave of Khaybar was subdued. At the same time, Meccan trade routes were cut off as Muhammad brought surrounding desert tribes under his control. By 629 Muhammad was victorious in the nearly bloodless Conquest of Mecca, and by the time of his death in 632 he ruled over the Arabian Peninsula.

Christianity is a monotheistic religion centered on the life and teachings of Jesus as presented in the New Testament. Christian theology claims that Jesus Christ is a teacher, model of a virtuous life, revealer of God, as well as an incarnation of God, and most importantly the savior of humanity who suffered, died, and was resurrected to bring about salvation from sin. Christians maintain that Jesus ascended into heaven, and most denominations teach that Jesus will return to judge the living and the dead, granting everlasting life to his followers. Christians call the message of Jesus Christ the Gospel ("good news") and hence label the earliest written accounts of his ministry as gospels.

The central tenet of Christianity is the belief in Jesus as the Son of God and the Messiah (Christ). The title "Messiah" comes from the Hebrew word (*māšiáḥ*) meaning *anointed one*. The Greek translation (*Christos*) is the source of the English word "Christ." Christians believe that, as the Messiah, Jesus was anointed by God as ruler and savior of humanity, and hold that Jesus' coming was the fulfillment of messianic prophecies of the Old Testament. The Christian concept of the Messiah differs significantly from the contemporary Jewish concept. The core Christian belief is that, through the death and resurrection of Jesus, sinful humans can be reconciled to God and thereby are offered salvation and the promise of eternal life.

While there have been many theological disputes over the nature of Jesus over the first centuries of Christian history, Christians generally believe that Jesus is the "unique or only" son of God incarnate and simultaneously "true God and true man" (or both fully divine and fully human). Now Jesus, having become fully human, suffered the pains and temptations of a mortal man, yet he did not sin. As a personified aspect of the Holy Trinity, he defeated death and rose to life again. According to the Bible, "resurrected himself," and ultimately ascended to heaven, and is "seated at the right hand of the Father." He will return again to fulfill the rest of Messianic prophecy such as the Resurrection of the dead, the Last Judgment and final establishment of the Kingdom of God.

In the early years of the expansion of Christianity, there were many different sects who had different understandings of Jesus' teachings including the Gnostics who believed that each man was to seek God within himself. According to the Gospels of Matthew and Luke, Jesus was conceived by the Holy Spirit and born from the Virgin Mary. Little of Jesus' childhood is recorded in the canonical Gospels, however infancy Gospels were popular in antiquity. In comparison, his adulthood, especially the week before his death, are well documented in the Gospels contained within the New Testament. The Biblical accounts of Jesus' ministry include: his birth, baptism, miracles, teachings, and resurrection.

According to the author Levi in "The Aquarian Gospel of Jesus the Christ" he suggests a peculiar claim

Chapter VI: The Origins of Religion

that I'll present, and you can decide for yourself. Abraham is the patriarch of the Jews and the Arabs. As we know from the old testament of the Bible that Abraham is supposedly the father of all nations. **"That in blessing I will bless thee, and in multiplying I will multiply thy seed as the stars of the heaven, and as the sand which is upon the sea shore; and thy seed shall possess the gate of his enemies; And in thy seed shall all the nations of the earth be blessed; because thou hast obeyed my voice." Genesis 22:17-18** The three religions of Christianity, Judaism and Islam are all sometimes referred to as the Abrahamic religions because they all trace their history to this biblical figure.

Now Abraham was originally named Abram prior to God changing his name. Abram supposedly means "exalted father" and Abraham means "father of many." Now Abram was originally from Ur of the Chaldees (Chaldea), which is supposedly somewhere in what was then Mesopotamia however no one disputes the cultural and religious influence of Chaldea upon Judaism and Christianity. Some argue Abram was in the northern part, which is current day Turkey. Some say he was in the southern part, which is current day Iraq. Regardless, Levi suggests that the name Abram was actually a name distinguished as A-brahm meaning that he was a very devout follower of a Brahmic Faith (Indian Dharmic Religion).

Primarily in India, they developed a caste system that originally had good intentions of attempting to identify an individual's basic characteristics. An individual belonged to one of four castes, which are the Sudra – interested in primarily satisfying the bodily needs who perform the manual labor; the Vaisya – more ambitious for worldly gain and become more of the thinkers in labor; the Kshatriya – who become the noble rulers, statesmen and warriors and finally the Brahmin – the spiritual leaders and clergymen. At the time, the Brahmin had supposedly become corrupt and ignorant of the true spiritual teachings and began idol worship. As stated earlier, Brahman is known as the Absolute Spirit or God. These teaching derive from the Vedas and the word Brahman comes from Sanskrit and means, "to grow." Brahma means "knowledge" and Brahmin means "learned."

A-brahm (Abraham) was supposedly a pious and virtuous Brahmin who had not become corrupted with the many members at the time. Let us recall that this is roughly around 2000 BC in which Judaism, Islam and Christianity had not existed at the time. With Mesopotamia being in the East and knowing that the only Brahmic (Dharmic – Hinduism, Buddhism etc) religions that could possibly date back that far, it is very conceivable that the culture and religious influence could have spread outwards towards Mesopotamia. Nonetheless, this may be justification why there seems to be an underlying unity of all religions stemming from the Vedas and Sanatana Dharma – Eternal Law.

Another concept of worship, not all that popular amongst the masses, is known as mysticism. Mysticism is the pursuit of communion with, identity with, or conscious awareness of an ultimate reality, divinity, spiritual truth, or God through **direct** experience, intuition, or insight. All the world religions have within them an aspect which believes that man is capable of directly knowing God in the here and now.

Mysticism usually centers on a practice or practices intended to nurture that experience or awareness. The masses of today are predominantly driven by their senses and the interaction with the outside world therefore these practices have been lost over the years but there are followers who pass down their techniques for realizing their relationship with the Creator. I think there are some misperceptions about the term "mysticism." Because of the name it sounds like its some sort of fantasy experience or witchcraft, but this is far from its purpose. Mysticism may be dualistic, maintaining a distinction between the self and the divine, or may be non-dualistic meaning all distinctions are illusion and only the Self experiences and realizes Self. Various religious traditions have described this fundamental mystical experience in some of the following ways:

- Nullification and absorption within God's Infinite Light (*Chassidic schools of Judaism*)
- Complete detachment from the world (*Kaivalya in some schools of Hinduism, including Sankhya and Yoga; Jhana in Buddhism*)
- Gnosis or Inner Knowledge (*Gnosticism in Christianity*)
- Liberation from the cycles of Karma (*Moksha in Jainism and Hinduism, Nirvana In Buddhism*)
- Deep intrinsic connection to the world (*Satori in Mahayana Buddhism, Te in Taoism*)
- Union with God (*Henosis in Neo-Platonism and Theosis in Christianity, Brahma-Prapti or Brahma-Nirvana in Hinduism*)
- Innate Knowledge (*Irfan and fitra in Islam*)
- Experience of one's true blissful nature (*Samadhi or Svarupa-Avirbhava in Hinduism*)

Regardless of your religious practice, the purpose of mysticism is to lead one towards enlightenment. *Enlightenment* or *Illumination* are generic English terms for the phenomenon, derived from the Latin *illuminatio* (applied to Christian prayer in the 15th century) and adopted in English translations of Buddhist texts, but used loosely to describe the state of mystical attainment regardless of faith. Mystic traditions generally form sub-currents within larger religious traditions – such as Kabbalah within Judaism, Sufism within Islam, Vedanta within Hinduism, Christian mysticism and Gnosticism within Christianity – but are often treated skeptically and held separate, due to their emphasis on living realization over doctrine. Mysticism is sometimes taken by skeptics or mainstream adherents as merely a distortion, though mystics suggest they are offering clarity of a different order or kind.

In today's world, the followers of these many religions consisting of many different denominations for the most part coexist peacefully. The individuals of faith tend to respect another's right to worship according to their beliefs. Although there are clearly differences in belief and practice, most conflicts of today are not necessarily a result of the contrasts in religion but more so a result of the intertwined issues of land, money, politics and power. Some of these issues are deeply rooted over the ages. However, if we look at the basic teachings of the various religions and the messages, they deliver they all acknowledge that there is a God and that He is the Creator of all.

If we study further into the practices of the messengers themselves, we see that they all seem to share a common link of direct contact with Spirit. All of the principles of these faiths encourage man to seek a more personal relationship with God. Unfortunately, the masses rather than studying the scriptures of their religion for themselves, depend on another "follower of the faith" to interpret for them. In most cases, we have the blind leading the blind. If we examine the lives of the spiritual figures from all the various texts, we see that they all, including Abraham, Jesus, Buddha, Muhammad, Krishna etc, exercised similar practices of fasting and meditation. There is a consistent theme that man is a three-part being that should purify himself physically through means of diet and exercise, expand his thinking with dutiful and righteous stimulating thought and should connect his inner being or essence with that of the Creator through some form of inward contact and devotion.

Unfortunately, we seem to have more religious followers who are more concerned with cleaning up

Chapter VI: The Origins of Religion

their neighbor's backyard rather than focusing on their own backyard. Regardless of your faith or your religious practices, we shouldn't be forcing non-believers to believe or convert to our way of worship. If you are a spiritual truth-seeker then your sincere search and effort to achieve salvation will eventually be found. What limits an individual is the idea that they already have the answers, although their life and personal relationship with God doesn't reflect this. Whether you are a Christian, Muslim, Hindu or other, you can get to know God with patience and perseverance. God created man in the first symbolic Adam and Eve. Man has always had a direct connection with the Creator prior to generations ever having created a religion or ever even having a need for one! This is what has unfortunately been lost over the ages.

      The eastern saints of old called this personal relationship with God – Yoga, which means "union." When man focuses his full attention and being on any goal, he is able to create great pieces of art, sculpture, monuments, writings, skyscrapers, etc. God is no exception! This process of centering your attention is called concentration when you're creating a song, drafting a sketch, playing a sport or anything else. Concentrating on Spirit is called dharana which leads to dhyana - meditation. There are scientific techniques that assist man in relaxing the body and calming the mind to promote greater concentration and clarity. But even without techniques, a consistent and devoted effort with reverence will allow you to feel His presence. When your concentration on God becomes great enough union is achieved!

      Anything we desire to do in life requires great focus and drive. If you want to be a successful business man, politician or artist it takes years to become great. Some studies have shown that it takes as many as 10 years to become great in any particular skill. If we can have that sort of focus and drive in getting to know our

Creator, then how much more will you be benefitted than by merely mastering an instrument. When you know God all of creation becomes your flute.

If you are a Christian, be a sincere and loving Christian.
If you are a Muslim, be a sincere and loving Muslim.
If you are a Hindu, be a sincere and loving Hindu.
If you are a Jew, be a sincere and loving Jew.
If you are a Buddhist, be a sincere and loving Buddhist.
And even if you are an Atheist, be a sincere and loving Atheist.

This is the essence of religion. Let love be your religion. Study your scriptures with earnest interest and one by one dissect them, pray on them, meditate on them and thus make the "words into flesh." Even the atheist who may not believe in God can appreciate the concept of loving his fellow man. The atheist just hasn't yet realized that it is the God within who is the true Lover. Regardless of your religious faith, it is your love for God, love for life and love for your fellow human beings that magnetically attracts God's blessing. To become great in your presence with God, being advanced in meditation techniques is helpful, but ultimately it is your loving devotion and God's grace that will manifest everlasting Bliss!

Chapter VI: The Origins of Religion

CHAPTER VII

Reconciling Science and Religion

What started off as a humorous question pondering the cyclic events of nature has now actually evolved into a truly thought-provoking "causality dilemma." That question is "Which came first the chicken or the egg"? If a chicken can only be hatched from an egg and an egg can only be laid from a chicken, then how could we possibly find a starting point for this never-ending circle of inter-dependent events? The obvious answer is – you can't! Mind-boggling concepts such as these cannot be explained with thought or scientific investigation. We may be able to find clues but that will not produce indisputable evidence.

Those attempting to answer this question will undoubtedly approach it from many different angles. Some may seek to solve this riddle by experimentation and available data. Others may search for answers through supernatural attempts to find the solution from the source, which they believe created both the chicken and the egg in the first place. These two approaches often times find themselves on opposite ends of the spectrum. What they don't realize is that although they are on two very different paths, they'll eventually end up at the same place, which will provide the truest answer. Mankind has classified these opposite points of view generally as the "scientific" community and the "religious" community. The majority of this book has been an attempt to equally balance the religious/spiritual perspective alongside with the more scientific angle.

Science is the effort to discover and increase human understanding of how physical reality works through knowledge. Using controlled methods, scientists collect data in the form of observations, records of observable physical evidence of natural phenomena and analyze this information to construct theoretical explanations of how things work. Knowledge in science is gained through research. The methods of scientific research include the generation of hypotheses about how natural phenomena work as well as experimentation that tests these hypotheses under controlled conditions. The outcome or product of this empirical scientific process is the formulation of theories that describe human understanding of various physical processes in addition to facilitating prediction.

A religion is a set of stories, symbols, beliefs and practices, often with a supernatural quality, that give meaning to the practitioner's experiences of life through reference of an ultimate power or reality. It may be expressed through prayer, ritual, meditation, music and art, among other things. It may focus on specific supernatural, metaphysical, and moral claims about reality (the cosmos and human nature) which may yield a set of religious laws, ethics and a particular lifestyle. Religion also encompasses ancestral or cultural traditions, writings, history and mythology, as well as personal faith and religious experience. The term "religion" refers to both the personal practices related to communal faith and to group rituals and communication stemming from shared conviction. "Religion" is sometimes used interchangeably with "faith" or "belief system," but it is more socially defined than personal convictions and it entails specific behaviors, respectively.

Science attempts to explain how things work. Science can tell us how molecules combine to form compounds. It tells us how gravity works and how the Earth moves through space and at what speed. Science tells us how babies are made and how a sperm

Chapter VII: Reconciling Science and Religion

unites with the ovum and then begins to multiply. It tells us how clouds are formed and what causes them to rain. Often the limitation with science is that it doesn't tell us "why" things work the way they do. It doesn't tell us why molecules combine to form compounds. It doesn't tell us why bodies of mass exert gravitational forces. It doesn't tell us why the Earth spins on its axis or why the solar system moves through space. It doesn't tell us why a sperm and ovum unite or why these cells then multiply or why certain cells become certain types of skeletal, muscular or other tissues. It doesn't tell us why water has several phases or why it rains or why we even need rain.

Religion does attempt to tell us why and the answer is always – God. However, this answer of God cannot be proven or experimented with by our current scientific methods. Because of this lack of proof, the scientific community attempts to not acknowledge this Spiritual Entity since it cannot be indisputably recorded and/or tested. Religion feebly attempts to justify the existence of God through a means of blind faith. This blind faith is generally based mostly on scripture and not so much on one's personal experience. Because scripture is based on the words of divine beings, we attempt to accept them whole-heartedly – for to question them would somehow mean a lack of faith. Thus, we have the ultimate dilemma: Religionists don't want to acknowledge that their understanding of scripture is truly limited. Likewise, the scientists don't want to acknowledge that their empirical evidence is still just a theory. That theory is just the most widely accepted idea until new evidence comes along to replace the current theory.

What is needed most is a marriage of the two. Anyone who disputes the significance of scientific data because it may appear to contradict their religious belief is simply being ignorant. Similarly, any scientist who believes this entire universe is simply the result of chance or coincidence is not only ignoring the laws of mathematical probabilities but they're not exercising much common sense either. To serve mankind the most, we need to bring science and religion into harmony. We must attempt to better understand the "how" as well as the "why." Ultimately, God is the greatest author, storyteller, poet, mathematician, scientist, magician, musician and artist. All attributes are the expressions of His omnipresent truth.

Essentially, every law of physics is merely the counterpart of a spiritual law. In fact, there really is only one law and it finds its expression differently depending upon the medium being examined. There are many laws in science ranging from thermodynamics, motion, relativity, magnetism and quantum physics to name a few. Although this is not intended to be a science journal, I think it is beneficial to understand some of the underlying spiritual laws that define these physical principles.

It helps to start with the basics regardless of whether or not science can prove it. In the beginning and in the end, there is only God. This source is Absolute and therefore in contrast, there is nothing that exists that can be separate or apart from It. In Absolute terms, even words like Omnipresence, Omniscience and Omnipotence don't truly have any meaning except on this level of dualistic creation. However, on the level of creation these terms have the next most significant meaning. We could start with any of these concepts, but they all have their outward expression of His consciousness, which are revealed as "laws" on the physical plane.

For example, if we take the truth of God being Omnipresent then that means that He is everywhere and there is no place that exists that He is not present. This in turn means He is infinite. Of course, if you're infinite then the word itself doesn't really have any meaning except in terms of there being limited space.

Chapter VII: Reconciling Science and Religion

Science has already "proven" that the universe as we know it is expanding. So, the next logical question is what is it expanding into? Or what is outside of the universe? The answer is – nothing! There's no thing, at least not in the terms in which we understand "something." There is in fact some *thing* outside of it and that is God. Science has told us that the universe started out as an extremely small point of dense matter no bigger than the tip of a needle. Well, guess what? Even though we now experience the universe to be an incomprehensibly massive amount of space, relative to an infinitely large Creator, it is still the size of the tip of a needle!

What the great scientists of spirit have come to realize is that all matter is simply energy. All energy is nothing more than God's thought in motion. The great sage Paramahansa Yogananda labeled these small sub-atomic particles "thought-trons." They could've just as easily been called idea-trons, life-trons or God-trons. The point is that the deeper we dive into matter the more we realize that it doesn't really consist of any particular substance. Ultimately, it is all only comprised of consciousness. Perhaps this is what the scientists are referring to when they attempt to describe a substance known as anti-matter. How do you measure or weigh consciousness? Thus, once we realize that consciousness is everywhere, we begin to better understand the laws of thermodynamics, which attempts to measure the effects of heat, temperature, energy, entropy and so on.

Heat or temperature is simply the measurement of how much energy a particular "substance" has. Energy is the measurement of movement of atomic particles. Atomic particles are composed of the simple interplay of positively and negatively charged particles, which are nothing more than ideas of God. If God removes the idea, then all the subatomic particles and matter "disappear." If we begin with these "assumptions" then we're better able to understand the laws of thermodynamics and the concepts of entropy and items seeking equilibrium. We also understand why science has yet been able to bring the temperature of a substance to absolute zero.

In order to bring a substance to absolute zero it would require a scientist to remove all of the energy from a substance. Since matter doesn't truly exist and energy is just a measure of a "thought in motion" it would require you to completely freeze a thought. But how do you freeze a thought? A thought is nothing more than an expressed idea and an idea only has meaning in relation to another idea. Therefore, to completely remove the "energy" from an idea means the idea no longer exists. Man doesn't have the power to completely remove an idea of God's. Only God can cease a thought and if He does then that idea and hence the physical reflection of that idea, which we call matter, no longer "exist."

If we examine Newton's Laws of Motion, we find there are certain observed effects of bodies of mass in motion in relation to one another. The most popular of these laws is the third law which in laymen's terms states that "for every action there is an equal and opposite reaction." In the physical world, this translates that if you were to push on a certain object such as a wall then that wall is pushing back on you with equal and opposite force. Now you may ask, "what if I push through the wall"? Well then this takes us back to the first law of thermodynamics, which states "energy cannot be created nor destroyed only altered in form." Essentially, the energy you exert in pushing through the wall was converted into thermal energy due to the friction of the wall, material breaking and sound energy in the form of the cracking noise emitted.

Similarly, the underlying spiritual principle for this physical phenomenon is the law of karma. Karma is the law of cause and effect. For every action you commit

Chapter VII: Reconciling Science and Religion

unto another, the same shall be done unto you. The reason for this law is based in the fact that all of the infinitely perceived objects in creation are really just expressions of the One God. Therefore, everything we do unto another we're actually doing unto God. God's exacting law of karma sees to it that you experience the same effect of what you commit against another. Unlike the physical equivalent of this law, which happens immediately, the law of karma can be instantaneous or may happen at a later time, but it is always unfailing. (Remember time is an illusion). Just because you strike another person doesn't mean that someone will immediately strike you, however, there will eventually be an equal and opposite "force" or experience that will be equivalent. There is one significant difference with the law of karma though. Through God's grace, it is possible to be relieved of a karmic burden if one sincerely seeks it or if the individual has a mediator who knows how to absorb or redirect that person's karma. This is what it means to have a Savior. That Savior intercedes on our behalf to assist our spiritual realization.

Albert Einstein was one of the greatest scientists ever. Part of his greatness was due to the fact that he was very creative and spiritual. He seemed to have an intuitive understanding that all things in creation were somehow connected. He used this notion in his approach to scientific experimentation. Through his investigations, he developed what is known as the theory of relativity. The basis of this theory is that energy and mass are equivalent and transmutable. This theory also had several consequences that became relevant such as the speed of light, black holes and four interconnected issues revolving around time, size, energy and mass.

What these conclusions in summary state is that no object, animate or otherwise, can travel faster than the speed of light. But it's very intriguing to analyze how these conclusions are drawn if we look at the four fundamental factors individually. The first deals with a concept called time dilation. This idea declares that the faster an object travels the slower its perception of time becomes. This is determined by the equation $D=\sqrt{(1-(v^2/c^2))}$. D stands for time dilation, V stands for the speed of the moving object and C stands for the speed of light, which is a constant. As the speed of the moving object approaches closer and closer to the speed of light, perception of time becomes slower and slower. At the speed of light, time perception goes to zero and slows down infinitely. What this means in simple terms is that if something were to be able to travel at the speed of light it would in essence be everywhere at once and its perception of time would be non-existent!

The next intriguing factor deals with a concept known as the "shrinking factor." What this states is that the faster an object travels, the smaller it becomes in its direction of motion. To an outside observer its length and distance become unnoticeable. Once the object reaches the speed of light, its size becomes zero and it in essence "disappears." This relationship proves that in essence, time and space are one and is thus referred to as space-time.

The last two factors are interrelated and are expressed with the familiar equation of $E=mc^2$. This formula is traditionally used for an object at rest but the variation of it is $E=mc^2/\sqrt{(1-v^2/c^2)}$ which is the theory of relativity divided by the time dilation. What this shows is that energy and mass are in direct correlation and fluctuate with changes in velocity. As an object's velocity increases, so does the object's mass and thus the energy needed to reach the speed of light becomes infinite. Likewise as an object's speed increases, an infinite amount of energy added makes the object infinitely massive. Now to tie all these conclusions together we must ask ourselves "What object has the ability to move at the speed light and thus become timeless, infinitely small to the point it

Chapter VII: Reconciling Science and Religion

disappears, possess infinite energy and be equally infinitely massive"? This "object" would be everywhere at once, all-powerful and all knowing – Omnipresent, Omnipotent and Omniscient! Hmmm... sounds like God to me.

This science proves that nothing can travel faster than the speed of light. This is true. However, the Creator is not a "thing." Rather He is Absolute and Pure Consciousness. It is not possible to comprehend or to describe such an Entity as this. Again, in order to make the jump from the laws of nature to the laws of Spirit a "thing" must realize that it is not actually a "thing" but rather ALL things and yet NONE of these things. The One becomes Many and the many becomes One! **"I am that I am!" Exodus 3:14**

Lastly, Einstein's studies in the theory of relativity led to a concept known as a black hole. A black hole is simply a region of space in which the gravitational pull is so strong that nothing including light can escape it. A black hole is difficult to identify because it doesn't look any different from any other area of black space. The only way a black hole can be identified is through its interaction with matter orbiting its event horizon.

"Event horizon" is an area surrounding the black hole known as the boundary in space-time inside which anything that passes through the horizon appears to freeze in place and get sucked in. According to Einstein, as mass is added to a degenerate star a collapse suddenly takes place creating an intense gravitational field causing the star to close in on itself. There are many theories on black holes, but they all seem to have one or all of these three properties of mass, charge and angular momentum. These observations are important but do not answer the questions of "why star's collapse upon themselves," "how does a gravitational field generate strong enough magnetism to even pull in light" and finally "where does all this matter go"?

Now I'm not a scientist and I've never read this anywhere before but based upon my own research and piecing together scientific as well as spiritual ideas, I've drawn some of my own hypotheses. From earlier suggestions concerning the cycle and ages of civilization we've seen that mankind seems to progress through various stages of spiritual growth. When a certain solar system has gone through a full cycle and the inhabitants have either become completely spiritual (good) or completely material (evil) then that solar system may be dissolved back into the abyss of the Absolute. After a certain amount of time that solar system may be "reborn" again to learn in the classroom of gross creation. As stated earlier, only God has the ability to freeze time, suspend an idea or magnetically draw creation back into Himself.

According to the concept of the yugas or cycles of man's virtue, mankind grows in its understandings of matter and electricities and I think this is reflective in society today with the technological advances we've made. The next area of major understanding will be in the fields of magnetism, which underlies all of the properties of man and creation. If you believe in an Omnipresent Creator, then all of creation has inherent consciousness and intelligence. These are attributes of the Creator. On the physical level this means that every subatomic particle (idea) is seeking greater expression. This expression evolves in form from individual atoms, to groupings of atoms in inanimate objects, to plant life and on to animal expression. Up to this point, the evolving expression is primarily influenced by outside forces of nature. When this intelligent expression finds its way into manifestation, as a self-aware man, then the consciousness has to "choose" further expansion through acts of free will. In due time, every man finds his greatest expression through a voluntary self-evolvement by uniting his consciousness with that of the Infinite.

Chapter VII: Reconciling Science and Religion

Hence, the experience we call life becomes complete and the individual expression becomes whole in Spirit.

I believe humanity will be best served when religious thought becomes less threatened by science. Likewise, science should not be used as some sort of weapon to disprove things beyond our intellectual propensity to grasp. Religion must learn to utilize scientific evidence to remove problematic dogma that has surfaced throughout the ages as a result of ignorance or lack of understanding. Scientists will most greatly flourish when they learn to become more creative and intuitive and accept, if even just for a moment, that perhaps **"There are more things in heaven and earth, Horatio, than are dreamt of in your philosophy." Shakespeare** All things under the sun cannot be understood simply from beneath a microscope. Art, music, poetry, love and life are all examples of human qualities that are adored and cherish and find their greatest value in the eye of the beholder and not as a result of a formula or equation. Balance between things seen and unseen is the key to truth. **"All religions, arts and sciences are branches of the same tree."**

Albert Einstein

PART II: LIFE

CHAPTER VIII

Who Am I?

Breishit is the original word used to name the first of five books of the Torah, part of the Holy scriptures upon which Judaism is founded and the word means "in the beginning." The Greeks later interpreted the word as **Genesis** and this word has been most popularly used since and means "birth or origin." This book symbolically describes the beginning of creation leading all the way to the birth and origin of man. Man becomes the highest expression in God's creation being made in His image. Thus, the interaction of man with God's creation and the experiences accumulated is what I call **Life**. Man's body was supposedly made from the Earth and upon death shall return to the dust. However, within the body is the *"living soul breathe into the nostrils by God."* This begs the question, "after this experience called Life, what happens to the living soul upon death of the body"?

The most fundamental and age-old question of any self-conscious being has always been "Who am I"? For an atheist who may not believe in a God, that answer may be that we are simply conscious physical bodies that evolved through a process of nature, born as a result of sex between two people of opposite genders, live a certain time period on this Earth and will cease to exist once the necessary bodily functions fail to operate. But every atheist must at least acknowledge that they themselves are not responsible for their own existence. Science tells us that for every effect there is a cause. If we are all simply the effect of our parent's procreation, and they are merely the offspring from their parents, and so on – then no one is responsible for their own creation. But what was the first cause that put this whole process into motion? How can you have a chain of events resulting in the population of billions of people on the Earth without something having started this domino effect?

A person of faith believes that God is that First Cause. However, even the majority of religious people's perspective isn't that far different from the atheist. Their visions of life and the after-life seem to be very much identified with the physical form. They imagine a life of good versus evil, heaven versus hell, God versus Satan; and the individuals who live a life approved by God will enter the gates of heaven in eternal salvation. Of course, those "not approved" will suffer in hell. But even the average person of blind faith remains unable to answer questions such as "Where is heaven"? "Will I still be black or white, American or Asian and male or female when I die"? "If I make it to heaven, will my family still be the same"? "Will I appear to be young or old"? "Are there still religions in heaven"? "Is everyone in heaven a Christian or will there be any Muslims, Buddhists, Jews or Hindus"? "Oh, and by the way, how do I know if I'll make it to heaven"? "Will I have done enough good to be worthy"? These sorts of questions are what lead most people on a path or search for answers.

Unfortunately, most people are told the answers by their parents or society at an early age and therefore believe they've found the truth without ever having actually done their homework themselves. The problem is that their parents were told the answers as well from their parents and people become fearful to question what they may have been told and thus no one actually takes the time to scrutinize their beliefs so that they truly understand their meaning. This leads to a form of outer worship and a mindset in which all I have to do

Chapter VIII: Who am I?

is follow certain rules and then I should have a place in heaven. Even more disturbing is the fact that the personal relationship that each and every one of us is capable of having with God gets lost.

Most people aren't even aware that they may get to know the Creator personally or are told to fear God so they probably wouldn't want to truly face God if they had the opportunity. God's universal laws may be exacting but as any loving parent who has a child can testify, love, grace and the desire to protect our children far exceed our wrath, anger or disappointment with them. But if you really think about it, what need would God have to be wrathful? I mean after all, if He were truly all-powerful and all-knowing, why would He be angry at His own creation? If any one of us were painting a picture and we didn't like how it turned out, we would simply scrap the painting and start a new one without any hesitation or afterthought, much less any attachment to it. Some may consider this blasphemous but if He gave us free will and we exercise it to His dissatisfaction shouldn't He be upset with Himself? If He didn't like what He was seeing, couldn't He just make it all disappear with the blink of an eye or just remove our free will from us? Fortunately, God is not so easily tested or tempted. Because He is all knowing and all seeing, this creation and man's interaction therein was to be expected and it is all by design.

The truth is we are made in God's image and to truly live up to that meaning we must have the free will He has as well. The goal is for us to consciously become like the Creator and utilize our free will guided by His wisdom. But since this Earth has been around for a very long time and there are billions of people on this planet, it is apparent that God is very patient. In actuality, it is man that has little patience and we have no control of our emotions because the ego is fragile and easily upset. So, man instead tries to impose our inability to accept and forgive onto God, when in fact it is only when our highest expression of love becomes pure and all-embracing that we are truly in tune with the Creator's nature.

Sometimes the best way to discover who you are is to first realize who you are not. Despite all of your interaction with the world, what society tells you, what you see in the mirror and what you feel... you are not your body! The universe is God's body although He exists beyond the physical universe. Likewise, although our bodies do serve a purpose, we are souls that exist beyond our physical frames. Our diversity in appearances is primarily due to exposure to different climates over time but more importantly is by design so that we may learn to embrace one another and to see God's universal presence everywhere. Variation is a result of relative creation. Singularity is the state of Absolute Spirit. The world we live in is no more than a testing ground for man to overcome and rise above. In rising above, we gain the realization of our divine birthright in Spirit.

However, most of us have lost touch with our true souls. Through identification with physical form we've become the "reflection in the mirror." Our bodies are like the shadows of our souls and yet we've become more identified with the "shadow" of flesh and no longer realize that we are the intangible consciousness within. We are not our thoughts or our race, gender, appearance or what the world sees us as. Now given, for this particular lifetime we must play the role we've been drawn to, but our outer physical appearance is no more than the equivalent of wearing a certain outfit on a particular day. At the end of the day, or the end of a lifetime, you are no more your body than you are your wardrobe.

We all spend a lot of time defining ourselves by our outer environments. In actuality, as a soul, you are not your circumstances or situation. Because you may have been born into poverty does not make you poor.

Chapter VIII: Who am I?

Likewise, because you may have been born into wealth doesn't make you rich. Everything we perceive in physical creation is temporary. A rich person today may be poor tomorrow and vice versa. When you learn to not identify so much with your situations then you learn to be less affected by changes in your life. As well, you learn to develop a level of even-mindedness and then empower yourself to create your own happiness from within.

Likewise, you are not your personality. Your personality is a result of your ego and your perceptions about yourself and your interaction with the outer world. You are also not your talents. Some children seem to be born with certain talents, but the truth is all talents are powers belonging to God. Individuals learn to develop these talents but are not the actual source of them. Since all talents are powers borrowed from God then every person has equal access to them as long as he or she learns to develop them. Every individual at some point in time had to develop his or her talent traits. It does require some willpower though. Similar to exercising, you have to work out the particular muscle or "talent" until it is strengthened. In time, it appears to be second nature as if you always possessed the particular quality.

Now it is always easier to talk about what we "are not" than it is to talk about "what we are." The reason is that God is ultimately indefinable. If you believe scripture, which states that man is made in God's image, then we are likewise – indefinable. Some say man is spirit-man, individuated spirit, a soul, God's thought, etc. but what does that really mean? If you've ever seen one of those stereogram paintings, then we can use that as an analogy to create an idea of God and man's relationship. A stereogram picture is one of those 3-D computer generated paintings that looks like a bunch of dots. When you stare at the picture and allow your eyes to relax, you're supposed to see an image appear. If we relate God to the painting, then He would be an infinitely large and complete image. God of course is truly formless, but this metaphor helps.

Now each dot within the larger image would be equivalent to an individual soul. Since God is eternal and without beginning then each and every "dot" or individual soul, likewise, is eternal and without beginning. Everything in physical creation, however, that has a beginning must ultimately have an end as well. Since every soul is made of the essence of God or to say that another way, since God's "Self" is what became each soul then they still retain the "qualities" of God – formless and eternal.

Now every "dot" or soul in the painting has a part to play but each soul desires to experience itself as a complete picture in itself. This is what causes the soul's consciousness to descend which causes the soul to believe it is a thing in and of itself. For a certain amount of time the soul imagines itself to be separate from all other things and it excitedly uses its new "freedom" to experience all sorts of things. The soul enjoys playing the many different roles of race, gender, status, career, leader or rebel. However, the soul in time comes to realize with all the experiences of good... there are equal experiences of bad. The soul intuitively knows and remembers the perfection of completeness and longs for that same realization as a separate entity. However, this is impossible because the only way for the soul to be perfect is in the role it originally played in helping to complete "God's total picture" in the first place. Each soul must then seek to regain its consciousness and oneness back in God. Until that realization is achieved, each soul will frivolously seek fulfillment from temporary things but will fail to find it until it returns home to its natural and eternal place in Spirit.

Therefore, every human being we meet is a brother-soul inwardly seeking happiness in this world. But like I already stated, an eternal soul can never find

Chapter VIII: Who am I?

complete fulfillment in temporary things. So, we are all equivalent to being pupils in a school. Depending on the individual's experiences we are in different grades. Some people will be ahead of us meaning "closer" to realizing their nature in Spirit. Others are further behind us, still seeking happiness in materiality but will ultimately come to learn the same lesson that all things in creation are imaginary like a dream and the only true reality is the Divine Dreamer! All souls, however, are inherently perfect as God is but we've become "sinners" based upon our attachment to things "ungodly." A soul more entrenched in the "dream" will tend to be more consumed in the idea of their separateness and therefore may appear "eviler" not because this is their true nature but because they're obsessed with pleasing themselves. Souls more advanced and closer to reaching the goal of union in God come to realize their connection with all other living things and appear "saintlier" because of their unselfishness and their desire to make others happy. Then there are those souls that have already "graduated." These master souls who have awakened come down into our dream world in order to tutor and guide all other dreaming-souls back to wakefulness in God.

Something I learned a long time ago that I had a hard time swallowing was the idea that "You are just as much a part of God now as you will ever be!" I couldn't understand how this could be the case. Most of us make many mistakes and we don't tend to feel very godly or divine. But the truth is the only thing that separates us from a divine being or saint is that the individual such as Jesus KNOWS his oneness with the Father. This "knowing" isn't just a result of imagination. The souls that overcome and are permanently fixed in their consciousness and awareness of their relationship with Spirit underwent a process of realization similar to the lives we all live. I like to think of God as an infinitely faceted diamond. Being made in God's image we are all individually little diamonds as well. But it is always God's brilliance that shines through us enabling us to shine forth as He does.

The main difference between liberated souls and the bulk of society is that we are more like diamonds in the ruff. Some of us are more like lumps of coal but we all have the potential to become diamonds. ☺ The trials and tribulations of life serve the metaphorical purposes of the heat, pressure and time that all lumps of coal experience to eventually be molded into diamonds – the hardest and most beautiful stone known to man! When we as individual souls overcome the tests of life, we then become one with the Father and then are more like an individual facet of His infinitely faceted brilliance. Always unique with our individual stories but eternally one with His Being!

There Is a God

If I could speak face to face to every person on the Earth
I'd seek to convey the true meaning of one's worth
Despite what appears on the surface within sight
Lies your birth certificate to prove your divine birthright

Chapter VIII: Who am I?

Whether big or small, rich or poor, short or tall
There's an unbreakable bond that unites us all
No surprise, you have free will to exercise without intrusion
But your sense of separation is only illusion

What you do unto another comes right back to you
You reap what you sow the law of karma is true
The power to create anything you want, just name it
Never rest till you obtain it, visualize, then claim it

Never seek pity or be a victim of circumstance
Just humbly go within, find your strength, take a stance
Then give to others that which comes to you from above
And the greatest gift to give is the power of love

Maintain a steady mind even when things get tough
The tests of time reveal the true diamonds in the ruff
So, as you seek the answer to life's mystery
To know the source of your essence just trace your history

The One became many, Infinity is the sum
Like pieces of a puzzle the big picture is still One
To realize Reality is your purpose it's true
To purify all things from what you say, think and do

Just be still and let the Light of the world shine through you
And know there truly is a God and He became you!

Lateef Warnick

CHAPTER IX

The Purpose of Life

Photo albums are like walks through time, a trip down memory lane. They tell the story of generations of family. Not only can you see the obvious changes over time of your ancestors, you can see the evolution of styles of dress, cultural practices, modes of transportation and even the advances in technology simply in the quality of the photos themselves. You may even see pictures of distant relatives whom you may have not even met during your actual lifetime. Photo albums tell of not only your own family history but also those of close friends, classmates, geographical areas, significant historical moments and entire world events. In fact, a well put-together album may tell a nicely choreographed story to an orphan who has never even met his family or to a complete stranger the roots and heritage of another family. Even a picture taken at a time that may not have been a highlight of your life will develop sentimental value to you over the decades. As our memories fade, photo albums help us to remember glimpses in time as cherished moments. As Gladys Knight stated in her song **The Way We Were** – *"Can it be that it was all so simple then or has time rewritten every line? And if we had the chance to do it all again, tell me, would we"*?

Life can also be like one huge photo album. Can you imagine all the billions of people who have once lived on this Earth? Look at all the mysterious faces we cross paths with everyday. We never know if a complete stranger will come to one day be someone we fall in love with. Or perhaps that person may be the paramedic, nurse or doctor who may save our life one day. Maybe that cashier at the grocery store may become the attorney who keeps you out of jail or reduces your fine. Perhaps that paperboy will become your child's schoolteacher. Could it be that your grade school classmate may become the next big movie star, professional athlete or even a world leader?

But for every unknown face that may play a vital part in our own life there are billions more that will never be significant to you. A person on the other side of the globe is no more important to you than the leaves that fall from the tree in the backyard that you'll have to rake up and dispose of in trash bags. Yet, for every individual who passes through this world their lives are just as important to their friends and family as you are to your own friends and family.

Many of these loved ones would quickly trade in their most precious items, wealth or status just to have another moment with their cherished friend, lover or family member who may have already passed on. Likewise, although no one ever wants to be the one to say it, there are people who have died and the people who knew them never shed a tear or missed that person. Even worse, there have been certain individuals whom the world is greatly relieved that they are no longer in the flesh. Of course, this is all relative because for everyone who may have been despised, there's another that loved him or her. But then, occasionally, there were those unique individuals who seemed to be loved by all!

With all the memories of life, good and bad, it is a shame that some people will have gone from the cradle to the grave without ever having asked themselves "What is the purpose of my life"? The answer to this question will obviously vary from one person to another. In fact, some may believe that life has no purpose whatsoever. A good majority of people envision the ideal life as one in which they become financially wealthy, find the perfect spouse, have the perfect children, live without ever having a problem, become

Chapter IX: The Purpose of Life

well respected by the masses, live a long healthy life and die a natural death surrounded by their loved ones.

However, most of us recognize that this is by far the exception and not the norm. As they say, the grass always seems to be greener on the other side. Life for most people is full of challenges. Those of us fortunate enough to have had involved parents know we've had more clashes than we probably would've liked to have had. We've been through most likely several "loves" of our lives. Our jobs are like roller coasters; we never quite get the gratification we expected and never seem to be able to capture that pinnacle of the moment where we can truly say "I've made it!" Life just never seems to stand still long enough for us to get out the right words, spend that quality time, accomplish that next goal or give us the proper warning that this may be the last time we see our beloved friend.

Most of us fail to realize that no goal, accomplishment, achievement, ambition, objective or intent can possibly be the purpose of your life. What you should realize is, in fact, life in and of itself **IS** the purpose! The majority of people spend their time blaming their parents, friends, family, co-workers, bosses, teachers, politicians or just society at large for all the problems of the world and their own personal lives. While we all may have legitimate gripes about the problems of the world, the truth is as far as our personal lives go; we are totally responsible for our satisfaction with it. The problem is that we all too many times allow outside influences to dictate our inner peace and happiness.

But if we could only realize that peace of mind and happiness is a choice and not contingent upon outer circumstances, our lives would be very different. I'll acknowledge that it is easier to have peace of mind and happiness when our lives are exceeding expectation. But the truth is, spiritually speaking, we have full control of our state of being regardless of the outside world. When you come to truly understand this reality, not only will you become a master over your life and attract all sorts of blessings to you, but even if an undesired experience comes your way you will remain above it and undisturbed by it. In fact, a spiritual giant has the ability to laugh at things that the most of us would be ready to slit our wrists over.

In order for us to truly try to grasp the purpose of life, we must retrace our footsteps back to the Source of life. Since God is the Creator of all life then His purpose must be the Supreme Purpose that trumps any of our own individual purposes. God's purpose for creating everything we know has often been pondered by man. Unfortunately, man often takes the approach that God was made in man's image rather than the truth that man was made in God's image. God is not a person with desires or a body or a being that could possibly want something that He couldn't have if He wanted it.

We've already stated that God is Absolute and what is absolute about Him is that He is Absolute Consciousness. Man being made in His image, therefore being eternal himself, is simply "expressed" consciousness! Man, and all of creation is merely "God in action!" Since all things of creation have a beginning, they will too have an end. All men who identify themselves with the things of creation will ultimately find his end as well when the physical cosmos is dissolved. But for the man who overcomes identification with creation and unites his consciousness with the Absolute, to him only is the eternal reality of "I Am" a truth! Hence, God's purpose of life is for all of His creation to lift up its expressed consciousness into Absolute consciousness.

All of life's experiences were never meant to be the end-goals themselves. They are intended to help awaken our consciousness and then for us to use our will to consciously become like our Father. It just so happens that if life were perfect then we would forever be lulled into complacency and remain asleep in this dream fairytale. The undesirable events of life serve their

Chapter IX: The Purpose of Life

purpose in "shaking" us out of slumber in what can oftentimes be a nightmare. But God knows that He is the only thing "larger than life" and thus all of creation must come to know as well that His Absolute truth as author is greater than the story itself. He is the Perfect Happy Ending! But if your consciousness remains attached to being an actor or player in the story, then your role will end when the story ends. In order to witness the end of the movie you must separate yourself from the character in the play and realize your true nature as a spiritual co-producer of the greatest story ever told!

Thus, man under the hypnotic spell of life may have many "purposes" which we see as the reason why we are here. Because we may have been born with certain talents, we come to believe that utilizing those talents is our purpose. Some people feel they were born to be singers, actors, leaders, athletes, creators, scientists etc but while I agree you should express your talents, none of these "expressions" can be your truest purpose. No matter how grand or noble your cause may be it cannot usurp your Divine Purpose, which is to realize your true spiritual nature and connection with God. Now obviously those unique individuals that helped to cure a disease, protect the innocent, lead nations, defend civil rights or inspire the masses deserve to be remembered for their contributions. But the crowning achievement goes to the minute few that have not only overcome all sin but who have shown those still suffering how to follow and find their own spiritual freedom.

Because of the strong influence of the material world, we all tend to succumb to "following the herd" and doing the things the world seems to dictate for us to do. We get caught up in trying to obtain what appears to be happiness in the accumulation of things from cars, homes, clothes, power, prestige and so forth but we seem to not recognize that each thing we gain we soon forget about and immediately begin looking towards the next object. The reason is that the fulfillment doesn't come from the objects themselves it comes simply in our thought of obtaining the item. If we were able to reprogram ourselves and maintain our inner fulfillment, simply as the result of our choosing, then our lives would become more enjoyable. You could then begin to have a more fulfilling life realizing that you are the source of contentment. If you've spent eons behaving in the former manner then it will not be easy to just wave the magic wand and say "presto, I'm a new person."

I often tell people to watch what you ask or pray for because when you ask for things such as patience, "patience" doesn't just suddenly show up at your door in a gift box ready for you to unwrap. Prosperity doesn't sneak in your window at night and hide itself in your sock draw. Serenity isn't going to tackle you on the sidewalk when you're on your way to work in the morning. Life mostly works on the premise of "opportunity." If you need to develop patience, then you will be faced with multiple opportunities that will test you until you learn to react patiently. Some people may be born with money, but prosperity is a result of your thoughts, beliefs and attitude. Man is like a conduit or channel for prosperity.

In order to always be prosperous, you must not hoard or be tight-fisted with resources. If you behave like a dam, then you will find yourself on the "dry side" by the time you've finished putting up your wall. But if you share your resources just as freely as it is shared with you then your thirst shall always be quenched even when the world seems to be in drought. **"Prove me now herewith, saith the LORD of hosts, if I will not open you the windows of heaven, and pour you out a blessing, that there shall not be room enough to receive it." Malachi 3:10** True serenity comes as a result of you being able to masterfully carry your inner temple, placid lake or mountaintop wherever you may go so that no one is able to ruffle your tranquility!

What is ironic is the fact that we all inherently know that all of the things of this world are temporary,

Chapter IX: The Purpose of Life

especially our lives and yet our minds are consumed in their pursuit. In fact, not to be morbid, but the only guarantee that we enter this world with is the truth that we will eventually leave it. It may be in a matter of days, weeks, months, years or many decades but death will ultimately come. Yet we all act like we're going to be here forever. If you actually compare what's considered to be a long life by most, say 80 years, to eternity it's like investing all of your attention to perfectly signing your name on a school exam without ever answering any of the questions on the test. It behooves you to actually try to solve some of the spiritual questions of life rather than spend all of your energy on temporary things that you know will not help you to pass the test but assuredly help you to get a failing grade. I'm not suggesting that we neglect worldly duties, but we all have to contribute towards the overall welfare of the planet and the people in it. When we not only serve ourselves, but we serve the masses, we develop a healthy balance between our body, mind and soul.

Each individual must live their life to the best of their current understanding but as they say, "your reach should always exceed your grasp!" As each of us grows in spirit, we become the propulsion to put the collective on the higher path to Truth. The spiritual pioneers are the ones who pave the "road less traveled" and through their experience and wisdom lead the way for others to follow. So instead of seeing a world filled with billions of people with their own agendas you should recognize each person as your spiritual kin with the same ancestral Father as yourself. When it all boils down, it's not your accomplishment that people remember the most, it's who you were as a person. So, in all your endeavors focus less on the temporary goals and try to maintain an air of helpfulness, joy and contentment in all you do. Time is never too pressing that you cannot take a moment to be polite, share a smile or lift someone's day by being thoughtful.

The day will come when we all must leave this Earth. This isn't just a cliché – no one is promised tomorrow! To truly live each day as if it were your last, you should remain anchored inwardly with God's presence. Remember to do unto others, as you would have them do unto you. Life is a god-making factory. We must use our experiences to develop the wisdom and consistency to express godliness! The first step begins with developing purity of heart. Next is learning to love all. If you can do these two then you shall find God or rather God will have found you. Thus, you become a perfect expression of God's consciousness. **"Be ye therefore perfect, even as your Father which is in heaven is perfect." Matthew 5:48 When** you are no longer in the flesh and are just someone's memory and they look at your picture in the photo album, what will they remember? The most remembered, cherished and adored will be the ones who most greatly expressed divine love to all.

CHAPTER X

The Power of Thought

Imagine you are quietly walking along a beach when suddenly you stump your toe on something. (You know the big hairy one with the ingrown toenail!) ☺ You look down to see what you've hit, and it appears to be a strange object unfamiliar to you. You reach down into the sand to pull out the unfriendly distracter and realize it's a foreign glass container of some sort. Out of curiosity you attempt to remove the cork from the bottle when a mysterious fume escapes. You reflexively drop the bottle and watch in awe as the ominous gas takes the form of a figure. That figure gradually crystallizes into a genie. By gosh, you've instantly been transformed into Aladdin and you're granted three wishes that can change your life forever. So... what do you wish for?

Well, regardless of what you wish for, what you **do** wish for tells something about the person you are. It also will symbolize your perception of yourself, the world around you and your understanding of your relationship with the Creator. The people that wish to do harm unto another are full of ignorance and are absorbed in "sinful" ways most would call evil. People who wish for things that only benefit them are still very much consumed with their ego and self-interests. Those who wish for something that benefits their family are not quite as ego centered but still have room to expand their concept of self. Those who wish for something that benefits the masses such as world peace are on the right track towards spiritual consciousness.

But why would anyone waste his or her wish on some material item that is only temporary. I know that these "genie scenarios" often come with the clause that you can't wish for more wishes but why wouldn't you just wish for the power of the genie itself? Then anytime you desired something, you could materialize it for yourself. Well, the good news is that you already have your very own "genie in the bottle." God endowed every man with this power since the beginning of time. The only question is "how to use it"?

Any religious person probably already has heard about the power of prayer. Prayer is oftentimes used to ask God for certain blessings. Other times it is used to thank God for current blessings. Now which do you think is the more effective prayer? Well, it so happens that the prayer, which is one of gratitude, has the greatest power but perhaps not for the reasons you might imagine. The reason the thankful prayer has greater potential is not because God needs to be flattered or likes to hear the words "thank you" but because it incorporates the affirmation that you already have that something! This is one of the first steps to understanding the Law of Attraction. Our thoughts are things and have creative energy.

    In other words, if you pray thanking God for your health then you're more likely to continue experiencing good health because you are already claiming and acknowledging that you have it! Our prayers are like a factory that produces exactly what you suggest. If you are saying thank you for wealth, health, love, careers, family etc then you are simply affirming that you possess these things in your life, which then sends out thought-waves to create or "solidify" even further your experience of these things. Likewise, when you pray that "I want a car" or "I want someone to love me" or "I want this job" then in essence you are reinforcing that reality which is an experience of you "wanting" which creates the reality of you not having it.

    Hopefully it's apparent that God doesn't take pleasure in playing mind games with us, but the goal is for all of us to live in His image, which means we're all

Chapter X: The Power of Thought

mini-creators. Now I don't expect your life to just miraculously change overnight and you never ask for anything ever again. What I am suggesting is that you start to take baby steps to re-approaching how you pray. Instead of asking for things, begin by thanking God for what you already have. Instead of focusing on what you want to do next, focus on what you have already accomplished. This does a couple of things for you.

First, it changes your mindset to make your situation more positive. Secondly, it helps you to strengthen the things that you currently consider good in your life. It helps you to go from a pessimistic perspective to an optimistic one. You begin to have more of a "half-full" attitude than a "half-empty" attitude. I don't prefer to use this cliché but it's true – "things could always be worse!" If your health is suffering, it could be worse. If you're lacking money, it could be worse. If are unhappy with life, it could be worse. Believe it or not there are other people in this world that have it a lot worse than you. So, when you acknowledge the positive things in your life it helps you to attract more of the same.

Now how do you make the next progressive step in materializing the things you want in life? Well, from the initial standpoint of recognizing and appreciating what you already have, no matter how small, then you can pray for your blessings to multiply. This is how you not only establish a more positive outlook but also you begin to tap into your creative abilities to deliver the desired result. It takes continuous monitoring to practice positive thinking. Next add the act of positive words to coincide with your thoughts and finally perform positive actions to truly put the "stamp of approval" on your efforts. One of the best ways to establish whatever it is you seek in life is to share that which you desire with someone else, perhaps someone that needs it even more than yourself.

Again, remember if you feel you need money then find someone that seems to need money a little more desperately than yourself. By sharing that which you have, you actually open yourself up to become a vessel for greater abundance in your life. **"For whoever has, to him shall be given, and he shall have more abundance: but whoever has not, from him shall be taken away even that he has." Matthew 13:12 What** this is really saying is the person with the attitude of prosperity, even when things may not on the surface appear to be abundant, shall always have simply because they believe and have the "faith" that things will come. Yet the person that feels that they never have, even if all their needs in life are being met, will continue to experience and create more of "not having" not because they're somehow being punished but because that is what they're creating and attracting for themselves. **"For as he thinketh in his heart, so is he..." Proverbs 23:7**

Now let me elaborate on this idea of prayer. Some people may feel they're just too busy to constantly be praying. But let's think about this for a moment... what really is prayer? A prayer is simply when a person attempts to speak with God by focusing their attention, concentrating their thoughts while blocking out other distractions, sometimes ritualistically by closing their eyes, getting on their knees, bowing or otherwise. But the true triggering factor is the concentration piece. Also, prayers are typically done in a very humble fashion. Actually, every thought we have has some creative power to it. So, to make your "prayers" more effective simply practice by being watchful of your thoughts and always maintain an attitude of humbleness in life because the truth is not one of us can even wake up in the morning unless it's God will. Next you simultaneously develop your ability of concentration by always maintaining a centered consciousness. The more centered you become and the more conscious,

Chapter X: The Power of Thought

"present in the moment," you are then every thought will have the power of prayer and you feed more energy into manifesting whatever life you desire.

Again, I don't mean to make this sound overly simple so let's start with the basic building blocks. Each human being in essence is just pure consciousness. This consciousness is sort of like a silent observer or witness of the events in life. Each of us, because of our idea of separation from God and separation from each other, has a "pseudo-self;" this is the part of us that identifies with our bodies and our interaction with our environments. We all have minds which, mostly driven by the senses, process and interpret information it receives. Based upon our innate nature in God contrasted with our long history of experiences, we all develop opinions about life events. Based upon our perspectives, we tell ourselves if certain things are "good" or "bad" depending on how they make us feel. So, in essence no event in itself is either good or bad because what may be good to one person may not be good for another. It is mostly a result of how we judge it. **"Judge not, and ye shall not be judged: condemn not, and ye shall not be condemned: forgive, and ye shall be forgiven:" Luke 6:37**

Most people who are familiar with this quote understand it in its most obvious meaning, which is to not judge other people, which of course is true. We have all been exposed to extremely critical people and every person surrounding them is waiting for the opportunity for that person to mess up so they can be ten times as critical in retaliation. No one likes to be judged but it always seems easier to do when watching other peoples' mistakes. Always remember there are layers to the meaning of scripture. Aside from the obvious meaning of being judgeless towards others it also means to not judge the events in our lives or *ourselves*. I know this can be a challenge, but self-judgment can oftentimes be the most damaging type of judgment because we have difficult times forgiving ourselves. Again, remember the power of thoughts. If you see yourself as not worthy, then others will see you as such and you will attract more of the same.

So, one of the first steps in reprogramming your thinking is to not judge the events that happen in your life, rather accept them and then decide how you want to move forward. Simply because something undesirable happens to you doesn't necessarily make it bad. Likewise, because something desirable happens doesn't quite make it good either. Only your judgment about it makes it so. There will be things in life that you didn't want but turned out to be good for you and other times something you may have longed for may have turned out to have been the worse thing possible for you. The more even-minded you become then the less power "bad" things will have over you. The less "bad things" are able to affect you; the more you realize you're able to control and create "good" things in your life. The more you grow spiritually, the more you'll realize that the only thing you really need that's worth controlling is your inner peace and joy; then outer experiences of the world won't be as important to you. Now you're on your way to becoming an enlightened being who understands that your greatest joy comes from God and helping to show others how to relieve themselves from suffering permanently!

Most importantly, realize it all starts with you. Our lives are simply a reflection of who we are as beings. If we are "being" generous then our lives reflect a generous flow of abundance. If we are being "loving" then our lives are filled with people who love us. If we are being "helpful" then those who surround our lives are willing to assist us. Likewise, if we are being "selfish" then our lives reflect a tight restriction of sustenance. If we are being hurtful to others, then we find others constantly out to get us. If we are being self-centered then we find our lives cut off from others' thoughtfulness.

Chapter X: The Power of Thought

If your perspective of the world is that people are cruel, heartless, harmful and out to get you then you will continue to experience that as your "reality." To change your reality, change yourself and your thoughts first and that begins with not judging.

Now I know there are a lot of people who feel like "I'm always nice to everyone but people are always two-faced." My response is that first because you believe this to be true then it becomes true. You're attracting those types of people to yourself. Secondly, your "being nice" cannot be conditional. You can't start out being nice to someone but then the moment you think they don't deserve it you suddenly become this cold and heartless person. If you want to be a nice person, then you have to consistently be that way with everyone regardless of whether or not you think they deserve it. You should be nice not for their benefit but for your own. When all you put out is good energy then you attract that in abundance to yourself. It doesn't mean that your life becomes perfect and no one ever wishes ill for you, but it does mean that your life is overwhelmingly filled with good cheer and you don't allow anyone's negative energy to ruffle your feathers. The people who are negative towards you are the people you should pray for even more greatly and send your loving thoughts their way. Ultimately, your blessings don't come from other people they come from God. He just uses others to deliver our blessings.

Now I would like to go a little further in depth on this whole "thought power" idea. There are a lot of writings today that are attempting to teach people how to think positive and create the world you want. I think it's important to recognize a few caveats with this perception. First, for the average person there are limitations to how much you can accomplish simply through your concentration abilities. There have been many charismatic people in history with great concentration skills that possessed the ability to influence the people around them and manipulate their environments. However, if your heart is not in the right place and your intentions are selfish then you will eventually have to face your karma of bad energy. Notice from **Proverbs 23:7** it says *"as he thinketh in his heart..."* It doesn't say as you think with your mind. The important distinction in your ability to create "like unto the image of God" is contingent upon the nature of your heart. A person with strong concentration abilities but without inner wisdom is like a kid with a gun. You may be able to attract certain luxuries of life but if your heart is not in the right place you will create situations that will come back to haunt you depending on how you handle yourself and treat others. You may, through your own self effort, create a financial kingdom for yourself. However, if your attachment is to your wealth without helping others then you will one day drown in your riches and realize that no one in your life is genuine or are only out for your money. For those of you who have heard of Bernie Madoff you know how someone can create an empire for himself but if it is done dishonestly then it will be a matter of time before you have to "pay the piper."

    So, let's see if we can truly understand why our thoughts create our realities. God being the original, unmanifested Beginning of all things created everything through the sheer will of His Thought. Everything that proceeds from God ultimately returns to God. Similarly, man being created in His image has His endowed abilities to create "reality" from our sheer thought and will. Likewise, what man creates returns to man as well. The difference is that God knows He is the Creator of this dream world. Man, under the spell of delusion, sees himself as separate from creation and forgets that he is the creator of his dream because he is stuck in the dream. When you are stuck in a dream and feel you are not in control but rather a victim of whatever the dream dictates to you then that is what we call a

Chapter X: The Power of Thought

nightmare. To truly alter the dream, you must raise your conscious above the level of the dream thereby stepping "outside" of it. Spiritual beings that have stepped outside of the dream are the only ones fully capable of manipulating this dream world of thoughts however they see fit or I should say as God guides them to do.

Even the person with great concentration skills and positive thoughts is still limited by the dream because they imagine themselves to be a part of the dream. The movie "The Matrix" attempts to play on this whole concept of self-awakening with the choice of the "red or blue pill." I personally like the scene where Neo asks Morpheus "So what are you saying, I can dodge bullets with my mind." And Morpheus answers "What I'm saying is that when the time is right – you won't have to!"

An awakened being is not limited in any manner by the dream because they see it for what it is – just a play of thoughts. Enlightened beings like a Jesus can create whatever they choose in the world but only do so in accordance with God's will because they realize Him to be the true Director of creation. When a master manipulates creation by his consciousness, he is merely materializing a "thought" into fruition, which is perceived by all individuals within the dream to be a miracle. In truth, everything we experience is in essence just a thought. Daily we eat "thought" food, perform "thought" acts and experience many "thought" events throughout our lifetimes. All of these things are simply the result of our minds ability to interpret stimuli through our senses.

But don't confuse the physical world, which is God's thought to be a result of your own imagination. Unless you have truly awakened from maya, the spell of creation, through your inner efforts and God's grace then you are limited by the dream and for you it is "reality!" Hence, if you think through your "positive thoughts" that you can fly by jumping off a building, rest assured that you will surely plunge to your physical death. In order to be eternally liberated from the restrictive laws of creation you must melt your individual "self" back into the true Self in Spirit. The laws of physics do not limit Spirit, being the Creator of physical laws. **"In the day of prosperity be joyful, but in the day of adversity consider: God also hath set the one over against the other, to the end that man should find nothing after him." Ecclesiastes 7:14 By** becoming one with the true Genie of creation you become eternally satisfied in Spirit and no longer have need for anything outside of Self.

The thought manifests as the word;
The word manifests as the deed;
The deed develops into habit;

Chapter X: The Power of Thought

And habit hardens into character;
So watch the thought
And its ways with care,
And let it spring from love
Born out of concern for all beings...
As the shadow follows the body,
As we think, so we become.

Buddha

Your beliefs become your thoughts.
Your thoughts become your words.
Your words become your actions.
Your actions become your habits.
Your habits become your character.
Your character becomes your destiny!

Mahatma Gandhi

CHAPTER XI

Free Will and the Law of Karma

"Ladies and Gentlemen... boys and girls... what you've all been waiting for... all the way from the city of Catchfools... I take great pleasure in introducing to you... the Great Pinnochio!" [Cue the Italian folk music; enter stage left; an 18-inch tall wooden marionette puppet held up by strings connected via a control bar.] Parents and children applaud together. The children smile with glee. [The magnificent Pinnochio goes into his first knock-knock joke] Five minutes later the parents begin to yawn by the ripple. [The wooden puppet Pinnochio then goes into his tap dance routine, clickety-click, clickety-click] Within ten minutes the parents are fast asleep, and the children become restless and begin to find more delight in poking each other. [30 minutes later Pinnochio, charioted by the hidden manipulator, prepares for his song and dance finale, clickety-click, clickety-click] The now squirming children, hungry and ready for the restroom, attempt to rouse their slumbering parents to leave for refreshments. [The great Pinnochio takes his bow before a non-attentive audience now attempting to beat the rest of the crowd out the doors.] "Thank you, thank you, our next showing will be in two hours! Come again!" says the Great Pinnochio.

If God had not endowed man with free will this thing called life would be about as exciting as a play starring a wooden puppet. It may sound like a cute idea at first, but it doesn't allow for much depth. Puppets are not dynamic creatures able to learn and grow. Fortunately, God gave us all free will to exercise, for good and for worse. God is fully aware of the consequences that come along with His creation and His children having the power to choose whatever they like whether or not it coincides with His divine plan for humanity. Truthfully, collectively speaking, it is in exact accordance with His divine plan; it is primarily individually speaking that we feel "out of control." To encourage man to learn to make wiser choices, God instituted a law of reciprocity, which allows an individual to know directly the effects of his choices. As we all know, experience is always the best teacher.

Unfortunately, certain people are slow to learn life's lessons and realize the consequences and experiences of their life are an exact result of decisions they've made. Because some people are more greatly engrossed in ego, meaning their idea of separation from everything outside of themselves, they tend to always feel like the victim when things go wrong never accepting responsibility that it is always a consequence of their own thoughts, words or action. You may not see it working but for every action we make, no matter how small or large, good or bad, a karmic effect generates that will eventually come back to us in like-kind sooner or later.

If the Creator had simply created humans and the universe to do His bidding as if He were a Master Manipulator, then it wouldn't have allowed Him the opportunity to fully experience His creation at its greatest potential in glory of Himself. God is the ultimate perfection. Therefore, everything in creation no matter how grand is still a "less perfect" expression of God. Hence all of creation not only has an opportunity to grow to express His divinity but also must eventually evolve to melt back into His perfection. So, in essence, everything man interacts with in creation is a blessing in disguise because the things that are "more divine" than himself serve as inspiration for man to aspire; and for everything that is "less divine" than himself will either be motivation to grow further or an opportunity to inspire those less developed.

Chapter XI: Free Will and the Law of Karma

So, do not judge because everyone can be an angel. Another reason not to judge is because everything has the spark of God in it regardless of its outward appearance. Even when you cannot find something loving about another individual you should try to separate the "evil" about them and realize that however distorted from truth they may be, there's hope for them because of the God within them. Since none of us are perfect (yet) the same empathy you show to another will someday be shown to you.

Now you may ask, "Isn't there an easier way to experience life and develop wisdom"? and the answer truthfully is "no." But realize that although this world will never be perfect it doesn't have to be hurtful. The issue is how quickly you can come to realize that you are at the source of your actions, your karma and your experiences. All of these may take some time to master but you can control your actions. The challenge is that most of us are driven by our senses. Our senses deliver information to the mind that we interpret as favorable or unfavorable. We all live through life trying to seek happiness and avoid sorrow. In due time, as long as you have the right desire to understand, you will come to realize that pain and pleasure are things that exist only in your mind. If you can learn to not be driven by the roller coaster of life towards extreme highs and lows, then through your balance you'll develop greater control to determine your happiness.

We all have our "hot buttons" that when pushed can get up under our skin and drive us berserk. Once we've lost our composure we literally become "out of our minds" and may through a fit of emotion do something that we didn't intend and produce a lifetime of regret. Our perception about a thing influences our internal dialogue and what we tell ourselves determines our actions accordingly. In order to change this dynamic, you must first learn to practice greater presence in the moment. When you become totally conscious of the matter at hand you develop the ability to separate yourself from the situation thereby maintaining a better frame of mind and hence make a better decision on how to act. If you learn to change your perception about a thing you can reprogram yourself to not be fearful or threatened and therefore less inclined to become overly emotional thus dictating your behavior. Once you learn to better control your perception, behavior and actions you then begin to create better karma for yourself. Again, this is a gradual process and you must be determined to control your emotions and do what generates positive intent and desire for a favorable outcome not just for yourself but also for all involved. Be aware though that you still have potentially past karma that will come to test your resolve. You cannot allow those tests to undermine your resolve to live in better accordance with righteousness.

Now the first level of free will is in the sense of just actually having the ability to make choices freely. The next aspect of this free choice deals with your actual will power. This basically describes your resolve to make a controlled choice and to execute that choice regardless of its ease or difficulty. We've all had experience with tough choices and sticking to them such as diets, exercise, schooling, work etc. We should accept all of life's tests as an opportunity to strengthen our resolve and will power. Developing strong will in one aspect of our lives is still strong will, nonetheless. That strong will can then be transferred to other areas of challenge producing beneficial results. Once you have the volition to see things through then by greater spiritual intelligence you learn to do things because they are more beneficial and not just because it pleases the senses.

Most of us become creatures of habit. Instead of trying to go from one extreme to another in either establishing or breaking a habit you should first try to

Chapter XI: Free Will and the Law of Karma

practice moderation. There are certain foods and drinks that most certainly have more of a detrimental affect on the body but if you've been indulging in them for a long time it may be difficult to stop. Try first to gradually cut back on your usage. There has been some scientific evidence that shows that the human brain develops electrical "grooves" that are in accordance with certain behaviors. The more you practice something the easier it becomes to continue to perform that behavior. It's almost like the movement of water. You become programmed to travel the route of least resistance. In order to stop the trend, you must create new "grooves" by establishing habits that better serve you. So instead of just trying to stop the bad behavior cold turkey, try to connect it with a better habit then gradually replace it until you can come to realize the old behavior no longer serves you.

    The next thing is to figure out how to develop the wisdom to make intelligent decisions and create new habits that serve you well. The first thing is to know that things that serve the soul are always of the highest priority. The mind and body are next in line consecutively. What serves the soul is anything that helps to inspire or connect you to the Creator. Often in serving the soul we get the mutual benefit of developing the mind and providing the body with spiritual energy. Of course, reading or watching programs that stimulate healthy thought are good for the mind while moderate exercise for the body keeps it healthy and lively. Now there are always numerous sources of information out there that will tell you contradicting things that are supposedly good for you. I always say to scrutinize all information you come across. Be mindful of whom the information is coming from and what motive might that person have for you engaging in their product or service.

    We are constantly bombarded with so-called information how good a particular food may taste when in truth it has absolutely no nutritional value at all. Obviously, that advertiser has a profit to gain by you purchasing that product. Most Americans have grown up with the concept of the food pyramid, which used to be four groups becoming five and now six. The suggested food portions and meals to eat are definitely more than what the average person's body requires. Depending on your age, gender and body structure what your body needs will vary from the next person. Americans are having a terrible time with obesity because of improper food portions, frequency of meals, type of food and lack of exercise. When we are young, we need certain foods because we are growing but as we age and stop growing, we don't need to still eat as if we are. Drink more water and natural juice; continuously try to snack on natural fruits, vegetables, nuts and grains. Eat meat occasionally if you desire but every meal should not be built around it.

Traditionally, we've all been trained to eat three meals a day. This honestly is not the best way to eat. It causes you to stretch the stomach and every time you eat you feel the need to "fill" it. When you snack throughout the day on healthy items it doesn't allow time for your brain to signal to you that you are hungry and yet it doesn't allow the stomach to become stretched. It also helps to speed up your metabolism. I'm not going to tell you to become complete vegetarians but do the research for yourself and decide. I constantly see test after test and new research showing how fruits and vegetables have favorable effects on the body preventing or removing various ailments, colds, sicknesses and cancer. Yet meat is continuously connected with high blood pressure, clogged arteries, constipation, heart disease, cancer, high cholesterol etc. The best argument for meat has always been that it provides proteins but truthfully you can get all the protein you need as an adult from other sources. Mostly the average person really just likes the way it tastes and how it fills our stomach. But that filled stomach and intestines is what leads to the feeling of lethargy, lack of energy, indigestion, over sleeping and constipation. Also, most people are turned off by the sight of blood and would probably go hungry if they had to kill an animal themselves. What gives meat its salty taste is actually bacteria growing in the decaying flesh. That's why it is important to cook meat properly and yet there are many who won't even do that claiming they like their meat raw. Often to enjoy a portion of meat we have to flavor it by loading it up with herbs and spices thus it's really not the meat we taste at all but seasonings.

As far as what is good for the body, oxygen is the number one most important item. The body can go days or even weeks without food. We can go days without water, but you can only go a matter of minutes without air. There are scientific studies, which show that proper deep breathing causes osmosis generating the pressure gradient necessary for the lymph system to work and remove toxins from the body. We actually exhaust many detrimental byproducts from our blood system just through breathing. Most of us have very shallow breathing. When possible, you should mentally practice and remind yourself to breathe in deeply to a count of ten or whatever number is comfortable. Hold it for a few seconds and then to exhale fully. Deep and smooth breathing not only fills the body with essential oxygen but also has a calming effect upon the brain and nervous system. This is one of the key factors for beginners in meditation. Animals that have slow breathing cycles are the longest living animals on the Earth.

As far as our minds go, we often spend our time filling it with entertainment on television or in observation of other stimuli putting our brains in an almost passive "sleep" mode. You should try daily to indulge mentally in some worthwhile thought-provoking subjects whether its science, social concerns, health, politics or otherwise. Don't get me wrong; having a good laugh keeps you young and pleasant. However, becoming a couch potato and going from channel to channel until you fall asleep is not stimulating. You can have a good laugh by sharing an upbeat demeanor with co-workers, friends, neighbors or family; just refrain from unnecessary gossip. You will serve your mind better to read good books or enjoy a hobby. Also, it is worthwhile to engage in either spiritual reading of scripture or engaging conversation. But don't just read verses from your holy book try to actually study it and comprehend it. Most holy scripts use language that is no longer in common practice, so it benefits you to read other interpretations and outside material related to the subject at hand.

Sometimes the best way to fully grasp something is to consider other writings, texts or opinions about your holy scripture. Don't worry this shouldn't be a threat to what you may believe. The sign of an intelligent person is not one who avoids other sources of information but one who is able to face different beliefs and still have sufficient understanding to clearly express and stand by their belief through proper reason and not just blind dogma. It is helpful to find other ways at looking at things and once you've examined a few different points of view inside or outside of your religion you can then draw your conclusions. But try to never get stuck in "having to only believe one thing." Allow yourself the opportunity to "change your mind" should new information come to light. And always listen to your life experiences. When you try to truly learn from experience, analyzing the event and praying to God for clarity, you will begin to gain the greatest insight intuitively from within.

Spiritually there are various ways to worship. The average person today praises God either at church, mosque, synagogue or temple. Group worship is always a beautiful thing and is better than no worship at all.

Chapter XI: Free Will and the Law of Karma

Singing song or listening to sermons can inspire us and stir the body. If you have a well-versed congregational speaker and you're listening closely then you can even learn quite a bit. However, there is outer worship and then there's inner devotion, which many have lost understanding in this concept today. All true divine messengers of God have always taught to develop a personal relationship with God. This doesn't always mean simply talking to God in our minds, out loud or through prayer but to learn how to listen to God as well. Often times He will speak to us through our experiences, but we may ignore it or not be present enough to recognize it. Therefore, you need to establish the habit of learning to still the body, quiet the mind and become inwardly tranquil. You can start with small increments of time, but you should at least once a day be alone, be silent and develop a serene place within. The better you become at this, the better you'll be able to begin to actually hear the Divine Mother.

For all parents it is important to continuously develop yourself in mind, body and soul. I'm a firm believer that you cannot give qualities to a child that you yourself do not possess. Therefore, if you want to teach your child perseverance then you must practice it yourself. If you want to teach your child patience, then you must be patient with them. If you want your child to be kind, thoughtful, courteous, hard working, disciplined, well behaved and so on then you must be the example and reflect all these qualities yourself. Every child won't become a professional athlete, doctor, lawyer, celebrity or entrepreneur but every child can grow to be a good person. Be the example by being a good parent first.

Lastly, I want to examine this concept of karma. As stated previously all things in creation are but mere reflections of His presence. Thus, everything you do unto creation you are doing unto God, good and bad. Since He is within you as well, you are in essence doing it to yourself. He sees to it that all you do unto another is done unto you with equally good measure. Some have the impression that karma is only the effects you performed in a previously life or that carries over to your next life. While it is true that if you have not found total liberation in Spirit then you are subject to all past karma recent or from ages ago, but karma doesn't have to be confined to a past life or future life. In fact, the more "aware" and spiritual you become, the sooner you will tend to experience your karma. For some their karma may come immediately. For those very spiritually evolved you have the choice to overcome your tests of this flesh in this lifetime and free yourself from all past karma. You may be able to work out past karma either through experience, meditation, intervention from a spiritual master or through prayer and God's grace.

The first step is to try to minimize creating further bad karma. You do this by strengthening your resolve to always try to do well no matter what. When in doubt ask yourself honestly how you would want someone to act towards you in any particular instance and that will hopefully guide you on how to treat others. While it is often easy to simply conclude that a person "deserved" your harsh treatment or that you're justified in acting a certain way, the truth is we always appreciate it when a person treats us with love and forgiveness even when we know we were "dead wrong" in something we may have done. Ultimately, even good karma must be overcome because karma in and of itself is binding to man's soul. Remember the concepts of good and bad are only relevant in physical creation. Spiritually you must overcome all karmic bonds by raising your consciousness and releasing it from all identification with the body. Until you've transcended all attachment to the ideas of ego and sense of separation from the Source then you are subject to experiencing karmic attachments.

The truth is God created all of us to be "real boys and girls." Yet we by our own doing make wooden puppets of ourselves. We create karmic strings and tie ourselves up to the control bar of the senses of the flesh. Then our worldly experiences dictate to us how to behave. Our lack of will power enslaves us to habitually follow the demands of the rituals of the same old tap dance day after day. You must gain the wisdom to change your reality. Through your wisdom you come to understand how to empower yourself to exercise your free will. Once your will is strong you can cut the karmic-tying strings of life and free yourself forever. The Great Geppetto rejoices and the heavens celebrate when each of His children realize their true freedom in Spirit and live as intended in perpetual Bliss at home in His kingdom of the Infinite.

CHAPTER XII

What Is Sin?

"All unrighteousness is sin: and there is a sin not unto death." 1 John 5:17 The symbolic Adam and Eve have the unpleasant distinction of being known as the first "sinners" in creation. This fall of man wasn't so much a punishment as it was a declaration stating that anyone who succumbs to the temptation of the senses removes himself from his spiritual presence with God. In fact, the soul is eternally present in God. It is man's consciousness that falls from the "Garden of Eden" of perfection. You may ask "why did God even provide an option to eat from the fruit of the center of the garden if He didn't want man to indulge"? The answer again is that man in order to live in the ideal image of God must have the free will to choose right and even wrong.

    The concepts of right and wrong exist only on the level of creation. God exists beyond right and wrong. This world of creation could not exist if there wasn't the duality of right and wrong. It would be like trying to define a word by using the word itself. Imagine trying to convey an idea to a group of friends and all you can use is white chalk on a white chalkboard. You need to have the contrast of a black board to give the white chalk its ability to be seen. Likewise, man must develop wisdom and learn to shine perfectly amongst the dark backdrop of an imperfect world. But no matter how much dirt and grime you pile on top of a diamond once the filth is removed a brilliant diamond still shines underneath ready to be revealed.

    Ultimately, God is absolute perfection. Everything in creation is imperfect. However, man being made in God's image, and even more being nothing more than an expression of God, is inherently perfect. The purpose of life is for man to journey through the maze of imperfection, travel the road of refinement and ultimately arrive at the destination of Perfection. The key is for man to realize his perfection within and through wisdom to consciously *choose* perfection. In truth, we don't "become" perfect rather we shed the delusive garbs of imperfection to reveal the already perfect soul within. So, in the strictest terms sin is ultimately choosing anything less than perfection. Now what causes one to choose anything less than perfection is "not knowing;" and thus *ignorance* is the greatest cause of sin. **"Be ye therefore perfect, even as your Father which is in heaven is perfect." Matthew 5:48**

Now clearly ignorance comes in many different variations. There is subtle ignorance, which may just be the result of selfishness or telling lies. Then there is gross ignorance such as blasphemy, theft and murder. In actuality, any sense of separation, seeing or doing unto others as if you are not doing it for God, can be construed as sin. For a liberated spiritual master, they see all of creation, even "sinners," as reflections of God and thus interact with all as if they're engaging with the Creator Himself. Even if they are sternly correcting a lost soul in ways of righteous behavior, they are doing such out of a center of love and virtuous intent to help uplift the individual. Loving someone means condemning the behavior but not the person! When you are a liberated soul who has overcome the tests of life then it is easy to see the Divine in all. But when we ourselves are still under the ignorant dream spell of delusion it can be difficult to see any good in those who appear "evil." Dealing with truly "evil" persons should be left up to the heavyweight spiritual masters who receive their direction directly from God. **"Know ye not that we shall judge angels? how much more things that pertain to this life"? 1 Corinthians 6:3**

Chapter XII: What is Sin?

As for yourself, you should not think of yourself as a sinner. I'm not saying that you should therefore make excuses for yourself to not even try to change sinful ways or to correct improper behavior. But what I am saying is if you see your core self as somehow being flawed then it becomes very difficult to ever see yourself in the light of perfection. Something imperfect cannot become perfect. You must come to realize that you were created perfect and you've simply lost your way. You must learn to separate yourself from your behaviors. If you are already inherently perfect, then you are just learning how to express that perfection outwardly. Be firm with yourself, hold yourself accountable but shift your perspective and know that you are a work in progress. And the same forgiveness you show yourself, show to others.

The truth is you are not yourself. **"What? know ye not that your body is the temple of the Holy Ghost which is in you, which ye have of God, and ye are not your own"? 1 Corinthians 6:19** What I mean by that is that you were created as the perfect eternal soul. However, under the spell of delusion you've come to believe that you are the ego. The time will come when you must face this "false self" and transcend it. The ego has a different agenda than the soul. The ego's purpose is to try to preserve itself by keeping your consciousness identified and attached to worldly desires. The soul is patient and is capable of enjoying the drama of this world but will eventually grow tired and then begin to reclaim its authoritative divine right. However, the ego will not go down without a fight. It will find clever ways to keep you confined to matter. God does forgive sin but keep in mind that you still create karmic effect for yourself and sometimes it is necessary that you learn lessons from your actions in order to grow.

Every true religion attempts to establish a certain moral code of conduct for followers to abide by. While certain religions may be a little stricter than others, their goal is essentially the same – to steer man away from sinful ways. Judaism and Christianity have popularized The Ten Commandments. These are a set of moral codes handed down from God to Moses to assist his people with a sign for them to follow. These "commandments" are known in Hebrew as either Aseret ha-Dvarîm or Aseret ha-Dibrot, which most closely translates to "the ten terms." I'm not sure how the translation of commandment came about but I feel it has had some unfortunate repercussions. These ten terms are more like indicators or identifiers of how a spiritually righteous person should or would live. I suppose the Lord could command our behavior if He desired to but that in essence goes against why He designed this creation. Giving someone free will and then commanding them on their behavior sort of contradicts itself. God wants us to utilize our intelligence to seek out and understand His spiritual laws and then abide by them willingly by wisdom but not by fear of retribution.

Now this next topic is a very important one to discuss. There are a lot of interpretations of scripture that man is born in sin and that there is nothing you can do about this. I believe this to be misleading. While it is true that for every breath you take under the spell of ignorance you are under the hypnosis of sin. But remember your true nature is the soul. You are just temporarily, due to a lowering of consciousness, behaving as one in sin. But the heights of your awareness have unlimited potential. However, your focus has to be one of positive growth and not simply one of avoidance of the negative.

Let me elaborate on what I mean. There are those that take the defensive approach to life which is to simply try not to "sin" and then I'll hopefully make it to heaven. This is not sufficient to become a heavenly being. This sort of mindset leads to mediocrity. It is not enough to just avoid sin to become blessed. It reminds

Chapter XII: What is Sin?

me of a joke by the comedian Chris Rock. He mocked how some people say things like "I ain't never been to jail!" or "I take care of my kids!" And his response was "You're supposed to!" In other words, no one is going to give you much credit for doing things that we're supposed to do. Similarly, we're supposed to "not sin." God created us to be better!

Now for some people simply "not sinning" may be their best start. However, it is and should not be the goal or destination. You have not arrived just because "I don't sin." Your approach needs to be a more conscious effort of actually becoming virtuous. Thus far mankind has "evolved" to its current state due to its interaction with nature and its surroundings. But the time has come for each individual to take up the mantle and take conscious responsibility for his or her own spiritual growth. This only comes as the result of a genuine desire to express your highest potential. This is more than just being "not bad." This is recognizing that there have been model persons who have walked this Earth and have stood for impeccable Love, Wisdom, Charity, Heroism and more. Each of us is a divine expression of the Creator and must rise to reach that highest status.

When you come to your "judgment day" your salvation will not be determined by how little you've sinned. Each of us have sinned innumerable times on every end of the spectrum. If God were counting sins, then none of us would be worthy based upon that sort of criteria to enter the kingdom of heaven. Your salvation will be determined by your purity of heart. Do you embody the Christ-like nature of the "only begotten son"? Have you lived in the "image of God"? If your answer to these questions are "yes" and you've lived your life as such then there will be no "judgment day" for you because you will have literally become your own answer. **"I have said, Ye are gods; and all of you are children of the most High." Psalms 82:6**

Something many people seem to have lost when it comes to understanding spirituality is common sense. When something doesn't totally sit right with us, we should trust our gut feeling to question that thing. It is our intuition that guides us instinctively to know when something may not be what it appears. It is our common sense, which tells us to scrutinize the information to find its validity. For example, our intuition may tell us that something may be lurking in the dark shadows of an alley and we shouldn't walk that way. Our common sense tells us that perhaps we should never walk down dark alleys because whether or not something is lurking in the shadows we don't know unless we walk down the alley. Thus, why take the chance? Unfortunately, the consequences one may have to suffer for finding out may be too high of a price to pay.

We are often guided by both our intuition and common sense in life. In due time, when one grows spiritually, he learns to trust his intuition more often. In the meantime, the average person should use his abilities of common sense to raise an eyebrow and know when to question things. If man had just accepted that the world as flat and never ventured into the massive oceans, we may have never learned the world was actually round. It was man's intuition that suggested the possibility. It was his common sense that led him to take the proper precautions before venturing out. Likewise, had man accepted that since we weren't born with wings we were just not meant to fly, we would've never conquered the skies. Intuitively we knew if birds could do it then there must be a way for man to accomplish this feat. However, it was man's common sense for trial and error, which concluded maybe we should do more than just strap some bird feathers to our arms and jump off a cliff.

But it seems when it comes to spiritual matters and studying scripture man appears to have a fear of using his intuition and common sense. I guess some think

Chapter XII: What is Sin?

to scrutinize holy texts makes one a non-believer, atheist or of little faith. I think questioning all things and utilizing common sense in the case of understanding God and man's relationship leads to greater faith. One should develop the practice of taking the initiative to examine and compare scripture, understand the laws within and then to figure out how to apply it to improve one's life and then hopefully for the greater good of all mankind. Even if you believe the holy texts were divinely inspired, if you research the historical evidence you would know that the people who compiled these holy books, edited them and disseminated them were not the same divinely inspired authors. Why trust another person's judgment to tell you what is meant for you to read, know and comprehend? Be sincere in your efforts, seek out as much information as you can find and use your own judgment to grow in your understanding.

Many of you, I'm sure, have seen the acronym for B.I.B.L.E., which stands for Basic Instructions Before Leaving Earth. I like that analogy and think that the Ten Commandments can be related as such... basic rules or guidelines towards becoming virtuous. The Ten Commandments are just the beginning of learning how to live in the "image of God." Since God is the only source in life, everything should reflect His universal presence. The commandments five through ten provide instructions on how man should deal with one another. When you do not honor your parents and/or commit murder, adultery, steal, bear false witness or covet then you are consumed with the ego and the sense of "I." The fact of the matter is all things of creation do not belong to man. They all belong to God. We don't come into this world with possessions and we will not leave here with them. Man must first learn how to interact with one another in a consciousness of unity. If man could simply learn to live by the Golden Rule of "do unto others as you would have them do unto you," then the world would be a much better place.

You wouldn't dishonor your parents because you wouldn't want your children to treat you in such a manner. You wouldn't murder because you wouldn't want someone to take your life. Likewise, you wouldn't want anyone to commit adultery with your spouse, take your belongings, and lie on you or secretly scheme on your livelihood. Unfortunately, we've created a world of "might makes right" and "survival of the fittest." Because of the heavy delusion of "divide and conquer" we find it suitable that some people in this world prosper while others suffer with not even having the most basic needs. We act as if it's the government's responsibility to address these problems but even when the government attempts to do this the greediest of society convince the public that its "welfare." Or we begin to think selfishly wondering, "what do I get out of this"? or "why isn't anyone helping me"? And again, we're back on the offensive to hoard as much as we can in case there's none left for poor little me; as if the Lord had decided it was our time to leave this Earth, we would be able to stuff our pockets and take it with us. I assure you that no man, statesman, president, prophet, pharaoh or king has ever taken one penny in his pocket with him into the afterlife. That penny is still sitting in those pants waiting for the first discoverers to kindly relieve him of those material gains.

Scholars of Indian scripture would follow the teachings of pravritti and nivritti as possibly another definition of sin. Pravritti is described as the "outward path" of creation. It is anything that pulls us away from God and towards greater limitation, worldliness, individuality and a lowering of consciousness. The Nivritti is the inner path back to Source. It is associated with the breaking down of individual barriers, greater spirituality, removing limitations and raising consciousness. These two qualities are correlated with Buddhi defined as spiritualized or discriminative intelligence and Manas known as sense-ensnared mind. Physiologically

Chapter XII: What is Sin?

speaking, Buddhi is said to draw its right discernment from the Superconsciousness of the soul, which manifests in the causal body of consciousness; the chakra centers in the spine. Manas is termed as a subtle magnetic pole, which is turned outward towards the world of matter. Within the body, this characteristic is connected to the Pons Varolii in the brain, (located in the brain stem between the cerebrum and medulla) which is responsible for sensory coordination of the body.

Again, these are just the basic starting points for man to follow on the road to virtue. However, a man may on the surface abide by all of these "commandments" and still not be an honorable or good-hearted person. Some people may not act on their temptations but still be filled with contempt, anger, hostility, and vengefulness or even hate within themselves. God can read the hearts of men and know their true character. These six commandments are the basic principles of the "arithmetic" of spirituality. Man must elevate his consciousness to the more advanced levels of "algebra, geometry and calculus" of divinity.

The first four "commandments" deal with man's relationship with God. If man has not yet mastered unselfishness and genuineness to treat his fellow man properly then he is not even close to being ready to develop a personal relationship with the Creator while still under the spell of the ego. The fourth commandment tells us to remember the Sabbath and keep it holy. Over the course of centuries there have evolved differences on what day is considered the Sabbath. There have spurned new churches to differentiate themselves just off of this one premise. Ultimately, it doesn't matter which day you keep as your Sabbath just that you do take some time to acknowledge your Father. The true importance of keeping the Sabbath is a starting block for man to remember the Creator, which gives him life. Without God no one is capable of any action or even breathing.

Out of our busy weeks we don't even take one day (some of us not even one hour) to simply acknowledge the Supreme source of life. Jesus lived his entire life in service of His Father's will. Yet many of us live as if our existence is a result of our own doing; ignorant of the reality that it can be cut short any second. True liberated masters live by the prayer of "Lord teach me to think of thee until thou dost become my only thought!"

The third commandment says "Do not swear falsely by the name of the Lord..." This doesn't just mean to curse or use God's name in an obscene way or sentence. This concept goes a little further to state that a truly virtuous person performs *any* and *every* act as if she were doing it for God. Especially when you are supposedly doing something for God i.e. worshipping at church, singing praises, studying scripture or whatever then it should be performed not only with your full attention but with the utmost love and desire in your heart. That also includes baptisms or other prayerful acts in the "name of God." You shouldn't "blaspheme" the act by not truly doing it with the purest and sincerest efforts at feeling God's presence.

The second commandment says, "do not make an image or any likeness of what is in the heavens above." Again, this doesn't mean to just not create graven images, wooden statues or objects intended to worship God. The true Lord of the heavens has no form. All you need to worship Him is your full attention and love of your being. But further, man should not give praise to any person, object, institution, preacher, church or idea without knowing that it is the hidden Lord behind all things that deserves the true praise. Do not worship the messenger. Worship the one who created the message and sent the messenger. **"And Jesus said unto him, Why callest thou me good? there is none good but one, that is, God." Mark 10:18** All things in life are temporary. Realize that when all things have been

Chapter XII: What is Sin?

taken away from this world, only the eternal God remains, and it is He you must eventually come to directly.

The first commandment essentially says, "I am the Lord your God and you shall have no other gods before me." When asked, Jesus answered accordingly and summarized the most important commandment as such **"Thou shalt love the Lord thy God with all thy heart, and with all thy soul, and with all thy mind. This is the first and great commandment. And a second is like unto it, Thou shalt love thy neighbour as thyself." Matthew 22:34-40** If you are capable of whole- heartedly living by this commandment then not only would it fulfill all the other commandments, but you would in essence be incapable of violating any other commandment or capable of committing any sin. When a man loves the Lord with all of his heart, mind and soul then God reveals Himself and takes that man into His bosom. Once a man truly finds God then he no longer is ever separated from His presence.

So, let us ask ourselves again, "what is sin"? Let us look to Merriam-Webster for the definitions of the word often times associated with sin – **carnal:** 1: relating to or given to crude bodily pleasures and appetites 2: bodily or corporeal (having, consisting of or relating to a physical material body; not spiritual) 3: temporal or worldly. So, in simplest terms sin is anything that places precedence on carnal things as opposed to Spirit. When man seeks pleasure and satisfaction from any material or worldly desire then he is acting against spirituality. In this world of duality there are "right" things that pull us towards God and there are "wrong" things that pull us towards greater carnal appetites. Carnal things are temporary and never satisfying. Things of Spirit are eternal and all-fulfilling. So, sin is any carnal thought, word or deed that places the "flesh" before God. Only when man is capable of placing Spirit in Its rightful place on the throne is he capable of living above sin.

"Who is made, not after the law of a carnal commandment, but after the power of an endless life." Hebrews 7:16

"For the law made nothing perfect, but the bringing in of a better hope did; by the which we draw nigh unto God." Hebrews 7:19

CHAPTER XIII

Reincarnation

"Jesus answered and said unto him, Verily, verily, I say unto thee, except a man be born again, he cannot see the kingdom of God." John 3:3

For centuries the concept of reincarnation has existed and perhaps for equally as long there has been dispute on its validity. Essentially every religion has within it a sect that adherently holds it to be true. Hinduism, Theosophy, Scientology, Buddhism, Norse mythology, Native American thought, Islam, Judaism, Gnosticism, Greek philosophy, Taoism, Sikhism, Jainism and Christianity all have within them followers who believe in reincarnation. And yet there are those that with equal adherence believe it to be heresy. The average person is somewhere in the middle. They've undoubtedly heard of the concept and are not totally offended by the idea and yet it may not be what they believe. However, the average person will probably also admit they haven't conducted any research or investigation to conclusively consider it to not be a possibility. I can see why some would profusely stand against it because this one concept has the ability to undermine certain religious faiths; at least in the way that they are currently understood and practiced. But if one truly understands the underlying principle of it then it can be a liberating idea that can only strengthen one's aspiration.

The concept of reincarnation has been around for about as long as civilized man has been around. From a time, immemorial the most ancient faiths have held it to be true. The Hindus and the Buddhists, although they have differing caveats to the issue, both hold it as a basic tenet of fact in their religious teachings. The essential idea of reincarnation is that each and every soul has been "here" before in another time, place and body. The essence of the individual, soul, ego or personality, remains the same but the experiences and family and outer environment all differ. The belief is that every person has a certain "I" ness that remains consistent eternally. But for the purposes of growth, which can only be nurtured through physical experience, a person must return to Earth for an undeterminable number of lifetimes. The number of lifetimes is undeterminable because it will vary from soul to soul. Essentially each soul must rise above the physical plane of life and its attachments to ascend to a more spiritual consciousness. One's attention and consciousness turn from "outwardness" to "inwardness."

Now of course the "traditionalists" will argue that when Jesus said a man must be "born again" he was simply talking about being baptized. And I would agree with them. But as well, we all know Jesus often spoke in parables and his phrases often had double meanings. As I've been stating, scripture very frequently has layers of understanding. On the surface Jesus was saying that a man in his particular lifetime in order to see the "kingdom of heaven" must be baptized. However, history and scripture tell us that the modern-day baptisms that are performed with water are a continuation of John the Baptist's ceremonial rites. Jesus on the contrary was known to baptize with "fire" or the spirit. Many yogis believe that this type of baptism actually has to do with an inner experience of raising the spiritual consciousness through meditation and not with a more outward experience of the familiar church ceremony. We will explore these ideas in more depth later but for now let's stay focused on this concept of reincarnation.

Now what is ironic is that the average person of faith that believes in God when challenged by non-believers are offended at the idea of trying to "prove"

Chapter XIII: Reincarnation

that there is a God. They say they just simply believe. And yet when it comes to the idea of reincarnation the same "people of faith" want proof as to its existence. As you may know trying to convince someone of something, they just don't want to believe is a very difficult task to say the least. The same way the challengers of Jesus' divinity tried to test him by begging of him to perform miracles in order to prove his spiritual stature is the same way the challengers of the validity of reincarnation desire some sort of indisputable evidence. Jesus, however, knew that the lust for miracles of the non-believer would be insatiable and they would continue to doubt no matter what his charities may have been. God never proves himself but only to the pure and sincere in heart who seek Him for His grace and nothing more. The truth is God, as well as reincarnation, can be proven to any devout and determined person who seeks to know the truth for his or herself.

Now there are certain "scientific" techniques that will help any person to find the proof they seek. However, like any good scientist you must be willing to do the "experimentation" identically as the spiritual scientists before you in order to achieve the same results. Once achieved, you'll be able to duplicate the experiment and outcome repeatedly. But in order to execute highly advanced scientific strategies you must first understand the very basics of Spirit. It is helpful to study and analyze scripture to see what subtle meanings it holds. You must know a little bit of history and be able to determine for yourself what the evidence suggests. You must be able to use your own common sense to decide how to separate dogma from deductive reasoning and be able to follow the most logical train of thought. Lastly, and most importantly, you must nurture your own spirituality in order to receive direct intuitive perception on matters concerning Spirit.

To start with the basics let's get a clearer understanding of the concept of reincarnation. The definition of reincarnation is "the rebirth (of souls) into new bodies or forms of life." The purpose of reincarnation is based in the doctrine that every soul is compelled to be reborn into progressively higher lives and experiences. Each soul being an image of God is drawn by spiritual evolution/ involution to be refined through wrong actions and elevated through right actions until ultimate God-union is attained. The physical world we live in serves two purposes: 1. to help mold and refine the soul through identification with flesh and 2. to test man in such a way that he must turn his attention away from materiality towards Spirit. Ironically, the same matter that helps us hinders us and ultimately must be transcended by the individual soul. Having overcome the limitations and imperfections of creation, the soul is reunited eternally in Spirit. Many believe this to be the prophetic interpretations from **Revelation 3:12 "Him that overcometh will I make a pillar in the temple of my God, and he shall go no more out."** Until a soul "overcomes" the carnal life, he is forced to "go out" again and again. Once he overcomes then he becomes a permanent "fixture" in the temple of God, which is Spirit.

Granted, this idea of reincarnation is debatable but let's start with a few phrases from the bible that seem to suggest its existence. One of the simplest concepts lies in the statement from Jesus **"...all they that take the sword shall perish with the sword." Matthew 26:52** If taken literally then it simply means an eye for an eye. If you take another's life by killing them then you shall be killed in an identical fashion. As we all know from watching the news that there are many murderers, statesman, soldiers and politicians that cause another to lose his or her life and yet they live long or die another way. This can only be true if man has multiple lives in which if he killed someone with a "sword" that he may in another lifetime lose his by the "sword." Yet the prisons are full of killers and murderers who may die in jail or be released and live a normal life and die of old age.

How can this statement be justified unless everyone who takes another's life by violence dies a violent death at someone else's hands? We've all seen many cases today where someone has spent years in jail for a crime, they didn't commit, only to be exonerated decades later by DNA. We can only imagine that some of these people may have lost their life through state "correctional facilities" for a crime they didn't commit as well. Some may argue that this statement wasn't meant literally and was simply a warning to get man to behave. Maybe so but couldn't it have been said another way to deter man from taking someone else's life other than to warn him that his life shall be taken the same way? You can decide.

From **Mark 10:29** we have **"And Jesus answered and said, Verily I say unto you, There is no man that hath left house, or brethren, or sisters, or father, or mother, or wife, or children, or lands, for my sake, and the gospel's, But he shall receive an hundredfold now in this time, houses, and brethren, and sisters, and mothers, and children, and lands, with persecutions; and in the world to come eternal life."** Again, if taken literally, how can a man have hundredfold "mothers"? We all know a child can only have one mother at a time. Only with reincarnation can it be said you may have had hundreds of mothers. Again, one may say that Jesus only meant this symbolically and perhaps a man may have a few "mother-like" figures, but hundreds? Not likely.

Now in **John 9:1-3** we have **"And as Jesus passed by, he saw a man which was blind from his birth. And his disciples asked him, saying, Master, who did sin, this man, or his parents, that he was born blind? Jesus answered, Neither hath this man sinned, nor his parents: but that the works of God should be made manifest in**

him." The essence of the disciple's question is, did the man himself perform some sort of act to cause his own condition or were the actions of his parents to blame. Jesus expresses that he is blind not as a consequence of his or his parents' actions. The underlying issue here suggests that the disciples may have believed in reincarnation by the fact that if the man was born blind then how could he possibly have done something to cause his own condition at birth?

This shows that the disciples must have believed in the preexistence of the soul prior to a man's birth. But what truly hints that perhaps Jesus himself supported the idea of reincarnation is the fact that he even tolerated the question as it was proposed. If he thought the disciples were totally "bonkers" in their understanding of action and sin, then why would he not have taken the time to quickly correct their thinking? Jesus certainly in the past was quick to scold his disciples at the same time being very patient with them to thoroughly explain things of Spirit. The fact that he even answered the question implies that he at the least was not offended by the concept. Now I must acknowledge that the same way Jesus didn't correct the disciples in this suggestion of "prior existence" he equally did not take the time to expound on the doctrine of reincarnation either. But nonetheless the question was posed and answered in this context without further elaboration. You can decide what it infers.

There are quite a few suggestions in the Bible about reincarnation that I invite you to investigate for yourself. We will touch on this last one and then discuss more specifically the relationship of Jesus and John the Baptist. In **Jeremiah 1:5** it states, **"Before I formed thee in the belly, I knew thee; and before thou camest forth out of the womb I sanctified thee, and I ordained thee a prophet unto the nations."** This clearly states that God knows each person even before they are born inside the womb of a mother. One of the main arguments of

Chapter XIII: Reincarnation

Orthodox Christianity is the belief that the soul is tied to the body and that it has its beginning along with the formation of the body in conception. This raises the question of when exactly God "knows" a person even before his or her birth. Some may argue that this is just a figurative statement implying that God knows no time and can predetermine a man even before he is born. Or it may suggest the idea of reincarnation – that a soul through many incarnations maintains its "individualized self" before, during and after its life on Earth.

Now for me personally the strongest case I've come across in support of the idea of reincarnation comes from the Eastern yogi, Paramahansa Yogananda. Most famously known for his best-selling book "Autobiography of a Yogi" he expounds in great detail his conviction of reincarnation in examination of Jesus and John the Baptist's relationship through two incarnations in his book "The Second Coming of Christ." In this book he claims that not only did Jesus and John support the belief in reincarnation but also that they themselves had prior lives documented in the Bible. John the Baptist was supposedly Elijah (Elias) from the Old Testament and Jesus was none other than Elisha (Eliseus), Elijah's disciple in that lifetime. The distinction in names is simply the Greek and Hebrew versions of these Old Testament prophets.

His initial support and evidence come from **I Kings 19:19-20** which says **"So he departed thence, and found Elisha the son of Shaphat, who was plowing with twelve yoke of oxen before him, and he with the twelfth: and Elijah passed by him and cast his mantle upon him. And he left the oxen, and ran after Elijah, and said, Let me, I pray thee, kiss my father and my mother, and then I will follow thee."** Yogananda states this description of "Elisha plowing the fields with twelve oxen" was foreshadowing of his future incarnation as Jesus with twelve disciples. The Eastern teachings state that every soul that is not yet freed from the karmic bonds of reincarnation must be liberated by another soul who has already overcome. In that lifetime, Elijah was the "guru" that assisted Elisha in his perfect attainment and liberation. Elisha recognizing the spiritual greatness of Elijah beseeched him to accept him under his guardianship for mentoring, study and ministry.

Later from **II Kings 2:11** it states **"And it came to pass, when they were gone over, that Elijah said unto Elisha, Ask what I shall do for thee, before I be taken away from thee. And Elisha said, I pray thee, let a double portion of thy spirit be upon me."** Elijah responds "Thou hast asked a hard thing: nevertheless, if thou see me when I am taken from thee, it shall be so unto thee; but if not, it shall not be so." Ultimately, Elisha is present to see Elijah rise up into the heavens in a "fiery chariot." Yogananda states that Elisha's request for a "double portion of spirit" to fall upon him was needed for his future incarnation as Jesus and the role he would play as a Savior for mankind.

Now prior to the end of Elisha's life he had overcome all material tests of the flesh and hence had achieved the perfect state of soul union with Spirit. When a soul achieves this permanent enlightened state of self-realization, he becomes one with the Christ consciousness, which is the "only begotten son" of the unmanifested Spirit reflected in all of creation. Elisha had become a spiritual master and no longer had anything to learn from life's experiences. At this state of perfection even the cells of the dead body of Elisha were vibrant with life-giving energy and the power of resurrection. Thus from **II Kings 13:21** we have **"And it came to pass, as they were burying a man, that, behold, they spied a band of men; and they cast the man into the sepulchre of Elisha: and when the man was let down, and touched the bones of Elisha, he revived, and stood up on his feet."** This biblical verse clearly states that another "dead man" was resurrected just by simply coming in contact with the dead body of Elisha.

Obviously, Elisha must have attained a level of divinity on a level few souls achieve in a lifetime.

Elijah and Elisha had achieved the ultimate state of being that every person must achieve sooner or later. This is the purpose of reincarnation. Until man reunites his soul with Spirit, he is drawn back to earthly experiences repeatedly until he reaches his glorious destination at the end of this road of perfection. Elijah and Elisha as prophesized in the Old Testament would return to Earth not for any personal compulsion of worldly desires but simply by the direction of God's will to play the ultimate roles of John the Baptist, the precursor of purity, and Jesus, the savior of mankind through love of Christ. In **Malachi 4:5** we have **"Behold, I will send you Elijah the prophet before the coming of the great and dreadful day of the LORD."**

After the prophecies of the Christ to be born of a virgin, we continue to see a link between Elijah and Elisha now known throughout history as John and Jesus through prior incarnations, death, rebirth, life and the crucifixion. Elisabeth was the mother of John and Mary was the mother of Jesus. While both of these women were still carrying their unborn children in **Luke 1:41 and 1:44** it states **"And it came to pass, that, when Elisabeth heard the salutation of Mary, the babe leaped in her womb; and Elisabeth was filled with the Holy Ghost"** and **"For, lo, as soon as the voice of thy salutation sounded in mine ears, the babe leaped in my womb for joy."** It is believed that the spiritual stature of these two unborn children was so strong and keenly aware that they could sense each other's presence even from the womb. Of course, after birth, each of these children would go on to totally dedicate their lives to the work of the Father.

Later, as adults they would cross paths again when John baptizes Jesus. In **Matthew 3:13-15** it says **"Then cometh Jesus from Galilee to Jordan unto John, to be baptized of him. But John forbad him, saying, I have need to be baptized of thee, and comest thou to me?**

And Jesus answering said unto him, Suffer it to be so now: for thus it becometh us to fulfill all righteousness. Then he suffered him." Recall that in his previous incarnation as Elisha, Jesus had requested a "double portion of spirit" and would need such in order to carry out his Divine plan in this life. Even though Elijah had served as "mentor" to Elisha previously, he was now playing a "less significant" role in this life as John to honor Jesus as the embodiment of Christ.

Eventually, towards Jesus' nearing of his crucifixion, he began to "wrap up" his life's work in helping to develop his disciples so that they may carry on his teachings. As witnessed in **Matthew 16:13-14 "When Jesus came into the coasts of Caesarea Philippi, he asked his disciples, saying, Whom do men say that I the Son of man am? And they said, Some say that thou art John the Baptist: some, Elias (Elijah); and others, Jeremias, or one of the prophets."** Again, here we have strong evidence that Jesus' disciples felt very comfortable talking to him about the possibilities of prophets returning to form and flesh as another person even the Christ himself! More strikingly, we see here that Jesus commends Peter for seeing him as the Christ and yet doesn't correct them for considering that he may have been a returned prophet from another time. Obviously, Jesus knew who he was and yet wanted to entertain the question to see if his disciples saw him as the embodiment of Christ, which was what his mission was intended to accomplish.

Now to me the most compelling argument for reincarnation comes directly from the book of Matthew. After John the Baptist's beheading and nearing Jesus' crucifixion, Jesus takes Peter, James and John up the mountain and there they witness him engage with Moses and Elias (Elijah). **"And, behold, there appeared unto them Moses and Elias talking with him." Matthew 17:3 Moses** as the forefather of God's commandments, Elijah and Jesus are key figures in the lives of the Jewish

Chapter XIII: Reincarnation

people and the world at large. As they descended the mountain, we hear some of the most compelling evidence on reincarnation directly from Jesus himself. **"And his disciples asked him, saying, Why then say the scribes that Elias (Elijah) must first come? And Jesus answered and said unto them, Elias truly shall first come, and restore all things. But I say unto you, That Elias is come already, and they knew him not, but have done unto him whatsoever they listed. Likewise shall also the Son of man suffer of them. Then the disciples understood that he spake unto them of John the Baptist." Matthew 17:10-13**

Now the "reincarnationists" would say that this is explicit testimony that John the Baptist was Elias (Elijah) in his prior life. If John the Baptist was to be the precursor to "make way" for the Christ then why did he not appear on the mountaintop with Moses and Jesus? Yogananda explains that John had achieved final emancipation in his incarnation as Elijah. As John the Baptist he played a "less significant" role with Jesus as the "starring actor." However, after John's beheading, his role had been fulfilled and in spiritual form he reappeared as Elijah (his liberated Self) with Jesus to assist in strengthening his resolve with the crucifixion at hand. It is said that a guru and his disciple always have an eternal connection, as the guru is the one who helps to free the disciple and "save" him from the karmic bonds of reincarnation.

Now those that argue against the idea that John the Baptist was actually the reincarnation of Elijah say that Jesus didn't mean to imply that Elias (Elijah) was actually John the Baptist. They say that Jesus only meant that John had the "power and spirit" of Elias. Either this or they argue that Elias never actually died in the Old Testament and rather that he ascended into the heavens in a fiery chariot. Eastern yogi's claim this "ascension in a fiery chariot" of a spiritual master is known as mahasamadhi, which is a divine saint's final exit from physical form. Regardless of Elijah's death, if John were truly Elijah then no one can argue that John was actually born in the womb of his mother Elisabeth which would mean "two births;" one as Elias and one as John and thus we have reincarnation!

Now again the orthodox still have a formidable counter argument, which comes from John the Baptist himself. In **John 1:19-23** it explains **"And this is the record of John, when the Jews sent priests and Levites from Jerusalem to ask him, Who art thou? And he confessed, and denied not; but confessed, I am not the Christ. And they asked him, What then? Art thou Elias (Elijah)? And he saith, I am not. Art thou that prophet? And he answered, No. Then said they unto him, Who art thou? that we may give an answer to them that sent us. What sayest thou of thyself? He said, I am the voice of one crying in the wilderness, Make straight the way of the Lord, as said the prophet Esaias (Isaiah)."**

The first thing that must be said is that these priests and Levites sent to question John obviously must've felt it was possible for him to have been the reincarnation of Elias otherwise they wouldn't have even posed the question. Secondly, the fact that John engaged the dialogue in a back and forth discussion makes it apparent that the concepts of reincarnation were fairly widespread during these times. Now this leaves the question of "why did John deny being Elias if he were truly him"? This leaves us with three possible options:

1. John was the reincarnation of Elias and knew it but denied it nonetheless for some reason.
2. John was the reincarnation of Elias but didn't know it or recall this prior life.
3. John truly was not the reincarnation of Elias (Elijah).

According to Yogananda, any liberated soul has the ability to recall details of their previous lives but often times choose to refrain from doing so in an effort to not impede on their current role on this Earth. Also, perhaps John didn't want to draw attention from Jesus and may

Chapter XIII: Reincarnation

have denied any connection of himself with Elias to minimize distraction and thus rendered a somewhat ambiguous reply that "I am the voice of one crying in the wilderness." The second possibility is that God by design limits any man's ability to recall prior lives to prevent him or her from becoming attached to the ego of "roles" they may have played before as householder, elitist, royalty, sinner or otherwise. Lastly, perhaps John just was not Elias at all. If this is true, then it still leaves the question of "what was his and Elias' connection"? Why would Jesus make a statement to his disciples suggesting the connection and then leave them with a misunderstanding knowing full well that he was preparing to leave this Earth?

Now there are other references to reincarnation in the Bible but let's now turn to a historical perspective on this matter. There were several early Christian leaders that supported this idea of reincarnation. Some of these were St Jerome, Clement of Alexandria and most prominently was Origen Adamantius. Origen was noted as one of the early fathers of the Christian church, was said to have been an Egyptian scholar and interpreter and lived around 185 – 254 AD. We must remind ourselves that the Old Testament is none other than the Jewish Holy Scripture known as the Tanakh.

The first five books of the Tanakh are known as the Torah and these include Genesis, Exodus, Leviticus, Numbers and Deuteronomy. The Jewish faith is senior to Christianity, which didn't evolve until after Jesus' life. So, in efforts to preserve Jesus' teachings and life for the ages to come his disciples, as well as others who were not his disciple, recorded his story and their experiences with him, which makes up the primary four gospels of Mark, Matthew, Luke and John. We also have the epistles mostly written by Paul. There are other gospels such as the one written by Thomas amongst others, which are not included in most of the orthodox bibles. In all, there are 27 books that make up the New Testament.

These original scriptures were written in Greek and Aramaic. At the time there were no typewriters or erasers so authors would often write on the sides or margins of the paper to omit or interject an idea. Translators later on would have a difficult time determining what the original writer's intent may have been to include or delete a sentence. Keep in mind that the books of the New Testament were being written by different people at different times. As we all know, different people witnessing the same event will have different descriptions depending on their perspective. Because there had been oppression by the Pagans and early Roman Caesars against Christianity many documents would have been kept secret and would also lead to different sects of Christianity. One of those sects was the Gnostics who still embrace reincarnation to this day.

However, later on as many of the emperors began to embrace Christianity the scales would begin to tilt in favor of an organized church. Hence, we have the early meetings or councils at Nicaea and Constantinople. The first one we're aware of on record was the Council at Nicaea in 325 AD. It helped to create the Nicene Creed, which is still in use today, and it was intended to solidify the Christian Church and unite its many different sects and followers. As we all know with human nature there would have been many bishops present with the purest intents at reconciliation but there would've also been those with ulterior motives and political agendas. The Roman Emperor Constantine convened this first council. So, we can only imagine what concerns an emperor would have with the people under his empire worshipping Jesus, King of the Jews, as the Savior.

Now keep in mind that Origen was no longer living at this point in time. But while alive it is said that he taught metaphysics, reincarnation and Gnosis. Gnosis means the spiritual knowledge of a saint or mystically enlightened human being. Gnosis was a special knowledge or insight into the infinite, divine and uncreated in all and above all. It indicates direct spiritual, experiential knowledge and intuitiveness through mystic means rather than simply from rational or reasoned thinking. Gnosis itself is and was obtained through understanding arrived at via inner experience or contemplation such as through an internal revelation or intuition.

    The Arian controversy began around the late 200's in which the question arose by Arius that if God begat the Son then the Son has a beginning which would make him "lesser" than the father. This seems like a simple and small matter but would actually become a huge debate spanning hundreds of years. The reason being is that if it is true then it raises the question was Jesus God in the flesh or a potentially imperfect human that became the Son of God. Well you can see the implications here because if Jesus was only the *son of God* then he couldn't be perfect in human eyes because he would be "less" than the Almighty above. Likewise, if Jesus was simply a man who became *"like God"* then perhaps any man could become a god as well. If any man, no matter how sinful he may be, could become a god then not only does that make Jesus more ordinary but it becomes impossible to control the masses. Not to mention what need would a person have for the church or an emperor if he could become a god?

    Again, the Gnostics being an early sect within Christianity had a term known as **Homoousian,** which meant "of same substance" now more commonly known as consubstantiality. This idea would become the basis for the Nicene Creed to establish that Jesus was God and the Son of God. Thus, Jesus never had a beginning but rather was "begat" of the Father and essentially one and the same. It also helped to separate him from being just another human and thus no man would be capable of attaining his God status. The Orthodox Church finally had its solution to the problem. The only issue at hand now was to try to persuade those who believed in gnosis or any other such idea to come into the fold and embrace this new church doctrine. However, Arius and a couple others refused.

Thus, began the "pressure" tactics to force all Christians to decide which side they were on. Once that failed to work, the Emperor essentially ostracized all objectors calling them heretics and gave the order to burn any writings by Origen, Arius, Gnostics or others sympathetic to any idea contrary to this creed. Your options now as a Christian were to either accept this new belief that Jesus was the "only begotten son" or be persecuted and put to death. Of course, the Emperor justified these actions with the purpose to "unite" the Christian church but obviously it was also to suppress any challenges to this new authority. Therefore, any idea of mysticism, soul preexistence, reincarnation or human's becoming like Jesus i.e. God was castrated. Books burned, heads rolled, and objectors were either silenced or forced to go into hiding. The Emperor Justinian would bring a final end to any Origenism thought at the Second Council at Constantinople in 553. He has a reputation far more ruthless than even Constantine.

Hence, we have somewhat of a historical record in dispute of the validity of reincarnation, man's relationship with God and Jesus' relationship with man and God. I encourage all those interested to do your own homework and draw your own conclusions. In modern times, we have many advocates of reincarnation. Henry Ford, the automaker, was a staunch supporter of reincarnation as well as General George S. Patton. There is also the works of Dr. Ian Stevenson. He was a Canadian psychiatrist who studied people and in particular children who purportedly had memories of past lives. He also studied near-death experiences, apparitions and out of body experiences.

Chapter XIII: Reincarnation

His studies are contestable but seem to raise serious questions as to why some people have visions or "memories" of experiences that are from totally different time periods. He conducted field research in many countries all over the world producing over 3,000 case studies. And there have been known to be many cases of individuals being put under hypnosis that recall scenes in their life that couldn't have possibly taken place in their current incarnation. Michael Newton a counseling psychologist, Ph.D., and hypnotist has many case studies as well. Is it all just a result of imagination? I guess one could conclude that...

Now all "evidence" aside we can attempt to use our common sense and deductive reasoning to make a decision. The opponents of reincarnation believe each person has a soul that is created at the time of conception and is eternally tied to the body. Each person lives one life in which they either fall into a "sleep" at the time of death and we all awaken to face a collective judgment day known as the Rapture or each person individually is particularly judged at the time of death determining whether or not they enter heaven or go to hell; and then an ultimate Judgment Day will take place "finalizing" those in purgatory that will go to heaven or hell eternally. The basis of the criteria for entering heaven is that you've accepted Jesus as your Lord and Savior and that you try to live a righteous life free of sin but knowing most importantly that Jesus died for our sins. This is the true determining factor of who shall enter the gates of heaven.

I don't think there is particularly anything wrong with this concept. It is a rather simplistic idea. However, I do believe it leaves some rather gaping holes that are left unanswered. The first of which is what is the criteria or standard for making it into heaven? What is God's scale? Since there is no one without sin, how much sin is too much sin? Are some sins worse than others? Does murder preclude one from entering heaven? What if it was self-defense? What if it was on the battlefield in defense of your country? What about stealing or lying? What about someone who steals billions of dollars from others putting them out of their life savings? What if you die without asking for forgiveness?

These are difficult questions to resolve but they get even deeper than this. If living a good life and accepting Jesus is the basis then what about the billions of people who practice other faiths? What about the people living in small towns, villages or even the rain forest? How can you assure that everyone has heard of Jesus at some point in their life? What about the obvious fact that everyone is born with advantages or disadvantages? How is that fair? Is the wealthy person who never has to work in his life on the same playing field as the person born into poverty? How can someone concern themselves with spiritual matters when they've been starving as a result of apartheid since birth?

What about babies born in stillbirth? What about the baby that dies from crib death after a couple of weeks? What about the toddler that slips into a pool and dies? What about the adolescent that gets hit by the car riding their bicycle? What about the teenager that gets hit by a stray bullet? What about the young adult that had just enough time to consciously make poor choices in sin and die in a drunken driving accident? What about the drug dealer who ruined many lives but at the same time saw themselves as the "robin hood" who was very generous with their riches? And yet the questions can go even deeper. What about the children born with physical ailments and diseases? What about the children suffering from paralysis, leukemia, retardation, deaf, dumb or blind? What about the ones who cannot even speak or express themselves and who never even had the opportunity to commit a sin because their life was filled with constant supervision? What about those mentally "deranged"

Chapter XIII: Reincarnation

since childhood? What about the many people who make mistakes everyday with the hopes they'll live long enough to get it right before they die? Where is this defining line that makes it too late for us to change?

As you can see this "one shot only" idea leaves a lot of questions unanswered. How can we believe there is a just and loving God when so many people are not born on the same level playing field? This is the belief of those opposed to the idea of reincarnation. To accept this means either you come up with an even more intricate explanation for what started as a simplistic notion or you acknowledge that life is unfair, and some may make it to heaven having traveled an easier path that gave them an advantage. But as we tend to experience in life, "lies" can be hard to keep up with because they always seem to lead to more lies.

Now let's explore the doctrine of reincarnation. This is not only the simplest explanation, but it is also by far the most loving and *just* answer possible. Reincarnation has two basic tenets to it: 1. The goal and criteria for "heaven" is one and the same, which is perfection. The criterion is perfection, and the goal is perfection. 2. Until you become "perfect," meaning Christ-like, you will continuously evolve and be given numerous opportunities of life and death until you succeed! Reincarnation is the great "equalizer" of life. Karma which is directly tied to reincarnation is the "leveler" of each man.

Thus, this concept explains all the apparent "unfairness" we see in different lives. Similar to a marathon, and I use this term loosely because I don't think life is a competition, every soul is at different points along the route of life towards the destination God. It is not a matter of "if" you will get there but simply a matter of "when." Obviously, some will get there before others. However, unlike a marathon there is no time limit and there is no cheating. Some will fly, some will drive, others will run, many will walk, and some will stop and rest and a few will even go "backwards" but ultimately everyone must reach the finish line because there is no other goal to reach. Remember God is infinite and omnipresent so by law there is no permanent place for you to stay because He is the only "permanency" there is!

Reincarnation explains why some seem to be born with a "silver spoon" in their mouth. Opportunity for growth and karma explain the discrepancies of every individual's life, even siblings. Everyone's lesson to be learned next is different. For some being born wealthy may be the result of good karma and yet at the same time may provide the best "classroom" for them to grow spiritually. Those who appear to be suffering may be experiencing that as a result of bad karma or that role may be affording them the best and most expedient path for them to graduate to the next "level."

With reincarnation, everyone has an opportunity to experience the things they desire and yet get the spiritual "grooming" they need. Reincarnation justifies the imbalances in life. It explains why some are born wealthy while others are poor. It explains why some are born healthy while others are sick. It explains why some live long lives while others die early. Reincarnation shows that no one is truly a victim in life rather we experience what we choose for ourselves and by what we create or need most in order to achieve our true goal which is to be eternally reunited with God.

Lastly, as I stated early in this chapter, there are many ways to explore the idea of reincarnation. We've attempted to venture into it from a biblical approach. We've analyzed it from a metaphysical viewpoint as well as touched upon some of the scientific examinations. We've tried to reason it from a logical stance. In spite of what correlations may suggest, based upon my research, I have not come across anyone who can indisputably prove that reincarnation is a fact. Nor have I come across anyone that can indisputably prove it isn't a fact.

However, I also have yet to come across anyone that can prove God exists. At the same time, I haven't met anyone that can prove He doesn't! At the end of the day, most importantly, I don't think your belief in reincarnation is of the utmost priority. The fact is whether we have multiple lives are not is irrelevant, in the sense that you can only live one life at a time anyway. Thus, it behooves each of us to make the most of the one we're living now. Seek your understanding the best way you know how so you may truly come to "know thyself."

Yet there are a few unique souls that say man can prove God and reincarnation if he only follows the instructions to get to that revelation. These individuals, mostly swami's, yogis and worldwide mystics, say that a man must go within himself to find the answers to these questions. With the help of yoga, a man reaps the benefits of deep meditation to raise his consciousness to the liberating point of soul union, which is called samadhi. When the time is right, God reveals himself to the devotee and all the questions of his heart are answered. Finally, you will have all the "proof" you will ever need. **"The secret things belong unto the LORD our God: but those things which are revealed belong unto us and to our children for ever, that we may do all the words of this law." Deuteronomy 29:29**

Know Thyself: To Awaken Self-Realization

CHAPTER XIV

Level I Consciousness

"Because that which may be known of God is manifest in them; for God hath shewed it unto them." **Romans 1:19**

Congratulations on your win! I'm sure you're thinking, "What win"? Well the fact that you are able to even sit here and read this book means that out of millions you were successful in even being born. Each of us was physically conceived as a tiny spark of the union of a sperm and ovum. Your entrance into this world began in competition amongst millions of other sperm striving for the same goal to reach the coveted egg. Amongst all others you were the only one to enter the fertile grounds beyond the membrane gates that quickly shut behind you locking out the other envious sperm to suffer a quiet death in defeat. That deserves to be applauded.

Little did you know what you had next in store – nine and a half months in a restricted space impatiently waiting your release. Just when you thought you couldn't take it anymore you saw a light at the end of a tunnel. You made a move for it. Suddenly, you felt someone tugging on your head. You were momentarily taken back by the intrusion but welcomed the needed assistance. Finally, after months of confinement, vibrations, flashes, jerky movements and weird noises you were free! This was just the beginning. Then the real fun started… welcome to the world!

Although not all of us entered the world this way, most of us fall into this category. Some of us are welcomed with tears of joy while others barely made it here by the skin of their teeth. Nonetheless, you're here now and as long as you're cared for, until you're capable of doing it for yourself, the world is yours. Despite the circumstances in which you come into this world, each man is God's highest expression and representation on this Earth. Man was given dominance over all the other animals on this planet. We have not only the ability to master our environments, but we have the unique abilities of awareness, self-consciousness and rational thinking. As stated earlier, all of creation is an expression of God. Veils of delusion separate various life forms. Mankind is under the persuasion of two remaining veils. However, each man's veil varies in density; meaning some people are more deeply engrossed in ego or sense of separation. While others through experience, have grown in better understanding their connection with all of life.

Remember God is Absolute Consciousness and man is expressed consciousness. Man expresses himself in three types of ways, which are thought, word and deed. Depending upon how deeply engrossed in ego an individual may be will influence how he expresses himself and thus is a reflection of his consciousness. Various religions have numbered these "levels" of consciousness differently. Most Eastern religions number these levels of consciousness as seven or perhaps five with two of them being transitional stages. Sufism in Islam speaks of nafs and man's ego. Christianity often speaks of three or five levels of man's consciousness. For purposes of this discussion I've identified them as seven. Every man may at times express a combination of these "levels" of consciousness but is still primarily identified with one particular level although he may fall evenly between two levels because he is at a transitioning stage in his life.

What I am reluctant to do is to label these "levels" because regardless if you find yourself to be predominantly identified with a particular level or not doesn't mean you're restricted to that level. These in no way should be thought of as "castes" and we should all recognize that humans are dynamic creatures. The nature of a man can change forever in an instant. With a sincere desire to grow you can ascend your being with effort and conscious choice. In addition, the truth is the bulk of society will mostly likely be in this "lowest" level described. Now this should not be cause to fret because on the scale of spiritual evolution you've come a long way already!

The various religious beliefs may name these "levels of consciousness" differently but they all share similar distinctions of characteristics. I will briefly name the seven levels and we will, for purposes of this writing, focus on only one level per book; for it is better to fully grasp and understand the details of this matter before moving on to more intricate spiritual truths. But your continued growth becomes more and more of a personal responsibility. You must take control, practice greater self-introspection and strengthen your will for the most accelerated growth. Later on, we will talk more about the benefits of meditation and yoga, which will give you the greatest spiritual benefits.

Again, there are many ways to describe the seven levels of consciousness as you will find out should you decide to research them for yourself. I've named them as such in ascending order:

1. **Bodily Consciousness** (Physical, Sleeping, Personal, Evil, Sinful, Survival or Ignorant)
2. **Emotional Consciousness** (Dreaming or Worldly)
3. **Mental Consciousness** (Waking or Paranormal)
4. **Intuitional Consciousness** (Awakening, Transcendent, Transforming or Subconsciousness)

5. **Spiritual Consciousness** (Superconsciousness, being with the Creator or the Source of manifestation)
6. **Realization Consciousness** (Christ, Universal, Monadic or the Creator within Creation) and
7. **Absolute Consciousness** (Cosmic, Logoic or God beyond Creation).

These levels of consciousness are correlated to the Chakras but are not directly identified with one particular Chakra or another. We will discuss chakras in greater detail later and explain the differences but for now let's examine the first level of consciousness.

The first level of consciousness is known as Bodily Consciousness in which the vast majority of mankind falls into this category. It is distinguished by a heavy sense of attachment to the physical form. An individual under this consciousness thinks of himself as the body and doesn't have much understanding or ability to grasp the concept of the soul. They can hear descriptions about spirit and perhaps define it but have a difficult time thinking of themselves as anything other than what they see in the mirror. They are completely identified with their race, gender, physique and bodily sensations. They see distinct differences between themselves and other races or genders. If they believe in a heaven or rapture, then they believe they will be "reawakened" the same as they appear now as a particular race or gender. They see themselves in worldly terms and feel superior or inferior based upon this identification.

This Bodily Consciousness is primarily driven by fear and survival. This sense of fear and survival causes the individual to make decisions, which are completely ignorant or "evil." This inundated absorption with the flesh makes the individual almost like a slave to satisfy all the body desires whether it be for sex, food or pleasure. The irony is that this lust for physical stimulation will be the cause of the very destruction of the body itself. People

Chapter XIV: Level I Consciousness

heavily under the influence of Bodily Consciousness will to an extreme degree eat food that is not healthy for it, which can only be called gluttony. These individuals will fill the body with smoking, drinking, drugs or other unthinkable indulgences for temporary pleasing satisfaction in spite of the consequences. These individuals may know that certain things are not healthy for them and yet they're not able to comprehend just how terrible the physical suffering may be one day and thus they "live for the moment."

Recall that every soul expresses itself in three basic ways in thought, word and deed. The thoughts of an individual under heavy Bodily Consciousness is consumed with thoughts to benefit themselves and in particular the lusts of their body. Essentially, all thoughts are indulged in how to please the flesh. In defensive thought they are trying to always protect the body, not just from harm, but also from anyone who gets in the way of their desire to please the body. Anyone who may interfere with their carnal desires is considered an enemy. They think of ways to satisfy their insatiable sexual desires and may become violent if deprived of this pleasure. In the worse case scenarios, their lustful thoughts can lead them to promiscuity, infidelity, obsession with pornography, rape, molestation, bestiality or even murder.

The person under Bodily Consciousness often has very restless thoughts. Their mind is fickle and is driven by whatever the body desires. This person tends to have little self-control. If they see something they want, then they are compelled to obtain it at whatever cost. They are barely capable of thinking of anyone outside of themselves. Their thoughts are driven by the senses that find things pleasing to the touch, smell, taste, sound and sight. This person doesn't understand that the overindulgence in sense gratification will ultimately just destroy any brief moments of peace or serenity they may experience. This person lacks the discipline to give the body what it truly needs, which are a healthy diet, exercise and adequate rest. When the body begins to fail this person, they will result to ways to cheat aging by extreme medical procedures or cosmetic surgery. This person is essentially controlled by their environment or "nature" similar to an animal. This person is barely aware of their "self-consciousness" and walks through life almost in a dream-like trance. Their wakeful and dream states are not much different. This person sees themselves painfully separate from every other person and his outer world.

In word, this Bodily Conscious individual often is only capable of talking about himself. In conversation, they only allow another person to speak long enough to steer the discussion back to themselves. If they find interest in others its mostly due to gossip or opportunity to make themselves feel secure by other people's shortcomings. It is difficult for this person to grasp any value or principle that isn't self-serving. Their politics mostly revolve around "what's in it for me"? They seek immediate sense gratification and want immediate results.

In deed or action, the Bodily Conscious individual wants all the things in life that give the body the most pleasure. This "lowest" level of self is controlled by ego, pride, greed, and lust; and is very much self-centered. It is important to note that when we are discussing the "self" we are not really referring to the soul but rather the "ego" which is masquerading as the True Self. But this ego can never be completely evil; rather it is merely misled into pursuing things that take him away from Truth or God. Also, no person is ever a static creature; rather we are all dynamic beings continuously being pulled towards Spirit or towards materiality. This ego is driven by impulses to satisfy desires. These "impulses" dominate any effort to reason or discriminate behavior. The actions of the ego under Bodily Consciousness are like a

Chapter XIV: Level I Consciousness

wild elephant and are uncontrollable and often unstoppable.

This first level of human consciousness is an expression of the sense-dominated individual subject to evil acts. It is reflected in complete selfishness with lack of compassion, morality or sense of community. It shows itself in collective form as "survival of the fittest," "might makes right," and the "strong take from the weak." These individuals often are not even aware of their lack of will unless they attempt to modify one of their behaviors. This will usually result in denial because they don't see a need to change. On a massive scale, many individuals under the heavy influence of Bodily Consciousness create a climate of domination, aggressiveness and territoriality. This undermines the very fabric of society and leads to war and the tearing apart of nations and planetary peace. Although, most people don't express a constant state of animalistic behavior, the average person will resort to this expression if threatened or when desperate.

It is important to note that even a Bodily Conscious individual may have a belief in God. However, that belief often expresses itself in the need for safety, protection, security and the fulfillment of bodily desires. This individual's religion has evolved from the primitive man's need to feel safe from his environment. They turn to God in need of protection from Mother Nature, to provide health to the body, basic survival needs and the attainment of desires. These individuals tend to believe in a wrathful God that needs praise and worship through fear of extinction or eternal punishment. Their desire to make it to heaven is more so due to the fear of Hell rather than a true desire of a heavenly life or the effort to spiritualize him or herself. Because these individuals see themselves as the body, they fear death and separation from the flesh. They seek to preserve the salvation of the body rather than the upliftment of a soul.

These people call upon God to help them to prosper in worldly matters. Their religious practice is one of insecurity, fear and anxiety. Their religious salvation is closely tied to the concept of sin, favoritism, rewards and punishment. These individuals very much believe in the "right side" and the "wrong side." They believe their God is the "right" God and anyone on the "wrong" side will be judged by God and shall ultimately suffer eternal damnation. These individuals are afraid to question any scriptural teachings for fear of not believing or showing lack of faith. These Bodily Conscious individuals will even betray their own so-called beliefs by committing the ultimate atrocities and justifying it by saying it was in the name of God. They fail to be able to see this contradiction that an all-powerful God would need someone to do His killing if He so desired it to be done. If you believe in the Judaic scriptures of the Old Testament, you will be fully aware of God's ability to cause floods, drought, famine, plagues or any other disaster if He so chose to eliminate any particular group of people; without the need of any one particular person's help.

What's most important about this level of consciousness is not to go around looking for people who appear to exemplify these characteristics. These identifiers are not meant for us to use as ammunition against our fellow man rather to help those grow who may need help. More importantly, we should look for these traits within ourselves to begin to attempt to overcome them. We must begin to learn to practice greater self-control and discipline. We must learn to use greater wisdom and discrimination in monitoring and later controlling our thoughts. Even when we succumb to vindictive or selfish thoughts, we should refrain from speaking these evils. Lastly, if we should lose control and voice aggressive, controlling, domineering and self-serving words, we should at least try not to act upon the situation to make matters worse.

Chapter XIV: Level I Consciousness

All things begin with our perception. If we see ourselves merely as physical beings, without a soul or consciousness unconnected to our fellow man, then we will behave in fearful ways that lead to ignorant, evil and "counter to Spirit" actions. The first step to raising the consciousness beyond Bodily Consciousness is to gradually change your perception of yourself and the world surrounding you. Regardless of your consciousness and connection to the body, your true "self" exists beyond the human flesh. As you begin to see yourself more as a soul that inhabits a body as opposed to being just a body you will then come to ask yourself the correct questions of "who am I" and "why am I here"? The pondering of these questions alone begins to separate your consciousness from physical identification. Knowing yourself to be more than a race or gender you will come to see others as more than just their race or gender. You can then come to see everyone as a part of a greater whole with more in common in Spirit than the differences of physical form.

When we are capable of altering our perception, then our beliefs expand as well. As your belief strengthens knowing that there is more than what appears between you and mankind, your thoughts become less self-centered and concerned with survival of the body. You become more greatly interested in things that will serve your inner being. Your words and ultimately your actions will fall in concert with your newfound thoughts about yourself and your relationship with others. As you begin to identify your connection with others you now recognize how your actions towards others affects them and your own well-being. Thus, you begin to practice greater self-control and learn to discipline your behavior. Remember all of mankind is still encased within this second to last veil or intelligent sheath. As man ascends his consciousness, this veil becomes more transparent and begins to "dissolve." As a man expands his "self," his consciousness advances gradually through the seven levels of consciousness and thus he enters the next level of consciousness known as the Emotional Consciousness.

PART III: REVELATION

CHAPTER XV

Armageddon or Apocalypse?

Thus far, we've discussed the makings of man from the very beginning in Genesis. Man, becoming a self-conscious "image of God," then journeys amongst God's creation apart from the Creator (in awareness). This journey is what we call life. Revelation is the completion of that journey, the end of separation from God and thus man's ultimate return to Spirit. According to Merriam-Webster's, **Revelation** is defined as 1a: an act of revealing or communicating divine truth; b: something that is revealed by God to humans; 2a: an act of revealing to view or making known; b: something that is revealed – an enlightening or astonishing disclosure; c: a pleasant often enlightening surprise; 3: an apocalyptic writing addressed to early Christians of Asia Minor and included as a book in the New Testament. According to Wikipedia, **Revelation** is described as the act of revealing or disclosing, or making something obvious and clearly understood through active or passive communication with the Divine. Revelation can originate directly from a deity or through an agent such as an angel.

What is now most popularly known as the **Book of Revelation** was originally found in the earliest writings as the **Apocalypse of John.** Some argue that it should be the "Apocalypse of Jesus as scribed by John" since these are the revelations revealed by Jesus to St. John, his disciple. According to Merriam-Webster the word **Apocalypse** is defined as 1a: one of the Jewish and Christian writings of 200 BC to AD 150 marked by pseudonymity, symbolic imagery and the expectation of an imminent cosmic cataclysm in which God destroys the ruling powers of evil and raises the righteous to life in a messianic kingdom; b: something viewed as a prophetic revelation; b: Armageddon; 3: a great disaster. However, the actual world **Apocalypse** is a Greek word, which simply means revelation or "lifting of the veil." It is a term applied to the disclosure, to certain privileged persons, of something hidden from the majority of humankind. Today, the term is often used to refer to the end of the world, which may be a shortening of the phrase *apokalupsis eschaton* which literally means "revelation at the end of the eon, or age." Again, the English word "world" comes from the Greek word "eon" which only means "age." It is important to note that there are actually other writings still in existence today known as the Apocalypse of Peter and the Apocalypses of Adam, Abraham and Elias. Again, these would simply mean the "lifting of the veil" of these personages in divine contact.

I'm not sure how or when the word Apocalypse evolved to suggest such an unappealing connotation as the destruction of the entire world. I personally feel it is the gradual result of years of ignorance and lack of understanding of metaphorical writings intentionally written as such to mask the deeper meaning and teachings of matters that the masses weren't ready to comprehend in order to maintain its sacredness. In other words, it is an esoteric truth passed down to a few ready to receive its message while hidden in allegory for the many as simply a prophetic story. When a divine person experiences an apocalyptic transcendence, the "lifting of their veil" means an end to their ignorance or "not knowing." Once a hidden truth is revealed, your experience of the world ends as you once knew it. But I can see how the words "eon" "age" "world" "end" "prophecy" "vision" "beast" etc can create a doom

Chapter XV: Armageddon or Apocalypse?

and gloom perspective for those lacking the proper understanding and context.

Since the word Genesis actually means "beginning" it is natural to conclude that the last book in the Bible must be the end. However, as noted the word *revelation* simply means to make something known and the word *apocalypse* means the lifting of a veil. Both words insinuate that man is to come to understand something from the Creator Himself. Any logical person can conclude that this "revealing" must pertain to man, God and our relationship with Him whether that means a happy relationship or a separation from His Blessedness. Because most people believe Revelation to be a futuristic telling of things to come, we tend to develop a nonchalant attitude of worrying about that "bridge" when we get to it. But what if we didn't have to wait for some unforeseen future event to take place? What if each of us was capable of having our own "unveiling" individually at any point in time? After all, we see people die everyday. Are they all having their "judgment day" upon death? Is it possible for the Creator to reveal His mysteries to us while we're still alive as a result of our own conscious effort?

Unfortunately, apocalyptic spiritual matters as such in the wrong hands of the ignorant are like nuclear weapons that can lead to colossal misdirection, misinterpretation and destruction of the potential enlightenment of the masses in what are actually Holy Truths for its salvation. The Book of Revelation contains significant imagery, symbolism and prophecy, some of which may have already occurred. Because man has free will it is extremely difficult to interpret prophecy since it is not "set in stone" how things will transpire. Certain secrets of the universe are hidden even from the most highly evolved spiritual beings. If man is to know exactly how things are going to happen, it makes it difficult to know if a person has any choice in the matter and makes it nearly impossible for him to make any decision for fear of bringing about an undesired result. God doesn't want to paralyze man from using his will rather develop his will, discipline his senses and through union of his soul transcend the training grounds of the world.

God's intent is for man to learn from his experiences and to gain wisdom for making better choices. Prophecies of the future are often only mere "glimpses" of things to come. While it is assured that the world as we know it will eventually come to an end, this is most likely so many years into the future that it doesn't have much bearing on your personal life. Instead of trying to figure out how the world will end, your time would be much better spent trying to decide how to live your life in the fullest harmony with God's will and thus the ending of the world shall be irrelevant to your personal salvation. So, for purposes of this book we will focus on the spiritual interpretations of Revelation as it pertains to the universal truths of Jesus' "unveiling" to each and every person's individual apocalypse. There are some important clues in Revelation that are pertinent to everyone's spiritual progress that must eventually come to pass.

As stated earlier, all of creation exists as separate entities as a result of various "veils" which are a result of mind, ego, ignorance and consequent bodies. Man being God's highest reflection of consciousness on Earth is still under the influence of two remaining veils. Man's ego through the influence of evolution has journeyed to his current state of awareness. At this point, man must consciously pick up the reigns and begin to "involve" himself by completing the circle of life and reuniting his soul with Spirit. This is the challenge and yet unavoidable goal of every person to redirect his consciousness which has thus far been attached to his physical form having its focus outside of itself directed through the senses to worldly desires.

Chapter XV: Armageddon or Apocalypse?

Man, through time, comes to realize that his outward pursuits even when attained only provide temporary satisfaction. The soul after witnessing many disappointments becomes disenchanted with worldly pleasures and begins to wonder if there is greater fulfillment to be found elsewhere. Thus far, man's ego has been almost in a dream like state simply absorbing input from the dictates of the outside world. Upon this new spark of dissatisfaction, the soul begins to consciously seek its way home towards Spirit. This shift in consciousness can literally feel like you've just awakened in life. You reflect upon your former consciousness as if you had been going through life almost in a foggy haze as if you were in a slumber.

However, the ego and the senses used to having their way and command over the body do not just relinquish control easily. They will try to find ways to pacify the soul and persuade it to not let go of worldly pleasures. Hence, a battle ensues for rightful control and dominion. You start to feel as though your life is in conflict. This shift in paradigm will make it very difficult for you to function and operate in the world in the same ways you were familiar with previously. You may experience difficulty in relationships, workplace, career choices, health, emotional feelings and psychological well-being. The length of these spells will vary from person to person. You may start to feel like you're going through a depression.

I advise anyone who may be experiencing these sensations to cling closely to good friends or family that you can talk things through with. Depending upon the advice you receive you'll learn who the people are that are in the best position to give you guidance and help you through these moments. Since the challenges you are having are of a spiritual nature, no physical or even psychological solution or treatment is going to remedy what you are experiencing. When you have a foot problem you go see a podiatrist. If you're eyes are failing, you go see an optometrist. Likewise, if you are having spiritual troubles then you should go see a spiritual "doctor." Of course, it is difficult to know if you have a properly trained and skilled spiritual doctor even if they are active high-ranking members of a church.

Many people may think they're qualified to advise others on spiritual matters but do not have true spiritual wisdom they've acquired on their own rather they're just parroting what they've always been told. You will come to know the difference intuitively based upon what you hear and the vibes you receive. Trust your instincts or rather intuition. There have been a lot of great books written on very diverse spiritual matters. I suggest you take the time to do some research and find a book that closely pertains to what you may be going through. In addition, be sincere in your prayers and God will direct you to where you need to be or bring the right people into your life. Refrain from becoming attached to the things that may enter your life because people, events and places may come into your life for a specific reason but are not meant to be there permanently or to become your crutch.

In essence, God is helping you to learn to "walk on your own." For the most part, He's been carrying us through life, the good and the bad, in order for us to reach this turning point. Now when you may seem to need Him most He may seem to not be there. What in fact is happening is that similar to a baby you've been totally dependent and cared for by the Parent. Now your soul has stirred and you're seeking to learn how to crawl. But the only way for you to truly learn to crawl is to use the "muscles" you've never had to use before. These muscles are actually your discrimination or judgment, your strength of will power, your inner wisdom or intuition, your self-control and discipline which all must be strengthened until you not only learn to crawl but also walk, run and ultimately "fly" in Spirit! Be patient and yet be focused and determined and you'll learn that many things in your life are simply the result of your perception. By changing your thoughts about things, you can actually change your experiences. With enough time, clarity of mind and purity of heart you'll come to realize that manipulating the events in your life actually becomes rather easy.

But keep in mind that this can be a dangerous time for you because what originally awakened your soul was the dissatisfaction with worldly things and relationships. Your ego will try to pacify the soul by showing you how easily you can now have all the things in life you've ever wanted. In the Book of Matthew when Jesus went into the desert to fast, he was afterwards tempted by the devil to make a kingdom for himself here on Earth. However, Jesus states **"Get thee hence, Satan: for it is written, Thou shalt worship the Lord thy God, and him only shalt thou serve."** Matthew 4:10 Later, prior to his crucifixion, when Peter deplores him to make his death not so, he responds **"For what is a man profited, if he shall gain the whole world, and lose his own soul? or what shall a man give in exchange for his soul"?** Matthew 16-26 **Now** what is hidden in symbols throughout Revelation is the secret of how man may save his soul. That secret lies within man's ability to turn his attention inward through meditative effort and through a science of Yoga or union.

As we discussed earlier, God symbolically breathed life into creation through the Holy Spirit and breathed life into the nostrils of man making him a living soul. As well, all know the breath is what most vitally sustains every human being. If you cut off the breath a person will suffocate and die within minutes. This breath of the Holy Spirit is also what sustains the cosmos and the expression of all creation. When God withdraws his "breath" all of universal manifestation shall dissolve upon his inhalation and shall remain suspended in "nothingness" until the Creator breathes forth again recreating the heavens and the earth. Man, as a microcosmic image of the Creator, must also learn to consciously "be still" by controlling the breath. Through repeated efforts and practice, man gradually learns to master control of the breath while still retaining consciousness. Over time he comes to understand that his existence is ultimately independent from the attached inhalation and exhalation of the breath to the flesh.

Now this Holy Spirit, which is the vibrational breath of the Supreme Lord, is what sustains the world and of course God is independent from His creation. The Holy Spirit is actively and consciously present everywhere in creation and nothing is made without this Word. Yet this consciousness of God appears in varying degrees and it is named differently according to man's differences in perspective, experience and language. On a macrocosmic level, the Christians call it Holy Spirit, Holy Ghost or the Word. The Easterners call it Aum, Hum, Amin and Amen. As a personification, the Hindus refer to it as Shakti. The West calls it Mother Nature. As energy, it is called prana meaning "breath" a vital life sustaining force that vitalizes the sensations of breath, speech, sight, hearing and thought. In the Tao faith it is called Qi or Chi. In Japan it is known as Ki. The Egyptians referred to it as Ka, the Greeks Pneuma, and the Native Americans "Great Spirit." The Africans knew her as "ashe" and in Hawaii the natives named it "Ha" or "Mana." All of these are just varying words to describe this universal presence.

This Holy Spirit, as energy in prana, is said to enter the medulla oblongata in the brain stem. From there it creates a reservoir in the brain and disseminates throughout the spinal and nervous system of the body. In the fertilized egg of a mother it is the Intelligent guiding force that directs the growth of all the blood, skeletal, muscular and operating systems of the body as it descends down the spinal cord, which becomes the "tree of life." As this energy travels downward, the spinal

Chapter XV: Armageddon or Apocalypse?

cord it leaves an imprint at various points within the body. These points are not physical organs but rather subtle astral energy spheres that are known as chakras. These chakras are numbered as seven and are occult energy centers that sustain life and consciousness while providing energy for the body and its vital functions. This conscious energy, after establishing the necessary energy organs for sustaining the body, finds its way to the base of the spine and once there becomes dormant and is said to be "sleeping." In this form, the energy becomes known as kundalini.

Kundalini is known as an evolutionary force when man learns to consciously tap into its source. Once awakened through meditative practice and breath control, this kundalini begins to ascend upwards through the spine activating the chakras in the process until it reaches the crown of the brain. Through repeated efforts man eventually experiences the union of this Kundalini (Shakti – the mother) with the Father (Siva) creating a blissful state of consciousness known as Samadhi. This internal process takes man's consciousness through the physical, astral and causal realms and becomes a literal, symbolic and metaphysical battle between good (the noble qualities pulling man towards God) and evil (the ignorant and sinful temptations pulling man towards materiality). It is through man's efforts and the help of one who has himself won this spiritual war that a man's soul becomes liberated into a "New Jerusalem."

Man must first purify his heart to pave the way for this spiritual development. It is actually man's own ego (sense of separate existence) that presents the greatest obstacle that must be conquered. It is through the "death" of the ego that man's soul is freed into eternal emancipation in Spirit. Once permanently fixed in Spirit the soul is "reborn" or resurrected. Hence, man experiences Armageddon or the "end" of the age of ignorance and separation from God. Man undergoes his individual Apocalypse or "lifting of his final veil" to see the Reality of his nature. Through this Revelation all mysteries of life, creation and the Absolute Truth of Spirit is revealed.

CHAPTER XVI

Keys of the Kingdom of Heaven

"And the disciples came, and said unto him, Why speakest thou unto them in parables? He answered and said unto them, Because it is given unto you to know the mysteries of the kingdom of heaven, but to them it is not given." Matthew 13:10-11 **Consistently** throughout the Bible Jesus speaks to the masses in parable. Even his disciples ask him why he does it. He replies that the masses are not capable of receiving his true message. He says, "he who has ears shall hear." He also says not to "give what is holy unto dogs or cast pearls before swine." No other book of the Bible contains greater parables, metaphors and symbols than the Book of Revelation. When it comes to matters of the spiritual realm, beyond this physical world, it takes an adept that knows from direct experience to properly interpret such deep truths hidden in secret imagery.

Based on the time and ages, Jesus knew that many were not yet prepared enough to understand his radical teachings in a way that they could easily apply. *"If I have told you earthly things, and ye believe not, how shall ye believe, if I tell you of heavenly things"?* **John 3:12** So rather than give the masses spiritual elixirs too "concentrated" for them to take, he gave them "diluted" spoonfuls they could better digest in hopes that one day individuals would be able to increase their tolerance and receive a greater portion of his "truth serum." The Book of Revelation deals with some of the highest scientific teachings of yoga and thus is the most misunderstood. Hence, knowing the proper interpretations of the allegories would benefit someone desiring to understand the underlying truths. In writing these apocalyptic (unveiling) revelations there needed to be a way to paint a story for the masses to comprehend, use analogies in that day's terms the people could relate to, make sure the underlying truths stay consistent capable of standing the tests of time and yet preserve the sacredness and sanctity of the scripture.

In order to understand any sort of encrypted message it helps to have a key or a legend that guides you on how to interpret the symbols. The Egyptians were able to tell stories through their hieroglyphics that still stand today, and which are still analyzed by scientists centuries later. There are intricately woven symbols in Revelation that have been understood by sages who can read the metaphors like a nursery rhyme. When you understand what things are represented in allegory it becomes easy to comprehend the message. We will gradually attempt to analyze some of the most important concepts in Revelation to hopefully present a picture that falls more in line with God's plan for mankind and man's responsibility in helping to fulfill His purpose. ***"And I will give unto thee the keys of the kingdom of heaven: and whatsoever thou shalt bind on earth shall be bound in heaven: and whatsoever thou shalt loose on earth shall be loosed in heaven." Matthew 16:19***

As we've already discussed, the first impression that really needs to be changed is the true meaning of Revelation that is derived from the Greek word Apocalypse, which simply means, "lifting of the veil." The next detrimental belief that needs to be erased is this idea that God is somehow in a battle with Satan and that the Creator can possibly lose this war. If there is a macrocosmic war being engaged, then it is mostly symbolic. You cannot on one hand say that God is the Creator of all things; He is omnipotent but yet somehow may be threatened by His own creation. If God were somehow no longer in control of His creation, He could simply undo it all as if it never existed in the first place. Thus, if you have any faith in God and His omniscience then you have to conclude that He knows exactly what He is doing and that there is a "method to the madness." It is absurd to think even for a second that God could possibly lose any battle, not have His will done or create something with an unintended outcome. It is impossible for God to make a mistake of even the minutest proportion. **"Are not two sparrows sold for a farthing? and one of them shall not fall on the ground without your Father. But the very hairs of your head are all numbered." Matthew 10:30**

You must understand that all things in creation are operating and functioning as expected. I can't say that God intends for man to suffer or that there has to be catastrophes, starvation or disasters. But you must grasp the idea that this is all a natural consequence of ignorance and free will. God's individual expression of consciousness in man and in creation becomes "lost" when that individual consciousness forgets its connection to the Source. In the X-Men movie "Wolverine," the main character is a mutant whose body has been altered through a scientific experiment where his skeleton is coated in metal and has claws that extend from his hands. He, however, loses his memory of the surgery and sees himself as some sort of freak show and an outcast of society. He goes on a rampage to find the persons responsible for his current condition. When he finally meets up with the scientists who performed the surgery, he begins to regain his memory and is reminded that he was not an innocent victim and rather he volunteered for the experiment. He is shocked to learn of this new revelation and cannot comprehend what he may have been emotionally thinking at the time to do such a thing to himself.

Similarly, man suffers in this world not because of things imposed upon him but as a result of his own ignorant choices. If you are unhappy with your life, then it is due to your own choice or is simply a judgment you've made in your own mind as to your experience. Either you've created a karmic effect that has come back to impact you or you've attracted a necessary experience that is intended to help you grow. If we go to the gym to exercise, the desired result is that our body becomes stronger, more flexible or healthier to serve us better. The free weights are neutral. You cannot get angry at the nautilus machine for making your muscles sore. Likewise, the world is designed to strengthen our wisdom, will and spirit. When a soul is grounded in Pure Consciousness then it knows this creation to be nothing more than an idea or dream. When that soul ascends to the level of consciousness such as a Jesus then he becomes master of all creation. Thus, he can say, **"unto this mountain, Remove hence to yonder place; and it shall remove; and nothing shall be impossible unto you." Matthew 17:20**

This is the true purpose of all the craziness of this world. This is why man suffers. In truth, man only suffers in his mind, but that suffering is to shake man out of this dream idea that he is a victim of this creation. God created the entire cosmos as a playground for every self-realized soul and as a testing or breeding ground for every "deluded" soul to awaken to his true greatness and glory in God! When a soul is truly fed up with suffering and being a victim of life then he shall begin to wake himself up as if he were trying to free himself from a nightmare. This is why God sent and continues to send His angels, great souls such as Jesus, avatars, martyrs and others to show man the way to free himself. Remember God gave each and every soul free will to choose. So, to free someone against his will, would be a violation of that free choice. When an individual is truly ready to seek God in a personal way then the appropriate people, events and guidance will enter his or her life as needed to point the way to spiritual freedom.

Chapter XVI: Keys of the Kingdom of Heaven

Now the war between good and evil in the Book of Revelation is mainly a microcosmic battle that each and every individual must fight. It is man, and not God, who is in threat of suffering evil due to a lack of consciousness, purity and repentance. Man, in his actions under the influence of the ignorance of ego, commits sins that pull him away from the Creator and towards sensory temptations. There is a similar story called the Mahabharata found in the Bhagavad-Gita, one of the Holy Scriptures of India, part of the Upanishads in the Vedas. In this story the main character, Arjuna, represents the devotee who is a dethroned prince. He has as a guide, Krishna, who represents the Godhead. Arjuna's family has lost their kingdom to his evil cousins as the result of a fixed dice game. Their punishment as a loss of the bet was to be exiled from rule and after a certain amount of time, they would regain their kingdom.

Of course, after they've served out their "sentence" the evil cousins refuse to relinquish the kingdom to its rightful rulers. This leads up to a war that Arjuna doesn't want to fight. But he is urged by Krishna that this is a battle he must engage in for evil is not meant to rule but righteousness is to prevail. Ultimately, Arjuna triumphs and regains his rightful kingship. The moral of the story is that each and every soul has lost its divine birthright as a "prince soul" in God and suffers at the hands of "evil cousins" (the body) and must fight and win the battle of regaining control of our desires, overcoming temptations and repenting for our actions in order to regain our spiritual kingship.

When examined from this perspective the Book of Revelation makes more sense because it gains more value as something of personal treasure that we can apply to our individual lives. We are not meant to just be bystanders in the fight for virtue. It is everyone's destiny to overcome the tests of life and the influence of avidya (personal ignorance), maya (cosmic delusion) and thus ego (separation from God). The first thing to do in preparing for any war is to know your enemy or the opposing forces. It is beneficial to know their strategies and weapons as well. Having this information allows you to develop and strengthen your counter-defenses. Anything that pulls you away from a consciousness of life and unity in God can be considered an "enemy" that must be overcome. Anything that directs your attention towards a love for God and all of your fellow mankind (God in creation) is a "friend" or alliance that will help you in your spiritual mission.

One of the greatest delusions in life is the idea that we are serving God or aligning ourselves with virtue but in defense of this "virtue" we become "wicked" in the process. Remember the Bible says, "thou shalt not judge." Only God knows the heart of anyone no matter how they may appear on the surface. The worst thing one can do is to condemn others because of their religious faith or practice. I don't believe all religions are inherently bad, but most tend to become self-serving and thus they all compete to make themselves superior to all others. Most religions position itself to be the "right" or exclusive path to God. I suppose if they didn't take this approach it would limit its ability for growth or at least in the church leaders' minds it would. Rather than attempt to convert other people to your religion you should be open-minded and show love to all for we should be more concerned with finding Truth as opposed to simply being right. Truth belongs not to any one person or religion but to any Truth Seeker determined to know the Highest Truth.

Even if you disagree with another's faith their belief may provide an opportunity to strengthen your own practice when received as an honest avenue for growth and communication. Certainly no one should be executing people of other faiths in the name of their god. This goes against every moral code of any religion. We should all try to live up to the golden rule of doing unto others, as we would have them do unto us. When you look at Jesus, even though he was firm in his faith and gospel, he only condemned evil actions or behavior and never the person. He also never raised a hand to hurt another human being no matter what he felt that person's discretions might have been. Even when it came to defending his own life, he gave it up freely in the name of Love.

Instead of killing others in the name of God maybe you should try to have the courage to give up your own life in service to God. This certainly is not to be confused with "suicide missions" intended to kill other innocent people in the process. There is nothing virtuous in that behavior rather it is the most cowardly act one can perform. That is not giving up your life for God. That is the murder of others and suicide – killing yourself! "Thou shalt not kill." Such an act creates a heavy karmic burden you will have to work out in the afterlife and any future incarnation.

However, when it comes to standing up for truth and facing evil you should always be firm and unyielding in your resolve to embody virtue and righteousness. You don't overcome evil or convert people to be good by expressing evil actions yourself. You must be the loving example. Even when we're not surrounded by other's ignorance, we ourselves still have the most difficult challenge of overcoming our own ignorance. Herein lays the purpose of utmost importance. Man having gone through what seems like an eternity of identification with matter and the senses must begin to turn his attention from all that he knows towards a life of spirituality. After seeking fulfillment in material desires and not finding that satisfaction, man must come to realize that all he desires and the only thing capable of completely satisfying all desires is God. Man, through conscious effort, steady practice and the help of another qualified to assist him begins his ascent through inner meditation.

Man faces certain outward tests and challenges as well as inner conflicts and distractions on his homeward journey towards spiritual perfection. Everyone's personal experience will differ but there are universal truths that every soul must need to master. Every beginning novice in the practice of meditation must first learn to relax the body. The body is the grossest form of man's consciousness and therefore is normally the easiest to influence. Next you learn to breathe in slowly. Hold the breath and then exhale slowly. The breath is the subtler form of man's consciousness and thus more challenging to regulate. Lastly, you learn to silence the thoughts. The thoughts being the subtlest are the most difficult to learn to relax. The breath and thoughts are tied together so learning to relax and control the breath will beneficially calm the thoughts. Any meditation will leave subtle beneficial effects on your spirit even if they go unnoticed. In due time, with the right effort, you will advance into higher states of consciousness. I will give you a synopsis of the elevated states a person transcends.

Through spiritual progression, man's inner consciousness advances through higher planes of existence known as "spheres" or Lokas by the Orient. There are seven lokas in total. The first three lokas are under the influence of maya or delusion. The last three lokas are part of God's kingdom of Light. The fourth or middle loka is known as the doorway between the material and spiritual worlds. Every individual, animal and living thing is exposed and aware of the gross physical state of matter. Regardless of your spiritual standing everyone is capable of interacting with this sphere of consciousness. This is the lowest level known as Bhuloka.

In man's efforts to turn back towards the Father he is spiritually baptized and begins to repent. His consciousness is elevated from the physical plane of existence and he inwardly becomes aware of a subtler consciousness consisting of internal electricities. He comes to realize that the external world is simply a coalescence of the finer objects of sense, sense organs and organs of action as a result of his mind and conscience. At this stage, man becomes known as the "twice-born." This sphere is known as Bhuvarloka.

As a man continues to ascend in the baptized state with regular meditation, he begins to lose all interest in matters of the external world and becomes more focused on his new inner reality. As he enters into the next Loka, the Swarloka, he becomes aware of an even subtler state of being. This plane of consciousness is able to comprehend the magnetic attributes of creation. As previously stated, this Loka is still under the influence of Maya but on this plane, man begins to comprehend his Heart, not the physical organ but the feeling aspect of man's consciousness. This heart is known as chitta and is the magnetic third portion of creation. At this stage, man is said to be part of a "nearly perfect" state of being.

With a steady resolve and continued meditation on the Supreme, man enters the state of Maharloka. This sphere is known as the region of the magnet or the Atom. On this level man becomes removed from all aspects of Ignorance. His heart becomes pure and no longer entertains any desires of an external nature. Man becomes able to comprehend the Eternal Substance, the Alpha and Omega – God. In Maharloka, man's consciousness becomes a pure reflection of Spirit.

In time, man's consciousness becomes of an even subtler essence and enters the sphere of Janaloka. At this state of being, man is no longer just a reflection of Spirit but manifests the Essence of the Creator as well. This is the level of existence known as the Christ Consciousness. Man, thus knows himself, merely as an idea of the universal Holy Spirit of God, the Creator of all creation. **"I and my Father are one." John 10:30** In a continued state of this consciousness, the soul eventually abandons any idea of a separate existence from the Source. The soul melts itself into Eternal Spirit. The soul thus becomes "dead" in any idea of the little self and realizes only the Sole Self. This unified state of being is known as Kaivalya Moksha. **"Him that overcometh will I make a pillar in the temple of my God, and he shall go no more out: and I will write upon him the name of my God, and the name of the city of my God, which is new Jerusalem, which cometh down out of heaven from my God: and I will write upon him my new name." Revelation 3:12**

A soul who achieves this perfect state of God union is called a Kaivalyam. This liberated soul can thus discard the three casings of his body and submerge himself in eternal Spirit or depending upon the Lord's will he may descend back into bodily form to assist in the cosmic plan of the Creator. This liberated soul, however, maintains a state of consciousness known as nirvikalpa samadhi, a changeless awareness of blissful divine union with God. This "pillar of God" may interact with the world to guide other souls or subtly bless the world with prayerful good vibes to lessen the karmic effects of the collective consciousness but he never loses awareness or union in Absolute Blissful Consciousness.

CHAPTER XVII

The Holy Spirit: Kundalini

"What? know ye not that your body is the temple of the Holy Ghost which is in you, which ye have of God, and ye are not your own"? 1 Corinthians 6:19

As discussed early, the Word is God's vibratory essence present in creation. As stated here in Corinthians the body is the temple of the Holy Ghost. Similarly, the created universe symbolically is God's "body" and the Creator in the process of making man in His image replicated everything on the macrocosmic level to reflect equally on the microcosmic level within man. On the universal scale, God's creative energy is known as the Holy Spirit. On the grosser plane of existence in man it is referred to as prana.

Scientists have been able to study man's body as well as the bodies of all living creatures and plants. They've concluded that small threads of genetic information known as DNA are the blueprint of organisms and responsible for the formation of bodily tissue and organs. However, they've yet to discover what sets these genetic catalysts into motion that directs certain cells to form specific material in formation of the body. As stated previously, all matter on the gross plane of physical substance are merely condensed manifestations of more subtle electrical energies on an astral plane. Thus, science will never be able to identify the "cause" of various physical phenomena until they begin to investigate the subtler energies underlying matter. Science is still very young in terms of understanding the finer qualities of light in the form of lasers, radio waves, x-rays, etc.

All of these energies are guided by God's intelligent presence known as the Holy Spirit and more specifically, termed prana in terms of energy. This intelligent energy is responsible for guiding seeds to become plants, directing DNA to store and then form the genetic coding for all species of animals and ultimately the formation of God's most intricate creation in the human body. One unique study of DNA shows that these molecules actually function as "transmitters" or antennas. It is believed that these structures actually learn from their environments and can communicate information to create a continuously evolving atmosphere. The human body is a miniature version of the universe with all the elements present. The human body contains the solid, liquid, fiery, gaseous and ethereal elements collectively. When the fertilized egg begins to multiply it is the prana energy that enters through the "mouth of God" known as the base of the brain stem, the medulla oblongata. This energy directs all the energies first on the causal level as "thoughtrons," then on the astral level of magnetic and electrical attributes and finally into the gross physical organs we perceive.

Man is unique amongst all other bodily forms as having a developed brain, erect spinal cord and nervous system capable of experiencing conscious spirituality. The prana energy during the nine and a half months of pregnancy in the mother's womb develops the fertilized egg into a full human being capable of housing a soul and experiencing independent living outside the mother once born. Even the mother benefits from this higher level of pranic energy evident in the growth of hair, nails and nutrients prepared for breastfeeding. As the prana energy molds, the human brain to serve as a reservoir and extends the spinal cord to serve as the electrical and support system, it eventually descends to the base of the spine. In its trail it leaves behind six energy centers known as the chakras. Each chakra is related to particular colors, sounds and

Chapter XVII: The Holy Spirit: Kundalini

functions. As the formation of the body nears completion the intelligent prana energy stores itself at the base of the spine becoming mostly "dormant" or asleep and thus becomes known as kundalini.

Science has not yet been able to confirm the presence of any chakras or kundalini and they never will if they continue to search for it by performing surgeries on living persons or cutting open dead bodies to look for it. The chakras and kundalini are not found on the gross physical plane but rather in the astral body of man of which the physical body is merely a condensed version. However, certain cultures have been able to find correlations of the chakras and the effects they have upon the body. The Chinese, credited for the science of acupuncture, have discovered that by stimulating certain pressure points within the physical body they can influence various effects on the nervous and psychological systems of a person. Science has been able to identify various glands within the endocrine system that seem to affect or control certain functions within the body that correspond with the descriptions given to us by ancient sages of India who mastered the science of yoga.

Now kundalini in most people is dormant and cannot be stimulated by merely pressing on the physical location at the bottom of the spine. It is highly unlikely that you're going to awaken it by accident or on purpose if you haven't developed the appropriate consciousness necessary. Depending upon the individual, kundalini may be active to varying degrees. It is said to be the cause of expression in different individuals manifested as genius in some, musical talent in others, charming personality, artistic expression, poetic ability and so forth. However, this same intelligent pranic energy responsible for the creation of all matter is also responsible for the continued spiritual evolution of man. But man must learn to consciously awaken it, preferably with the help of a guide or someone who has mastered control of it. When the kundalini becomes active it is known as Kali amongst other names.

The kundalini is consciously awakened through a few different means. It can be stimulated by mantras, which is the devoted expression of certain sounds or vibration. Also, by asanas, which are various yogic postures that gradually stimulate parts of the body in order to awaken the kundalini in a healthy way. The kundalini can also be awakened through the practice of pranayama, which is most commonly thought of as breathing exercises but is more directly tied to the control of the prana in the body through the breath. Lastly the kundalini can be awakened through the assistance of a guru or a spiritual adept qualified at guiding the practicing devotee in the proper methods. This is the best path of awakening kundalini since there can be certain effects that can create problems for an unprepared practitioner.

As the kundalini gradually awakens it ultimately begins to ascend up the spinal cord towards the crown of the brain. This can happen in a controlled manner when under the proper supervision or it can happen unexpectedly by the devotion of a sincere devotee. Either way the kundalini now described as Kali is symbolically represented as Shatki (Holy Ghost) reunited with Shiva (the Lord) and results in the blissful experience of samadhi in the devotee. As the Kali ascends up the spinal cord it awakens the chakras symbolically represented as lotuses. Once the lotuses are stimulated the "petals" are said to turn upright in full bloom. Certain psychological and mystical experiences may be had in the process, thus again why it is important to be able to relay the experience to someone able to assist you in understanding it.

Kundalini is most popularly known as the "serpent power." This is supposedly because of the word *kundal*, which in Sanskrit means "coil." The kundalini is coiled at the base of the spine. Others say this interpretation isn't

Chapter XVII: The Holy Spirit: Kundalini

quite accurate and that the word actually comes from *kunda*, which means a "deeper place, pit or cavity." Thus, kunda suggests the concave cavity in the brain which if dissected resembles a snake curled upon itself. Either way this kundalini is famously related to a serpent energy that climbs the "pole" of the spine towards the brain. You will find images and references to serpent energy in essentially all cultures from the Mayan temples to the Egyptian hieroglyphics. References can also be found amongst the Tibetans, Chinese, Native Americans, Africans, the Koran, works of Plato and other Greek philosophers as well as Hermetic, Kabalistic, Rosicrucian, and Masonic writings.

The symbol of these curling snakes going up a pole have evolved from as early as 3000 – 4000 BC. The Greeks were credited with the image that is known as the caduceus. At the top of the pole are normally seen two wings. These wings at other times were also shown with a dove in their place. Of course, we know from the Bible that the dove was often the symbol for the Holy Spirit. The caduceus today is very often used in reference to the medical profession. There are a lot of private as well as government organizations, which still use this symbol. The Army and Navy Corp both have adopted this symbol. In the Bible we also see the phrase **"Be ye therefore wise as serpents and harmless as doves" Matthew 10:16** when Jesus was speaking to his disciples.

Caduceus

Symbolically, kundalini is represented as a snake coiled three and a half times. The three coils according to Swami Satyananda Saraswati in his book Kundalini Tantra represent the three matras (creation, preservation and dissolution) of Aum; past, present and future; the three gunas: sattva, tamas and rajas (positive, negative and neutral attributes respectively); three states of consciousness: waking, sleeping and dreaming; and three types of experience: subjective, sensual and the absence of experience. The half coil represents a state of transcendence and thus the three and a half coils collectively represent the sum total experience of creation and the transcendence of it.

When man learns to ascend the kundalini, his body and being literally begins to undergo a metamorphous. Science has shown that man supposedly uses less than 10% of his brain. Well kundalini is the "active ingredient" that awakens the other parts of the brain and the abilities that come along with them. When the Kali energy becomes unified permanently in the brain, man's consciousness transcends physical identification and man realizes himself as an immortal soul. **"And as Moses lifted up the serpent in the** *wilderness, even so must the Son of man be lifted up: That whosoever believeth in him should not perish, but have eternal life." John 3:14-15*

As anyone who's every taken a Biology or Physiology class has seen, the body contains a very intricate nervous system. Likewise, the astral and causal bodies have an "electrical" system known as nadis which are said to be as many as 72,000 of them within the "astral" body. The word nadi simply means, "flow." Now the spinal column in man is said to contain three main nadis instrumental not only to the involuntary functions of all the organs in the body but also to the ascension of the kundalini. In the center of the spine is a nadi referred to as the sushumna. Starting at the base of the spine there is another channel to the left known as Ida. This Ida is known as the lunar or moon and is responsible for the flow of a cooling energy also known as the negative or female aspect. The Pingala starts out on the right side of the spine at the base and is known as the solar or "sun." It channels the positive or male flow of energy. The Ida and Pingala criss-cross at each chakra up the spine and all three, the Ida, Pingala and sushumna all meet up at the ajna chakra correlated with the spiritual eye. These criss-crossing nadis are often symbolized as well as serpents climbing up the spine.

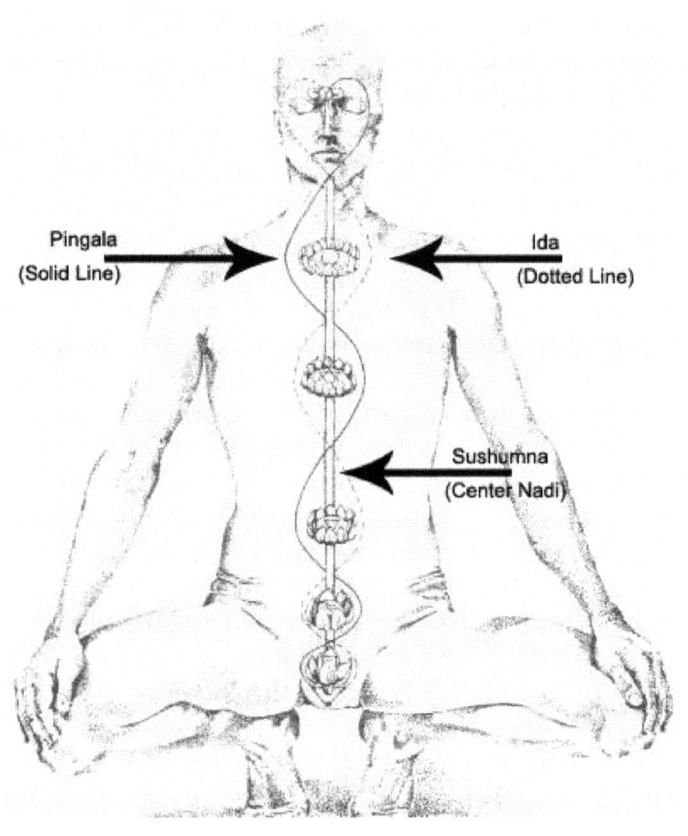

The Ida is said to control the mental processes while the Pingala controls the vital processes. Also, the Ida (lunar) is connected to the left nostril and the Pingala (solar) to the right. Thus, the left nostril, Ida, stimulates the right side of the brain and the right nostril, Pingala, stimulates the left side of the brain. The left side of the brain is most commonly associated with verbal, logical and analytical thinking. The right side of the brain is mostly associated with creativity, intuition, ambiguity and paradox. Since the Ida and Pingala function alternatively, we tend to experience breathing usually through one nostril predominantly and likewise activity of the brain. The sushumna with the ascent of

Chapter XVII: The Holy Spirit: Kundalini

kundalini helps to unite all three nadis at the medulla oblongata thus bringing all brain activity together simultaneously. These lunar and solar images are symbolized in many cultures and writings. **"And there appeared a great wonder in heaven; a woman clothed with the sun, and the moon under her feet, and upon her head a crown of twelve stars:" Revelation 12:1**

In all people, the pranic energy still enters the body at the point of the medulla oblongata in the brain. From here it is stored in the brain and typically descends down the spine and is "regulated" at all the various chakras below to enliven the body and energize the vital needs of the bodily functions. This pranic energy is often released during the sex act in concentrated forms to produce semen or vaginal fluids. So, in most people this energy is dissipated outwards and is directed to the surface of the body towards the extremities. Often times this life current is "wasted" similar to a house with poor insulation. Part of the process of yoga is to learn to redirect this energy away from the senses and extremities back towards the spinal column. From here the bodily functions become very relaxed and man's attention directs this pranic energy back up the spinal column into the brain vitalizing the concentration allowing for deeper experiences of consciousness.

The ascension of consciousness up the spine has also been symbolized as "climbing a ladder." **"And he dreamed, and behold a ladder set up on the earth, and the top of it reached to heaven: and behold the angels of God ascending and descending on it." Genesis 23:12 Through** meditation and yoga practice, man eventually learns to master the breath and thus the ascension of this pranic energy. In time, man's consciousness becomes angelic when he's able to climb the spiritual ladder at will.

Anyone seeking to awaken kundalini should do so only with the intentions of humbly seeking God. I invite you to do your own research to educate yourself more on kundalini. There are sufficient enough resources to gain a better understanding of this mystical catalyst. It is important to have a disciplined diet, good heart and pure thoughts as a prerequisite to any sort of yoga designed to awaken kundalini. The effects of active kundalini will cause permanent changes in the psyche and consciousness of the individual. These will impact your outward and social life. The awakening of kundalini is primarily for the transformation of the body to prepare it for higher states of spiritual experience.

The body will begin to purge itself of toxins and poisons in the system from the foods you intake. Many things will start to disagree with your body, and you won't be able to indulge or enjoy them as you may have in the past. You shouldn't fret your body is just letting you know what things are best for its spiritual development. You should also be mindful of your surroundings and the company you keep as well. When the kundalini, kali, ascends to the highest spiritual center it precludes the concept of duality. The knower, object to be known and the process of knowing all become One. Man's consciousness achieves the goal of yoga, union, with the Father in Heaven. **"He that dwelleth in the secret place of the most High shall abide under the shadow of the Almighty." Psalms 91:1**

CHAPTER XVIII

The Seven Churches: Muladhara

"Unto the angel of the church of Ephesus write; These things saith he that holdeth the seven stars in his right hand, who walketh in the midst of the seven golden candlesticks; I know thy works, and thy labour, and thy patience, and how thou canst not bear them which are evil: and thou hast tried them which say they are apostles, and are not, and hast found them liars: And hast borne, and hast patience, and for my name's sake hast laboured, and hast not fainted. Nevertheless, I have somewhat against thee, because thou hast left thy first love. Remember therefore from whence thou art fallen, and repent, and do the first works; or else I will come unto thee quickly, and will remove thy candlestick out of his place, except thou repent. But this thou hast, that thou hatest the deeds of the Nicolaitanes, which I also hate.

He that hath an ear, let him hear what the Spirit saith unto the churches; To him that overcometh will I give to eat of the tree of life, which is in the midst of the paradise of God." Revelation 2:1-7

    Throughout all world cultures and spiritual beliefs, we often come across terminology that may seem to suggest one idea if taken at face value. Most people will never think twice about what they're reading to possibly have any meaning other than what appears obvious. Even if we ignore the legends of sunken continents such as Lemuria or Atlantis, if we simply look at the historical evidence of more recent lands such as India, Egypt, the Middle East, South America, Europe and North America amongst others we can still find ancient relics with similar symbols immortalized in their history. In the system of Yoga there are said to be seven astral centers in the spine and brain. The six lower centers are known as chakras while the seventh one at the top is simply called the crown energy center, which enlivens all the others.

    In the book of Genesis, we hear of images of cherubs, rivers, trees of life, serpents, bows, ladders and flaming swords. In Revelation we hear of churches, angels, seals, candlesticks, stars, heavens and other vivid symbols. Many may take these simply as poetic metaphors, and this may suffice if you're a Jew or Christian. But if you ever take the time to study other cultures you may be shocked to find the same symbols used elsewhere. Now some may say those other cultures just borrowed from the Bible, but the fact is many of these cultures were using these same symbols well before the Bible was even written. The differences numbering may vary but their symbolic connection is uncanny. I'll explore a few.

    The Mahabharata is an ancient tale that was passed along for ages by word of mouth before it was

Chapter XVIII: The Seven Churches: Muladhara

ever written. It predates almost any other scriptures known to man. This story tells of an epic battle between family members, clans, cousins and dynasties. Although many accept this battle as an actual event, many others take the story as a symbolic story perhaps based on actual events but is more about the individual battle every person must face to overcome evil and achieve spiritual liberation.

The Mayans to this day have pyramids that still stand which contain mind-boggling astronomical significance. There temples even contain serpent like structures that 'light up" casting bizarre shadows at certain times of the year in accordance with the solstices. It is apparent the ancient Mayans were extremely advanced in the understanding of man's relationship to spirit and nature. Unfortunately, many have become aware of a darker period of the Mayans that included human sacrifices, but this generation came many years after the decline of this great civilization.

The Ancient Egyptians were also very knowledgeable of the chakras and kundalini. Their understanding of the serpent power is evidenced in the headgear of the Pharaohs. Many of their ancient manuscripts have been destroyed over time. There is one significant scripture by Hermes called the **Divine Pymander of Hermes Trismegistus**. Hermes was a mystic and relays the story upon which there was a time when in meditation he was beckoned by a great dragon Poimandres referred to as the Shepherd. This shepherd allows him to ask his heart's desires about God and creation. The shepherd describes to him seven spheres governed by "administrators" or governors. They are deities to assist man in being purged of sinful ways and prepared for ascension through the seven spheres to the eighth sphere known as the highest consciousness of pure "white light."

Upon being spiritually freed Hermes declares his efforts to help others through his own experience with the following words, **"I, with thanks and blessings unto the Father of the universal Powers, was now freed, full of the power the Shepherd had poured into me, and full of what he had taught me about the nature of All and of the loftiest Vision. And I inscribed in my memory the benefaction of the Divine Mind, and I was exceedingly glad, for I was full with that for which I craved. My bodily sleep had come to be my soul's wakefulness; the closing of my eyes, true vision; my silence, pregnant with good; and my barrenness of speech, a brood of holy thoughts. Becoming God-inspired, I attained the abode of Truth."**

In the Bible, Enoch is found in Genesis as the seventh generation from Adam and as the great grandfather of Noah. The Book of Enoch not only gives a fuller explanation of Adam and Eve but also tells of fallen angels also known as Watchers and Satan. From **Genesis 5:22-24** we have **"After he begot Methuselah, Enoch walked with God three hundred years, and had sons and daughters. So all the days of Enoch were three hundred and sixty-five years. And Enoch walked with God; and he was not, for God took him."** And in **Hebrews 11:5 "By faith Enoch was taken away so that he did not see death, and was not found, because God had taken him; for before he was taken he had this testimony, that he pleased God."** Now some of you may ask if Enoch pleased God then why was this book taken out of the Bible? Well, perhaps because his writings sound more mystical in nature than orthodox.

In this book, Enoch is a sage who raises his consciousness through ten heavens. The numbers are not important because the body has many chakras but the most predominant are often spoken of as seven. Enoch, similar to Hermes, reaches the "throne of the Lord" located in this tenth heaven. In the Book of the Secrets of Enoch discovered in Russia it says of him

Chapter XVIII: The Seven Churches: Muladhara

"There was a wise man, a great artificer, and the Lord conceived love for him and received him, that he should behold the uppermost dwellings and be an eye-witness of the wise and great and inconceivable and immutable realm of God Almighty, of the very wonderful and glorious and bright and many-eyed station of the Lord's servants, and of the inaccessible throne of the Lord, and of the degrees and manifestations of the incorporeal hosts, and of the ineffable ministration of the multitude of the elements, and of the various apparition and inexpressible singing of the host of Cherubim, and of the boundless light."

In Islam, there is a story of Mohammed's Night Journey. This story explains that the angel Gabriel awakened Mohammed and purified the prophet's heart and cleansed his being. According to the story, Mohammed passes through seven heavens guarded by one of the patriarchs to whom Mohammed paid due respect. Adam stood at the gate of the first heaven, John at the second, Joseph at the third, Enoch at the fifth, Moses at the sixth and Abraham at the seventh. Upon entrance into the seventh heaven he approached the throne of Allah. Many Sufis, Islamic mystics, suggest these heavens are actually the chakras.

The word chakra is a Sanskrit word that means, "wheel." Each chakra is said to be like a spinning wheel or vortex of energy that enlivens the body. Each of them is also known as a lotus. A lotus flower is a plant that grows in the water. Its roots are embedded in the soil bottom of a pond or river. Its stem is capable of growing upward through all sorts of murky water to reach the surface in which leaves then sprout upon the presence of sunlight. They are known to produce beautiful flowers that sit on top of the surface of the water.

The chakras and the spinal cord are equated to the lotus because of the similarity of the root of the spine and its upward extension into the brain where the "thousand petal lotus" is found. Some also suggest if you were to cut a cross section of the gray matter of the spinal cord it would resemble the lotus flower. Each petal of the chakra or lotus is referred to as a "ray" and is associated with a particular sound or vibration and is also directly connected to a particular part of the brain. Each chakra serves as a power dynamo that radiates rays of light and energy to the body. These chakras are also strategically located stations that serve sort of like valves. The soul's consciousness has descended into the body through these hubs and must ultimately reascend up the spine redirecting the flow of these chakras allowing the consciousness to be raised to the brain. Each chakra not only serves specific functions for the body they also have psychological and spiritual qualities pertaining to the soul as well.

    The first church of Ephesus in the system of yoga is equated with the first of the chakras (starting from the tailbone) known as the Muladhara. It is believed this mystic system was hidden in allegory of landmarks at the time to disguise the true inner meaning of these cerebrospinal centers. The word *moola* means root or foundation and it is located at the base of the spine. Each chakra is correlated within the body to the endocrine glands and also to certain levels of consciousness, colors, sounds and stones found within nature. The Muladhara, at the base of the spine known as the root, is associated with the Earth element and thus the Bhuloka sphere. It is physically correlated with the sacrum bone at the tail of the spine, which derives its name from the word "sacre" meaning sacred. This chakra is related to the physical functions of excretion, survival, sexuality as well as smell. Ironically, the adrenal glands are connected to this chakra and scientific study has shown that these glands are involved with the "fight or flight" sense in man. The stones associated with this chakra said to have beneficial effects on the body are

Chapter XVIII: The Seven Churches: Muladhara

Hematite, Black Obsidian, Black Tourmaline, Red Zincite, Garnet and Smoky Quartz.

The Muladhara has the color of a deep red and has four petals on it. The four petals represent rays that are directly connected to parts in the brain related to specific functions. Our root chakra involves all of our physical and material security. It "grounds" us to the world and yet connects all three nadis and the kundalini directly responsible for spiritual awakening. During meditation, the chakra is said to emit a sound similar to a drone of honeybees. As a side note, many believe that since the Earth is a living organism that it as well has "chakras" that influence its activities. The Root Chakra for our planet is said to be located at Mt. Shasta in Northern California.

The root chakra in man is also our first energy center and guides us in our most basic survival needs and our sense of belonging to a family or larger group. This chakra when functioning in a balanced sense helps us to feel secure and confident. When we allow anxiety and worry to dominate our consciousness this chakra can become "blocked." Because this chakra grounds us to the earth it assists us in our decision-making process in making beneficial choices and "alerts" us whether something poses a threat to us. This chakra also gives us the ability to succeed in our relationships in the world. When we have a healthy, balanced chakra it helps us in material pursuits, business matters and undertaking new ventures. In an ideal balance, this chakra brings us health, prosperity, security and dynamic presence. When this chakra is blocked it can cause one to feel fearful and frustrated.

The muladhara is affiliated with the elephant, which we know is the largest land animal representing great strength and solidity. Hence, the Muladhara can be a great dormant power when kundalini is resting in a stable and solid place. When kundalini is awakened it helps the spiritual person to interact successfully with the world. This chakra is also said to aid man in mastering speech and language. A healthy Muladhara helps in preventing knee, hip or joint problems in this area.

Now it's important to recognize that every chakra has a dual nature aspect to them. If the chakra is not balanced or awakened, then it disturbs the flow of energy in man. Also, this chakra regulates the sex drive so if an individual doesn't practice self-control, they can become consumed with lust. This lust in fact is the greatest challenge that must be overcome pertaining to the muladhara. In children and in awakened individuals this chakra expresses itself as innocence and wisdom. This innocence allows us to experience fulfillment and joy without any selfish motives. For the average person the qualities of innocence diminish due to man's perception of a cruel world, which leads the individual to become more self-serving and ego-centered as a defense mechanism or as protection of the feelings.

As pertaining to the book of Revelation the **"angel of the church"** is the purifying qualities and self-control that enhance the chakras to open and bloom sending the kundalini power upwards towards the brain. The **"seven stars in the right hand"** represent the seven chakras by a person who has control and awakened his consciousness. The **"seven candlesticks"** likewise represent the chakras or metaphorically the low light of the average person's chakras that merely serve the bodily functions. The chakras are typically in a neutral state but can be pulled in either direction depending on the awareness and perceptions of man. The advice given to all is to repent. When man begins to repent and humbly ask the Creator for assistance it begins to transform the chakra and allow for passage of the kundalini. As one gains greater control of his chakras and his choices, he becomes an asset to God. His **"works and labours"** are thus to serve God.

The creator has **"somewhat against thee"** because every man has **"left his first love;"** his

Chapter XVIII: The Seven Churches: Muladhara

relationship with God in pursuit of material desires and sensual pleasures. As man awakens his chakras and repents, he goes through a purging process that not only eliminates physical waste from the body but also spiritualizes the chakras to do **"the first works"** for a higher purpose. Most religions serve a basic function to assist in providing mankind with a moral code in which to live by. However, man can still practice morality without being a religious follower. Atheists may be skeptical of a living God but that doesn't make them inherently bad or evil. The system of yoga even starts out with basic do's and don'ts. These are known as Yama and Niyama.

The Yamas are essentially the "don'ts" of universal morality as follows:

1. **Ahimsa** – Compassion for all living things (don't kill)
2. **Satya** – Commitment to Truthfulness (don't lie)
3. **Asteya** - Non-stealing (don't take)
4. **Brahmacharya** - Sense control (don't lust)
5. **Aparigraha** - Neutralizing desires (don't hoard)

And the Niyamas are essentially the "do's" for personal observances:

1. **Sauca** – Purity (Practice inner and outer cleanliness)
2. **Santosa** - Contentment (Be faithful and satisfied)
3. **Tapas** – Disciplined use of energy (purge the body)
4. **Svadhyaya** – Self study (Seek self-awareness)
5. **Isvarapranidhana** - Celebration of the Spiritual

These are typically the first qualities to practice and embody on the path towards Self-Realization. There are some writings pertaining to ways to open the chakras as well as discuss some metaphysical abilities associated with awakened chakras. All spiritual masters advise people to not seek to awaken the chakras for the purpose of mystical powers. These abilities will only distract the devout meditator and serve as a hindrance. Those of you interested in awakening the chakras, I invite you to search for the appropriate reading. I will not venture into describing spiritual powers associated with chakra awakening and encourage those interested to work on first cleansing your heart and mind by using your life experiences and evaluating yourself to see how well you handle trials and tribulations. Those who have not begun to somewhat transcend the selfish ego may create greater difficulty than they're able to handle by stirring up abilities they don't have the discipline to control.

CHAPTER XIX

The Seven Seals: Bhuloka

"After this I looked, and, behold, a door was opened in heaven: and the first voice which I heard was as it were of a trumpet talking with me; which said, Come up hither, and I will shew thee things which must be hereafter." Revelation 4:1 Up to this point, the affairs being revealed unto John were focused on the earthly realm. Many things are revealed to John that gives man guidance on overcoming temptations of the flesh. At this point forward, John is shown things on the heavenly plane. This is where man begins to transcend the flesh and experience the subtler stages of consciousness on the heavenly or astral plane. The chakras independently assist man in raising his consciousness within the body. But once they are collectively awakened, they project man's consciousness upward through the heavenly realm. The lowest chakra, the Muladhara, being the earth element is correlated with the Bhuloka sphere, which is the physical gross stage of manifestation.

"And no man in heaven, nor in earth, neither under the earth," Revelation 5:1 This line here refers to the idea that there are three manifestations of God's creation. However, within each of these three levels there are different stages of consciousness as well. Each level has seven stages within that plane. **"In heaven"** there is what's called seven Lokas. Some differentiate that there are also stages within these stages, but I believe the sub-stages are less important. The reality of creation is that there is "no reality" in matter. For example, if you were to keep dissecting a particular distance in half there would be an infinite number of "halves" you could take without ever reaching a bottom

or "lack of distance." While it may true that lower levels exist, they all will serve the higher spheres of consciousness. Similarly, the body has seven main chakras, but some refer to more than seven and include smaller chakras that are present in other parts of the body and limbs. So, the main seven Lokas known as "spheres" are the Bhuloka, Bhuvarloka, Swarloka, Maharloka, Janaloka, Tapaloka and Satyaloka.

"*In earth*" we have the seven chakra centers: the Muladhara, Swadhisthana, Manipura, Anahata, Vishuddhi, Ajna and Sahasrara. Every man has within him these seven centers; however, each man individually has various levels or degrees of consciousness at each chakra. These chakras also have distinct characteristics and abilities that come along with awakening. Collectively, these states of awareness influence man's thoughts, words and actions thus making up the perception of his personality. We must remember that each man while still under the influence of ego has not been "unveiled" and thus continue to be tied to only consciousness of earthly awareness.

"**Under the earth**" refers to planes of existence that sustain lower levels of consciousness. Not only do animals and lower forms of life "exist" on these planes but also there are lower realms scripture and mythology has referred to as "hells" or places that house life not yet evolved. These seven planes are referred to Patalas. In descending order below the Muladhara chakra we have Atala, Vitala, Sutala, Talatala, Rasatala, Mahatala and Patala. Souls that are not yet developed, strongly under the influence of ego or paying karmic debt may descend to one of these planes until they as a result of conscious growth, grace or repentance "evolve" or reascend to a higher state of being.

We shall currently focus on the lowest level of the "heavens" (in this case the earth realm), which is the Bhuloka. As you can see this is a transitioning sphere between the heavens and the earth. On this gross level of existence, we see many different forms of life and expression. On the lowest level we have the inanimate objects such as rocks, minerals and earth. Even though these objects appear not to move or express life, there is still consciousness present. We then begin to see the smallest signs of life through movement and thus have microorganisms, bacteria, viruses and such. These small moving organisms through time evolve consciousness into higher expressions of interaction with their environment and become all the things we see within the plant kingdom. Consciousness continues to evolve till we see the animal kingdom and their sense of attunement with nature and environment awareness.

In time, this consciousness evolves into man who possesses self-consciousness as well as freedom from nature to make choices and exercise rational thought. However, at this stage man still identifies his consciousness with material substance. Only through conscious effort can man evolve his consciousness to become aware of finer, subtler experiences on a heavenly or astral plane. The irony is that, thus far, man's consciousness has evolved mostly as a result of "awareness" of his environment and interaction with his surroundings. Now man must "evolve" not by engaging his surroundings but by "involution" or going within himself to engage his own thoughts, awareness and consciousness.

Now in order to understand how man raises his consciousness above the physical plane, we need to first have a basic understanding of what makes up the things we perceive as "physical." So, let us go a little deeper into the aspects of creation on the subtlest plane. **"and in the midst of the throne, and round about the throne, were four beasts full of eyes before and behind." Revelation 4:6** One of the mysteries of Revelation is the "four beasts full of eyes before and behind." As stated repeatedly, God in His Absolute state exists as stillness and silence, just Pure Consciousness and Oneness undisturbed.

So, with the first aspect of creation, His/Her Omniscient Feeling manifests Its Presence along with its complementary Repulsion the desire less-desire to express and thus becomes the Creator. This ensuing effect appears as the vibrating "breath" producing the Word/Aum/Holy Spirit. This Word is the first "idea" and manifests with varying aspects.

The second aspect of the Word gives the idea of change. The illusion of change leads to the concept of time. Everything man attempts to measure with time, in truth, is just an assessment of change. For instance, if everything instantly stood still, how could you measure time? If we were able to stop the movement of all objects, Earth, moon, sun and heavenly bodies there would be no change. If there is no change to measure, then the illusion of time disappears. This idea of change or time is known as Kala. However, God is unchangeable thus time doesn't exist for Him.

Thirdly, the Word also creates the idea of division as the result of attraction/repulsion. The effect of division creates the illusion of space. If there were no division then everything would be One and thus you have God. God is indivisible. Without the idea of division there is no space, distinction or contrast and thus experience. This idea of space or division is known as Desa.

Lastly, as a result of division, the idea of a particle is manifested. These particles become innumerable and are known as the fourth aspect the anu or atom. So, from the One we have four original ideas, which lead to what we perceive and experience as creation. These four ideas are the Word, Time, Space and the Atom which all lead to the creation of the heavens, earth and that which is beneath the earth. The atom becomes the "throne of God" as it is the representation of these four ideas within and without; "before and behind." The oxymoron of the atom is that it is the building block of all matter and substance and yet in and of itself it has no true substance. Remember these are all just aspects of the One Creator.

However, these ideas are not able to manifest or absorb the Light of God. If the atoms were to manifest the same Light as the Father, then they would be revealed as immaterial and hence non-existence. Thus, the existence of the atom appears only as a "reflection of the light" and they are referred to as Darkness and en masse known as Maya. **"And the light shineth in darkness; and the darkness comprehended it not." John 1:5**

Now recall that these "four beasts" are nothing more than ideas of the Creator and are thus one and the same with Him. Now some people may have trouble relating the word "beasts" in the same sentence with God. Let's be clear we are not calling anything related to God as a beast but rather these original four ideas. From God's perspective they are just ideas but from man's perspective they are "beastly" because they lead to all the confusions of the world. Man, whose consciousness is identified with the physical creation, is subordinate to the four beasts for they "dominate" man until he is able to raise his consciousness above the level of these four primal aspects of creation.

"And round about the throne were four and twenty seats: and upon the seats I saw four and twenty elders sitting, clothed in white raiment; and they had on their heads crowns of gold." Revelation 4:4 Now from these four original ideas evolve other ideas that descend to manifest what appears as grosser and grosser manifestations of matter. But ultimately all of matter is nothing more than an extended idea of these four original ideas, which are aspects of the One but only as Creator. Again, God sits on the "throne" and is therefore above any of His created aspects.

The atom, "throne of God," is comprised of the original four ideas. This atom becomes magnetized as a result of the pull of two opposing forces that produces "poles." The one force, which is Universal Love attempts to pull the atom back towards the One Truth being God. The other force is a repulsion, which attempts to pull the atom towards the enjoyment of creation. This first pull, the attraction being known as the Heart or Chitta, when spiritualized is known as Buddhi or Intelligence (two aspects of the same idea). The other pull, the repulsion known as Manas or Mind when under the influence of Ignorance (separate existence) is known as ego; the **son of man** (two aspects of the other idea).

Now to summarize, the Atom (Anu, four ideas - beasts) is under the influence of four other ideas Chitta (Heart), Buddhi (Intelligence), Manas (Mind) and Ego (Ahamkara). The activity of these pulls or energies (ideas in motion) manifest the idea of a body for the ego (idea of self). This idea of a body, also known as a "causal body," consists, as well, of two extreme pulls in opposing directions, a center or neutral middle point between the two extreme poles, and two midway points between the center (neutral point) and the positive and negative pole extremities. Thus, you have five points also known as the five Root Causes or five instruments of knowledge and they function as "electricities" creating the idea of a causal body, which is nothing more than a magnetic field. Thus, the "ego" has its "first cause-all" body made up of *nine ideas*: Heart, Intelligence, Mind, Ego and five instruments of knowledge; the subtle *ideas* of sight, hearing, smell, taste and touch.

From this causal body, the ego (idea of self) made up of nine ideas develops fifteen more ideas, which all fall under the influence of the three aspects sattva (positive), rajas (neutral) and tamas (negative). The first five under the positive influence are called Jnanendriyas and they are the *mental organs* of the senses or instruments of action known as the abilities to procreate, excrete, speak, move and perform manual skills. The second five under the neutral influence are

Chapter XIX: The Seven Seals: Bhuloka

called Karmendriyas and they are the five instruments of prana (energy) or *organs of action* and are the crystallizing, assimilating, eliminating, metabolizing and circulatory functions of the body. Lastly, you have the five under the negative influence called Tanmatras that are the *objects of the senses* of smell, taste, sight, touch and sound. These twenty-four ideas comprise the astral body of man.

All of these attributes in total combine to make twenty-four ideas that are referred to as the "four and twenty elders." These four and twenty elders are "round and about" the *throne*, the atom. Without the original four ideas you do not have the atom. Without the polarizing action of the forces acting upon the atom you don't have the ego. Without the ego you don't have the attributes or electricities that comprise the causal and astral bodies of man. Finally, the negatively influenced attributes, Tanmatras, combine with the neutral attributes (Karmendriyas) to form the five elements of solid, liquid, fire, gas and liquid. These primary electricities, elements and other chemical elements comprise the gross physical body and matter. Of course, without the five elements the gross body cannot exist. Keep in mind that the body and all of gross matter are just ideas born of underlying ideas that originate from God.

The soul, however, is the omnipotent spark of the Almighty. It is God's original consciousness that creates the ideas of division. So, in truth, it is God who becomes man under the influence of ego. It is the ego that experiences, changes and evolves. Ultimately, it is the ego that ascends in consciousness to realize that it is again the Sole Self and not the individual self it imagined itself to be. This is the purpose that each and every man (ego) serves, to live, experience and reunite with its true Self – God. Now the aspect of God that became the "dream self" of Joe, Susie, Raheem, Tariq, Gwen, Cho, Juan and so on, always remembers the unique soul's journey and path it traveled and thus can retain or preserve identity but as a reunited One realizes that this soul-self was just a wave riding on the surface of the infinite ocean. The cliché is our "reality" of this world is in fact an illusion and our "illusion" of God is the only Reality.

Now man's duty is to return to his truth in Spirit. Thus, we have the "roadmap" to trace our path home. This physical world we identify with is called the Bhuloka. Its "reality" resides in the ego's negative sense actions and the objects of those senses. Our desires are what attract (spiritually repulse) our consciousness "downward" to remain confined to gross matter. As we begin to lessen our sense desires, we loosen the gross hold of matter on our consciousness. Thus, we can break the attachment. By turning our attention inward, we begin to allow the Heart (spiritual attraction) to ascend the consciousness towards the True Substance – Spirit. The book of Revelation talks about the Lamb, which is Christ Consciousness "the only true begotten son" as the soul, Jesus, which overcame.

However, this was not a unique disposition that belonged only to the persona or ego of Jesus. Keep in mind that Jesus came to earth not because he was in the "same boat" as the other people he came to save. Jesus had already overcome the ego (sense of separation) from God and thus had truly realized his oneness with God and could hence declare that oneness, as "my Father and I are one." His highest purpose was to save mankind by serving as the ideal example of how man can save himself. Contrary to popular belief, God has given every man the opportunity to save himself. Man, through his conscious effort, self-control, humility and prayers will have all the tools needed for salvation. When you sincerely seek God then He will send you the Savior of your heart, which may be Jesus if you so desire, another saint of any religion or perhaps a personal guru to guide you home.

Jesus is eternal life and he is capable of appearing in thought, dream, and vision or in the flesh for earnest devotees who seek him.

"And I saw when the Lamb opened one of the seals, and I heard, as it were the noise of thunder, one of the four beasts saying, Come and see. And I saw, and behold a white horse: and he that sat on him had a bow; and a crown was given unto him: and he went forth conquering, and to conquer." Revelation 6:1-2 The mission of every man (ego) is to open the seals for him or herself. When they have opened a seal then they become one who has conquered the challenges and tests that come along with that particular state of consciousness. It takes desire, will, self-control and the grace of God to raise the awareness. Of course, the assistance of God also comes through the medium of a helper, angel, savior, guru or the Lamb. We will explore in greater depth this concept in the next chapter. But the basic means as to raising the consciousness starts with a shift in the ego's understanding and perception.

"For as he thinketh in his heart, so is he:" Proverbs 23:7 Man under the influence of ignorance doesn't realize the power and potential that lies within him. Our thoughts actually define our experience. When we have inaccurate or false perceptions about spiritual reality then we tend to create worldly experiences that are detrimental to our peace and happiness. Yet we don't realize that we are the source of those problems, so we don't know how to fix it hence we feel like victims of the world. Man must learn how to change his belief system, and this starts with understanding our selves and our relationship to God. Being made in God's image, in truth, has really little to do with our physical appearance and much more to do with our spiritual potential.

When man understands himself as a spiritual being, he learns to conduct himself in spiritual ways. Thus, man must learn to seek answers within. When a man's interests shift from outside phenomena to internal truths he then eventually "becomes" that which he seeks or identifies with. As an example, if you place a crystal next to a red object, the crystal seems to take on the color of the object. If you change the color to purple, blue, yellow or otherwise then the crystal changes the same. Likewise, man becomes that which he identifies with. To become spiritual, you must identify with Spirit. Thus, we have **"But seek ye first the kingdom of God, and his righteousness; and all these things shall be added unto you." Matthew 6:33** The way to open the seal of Bhuloka; you must first learn to go within by meditation. You begin to repent for your transgressions against Spirit and learn to honor God's truth and His truth about you. You become spiritually baptized and your heart becomes purified. In time you "awaken" to a new spiritual world that transcends our physical plane consciousness and yet you remain able to function and interact with the world but just from a new heightened position.

Illustration of how the Formless takes Form

Chapter XIX: The Seven Seals: Bhuloka

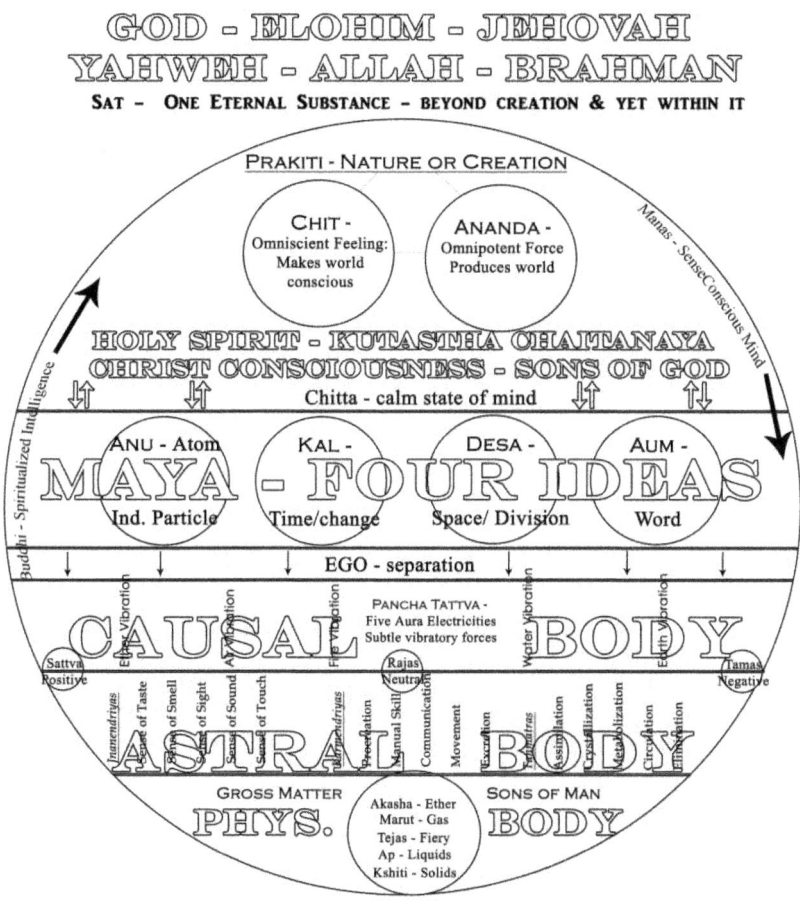

- Four Beasts constitute Maya: Time, Space, Aum & Atom
- Four and Twenty Elder – Five gross matters along with 15 attributes plus the four beasts.

CHAPTER XX

The Lamb: Savior or Guru?

"Then said Jesus unto them, When ye have lifted up the Son of man, then shall ye know that I am he, and that I do nothing of myself; but as my Father hath taught me, I speak these things." John 8:28

In all of history, there has probably never been a figure more controversial than Jesus Christ. Prior to even being born, he was foretold to come unto the world. With this prophecy, even before he was born, there was an attempt to end his life through execution. His birth itself was said to be an immaculate conception from a virgin mother and a father none other than the God "up above." I guess his child life was fairly normal except for the fact that he was known to perform miracles, quote scripture by heart and challenge the most scholarly High Priests of his time. He was born a Jew and yet not accepted by many of them within the church at the time. In due time, mostly non-Jews would carry on his legacy. A new religion would be born from his teachings known as Christianity separating itself from Judaism. He was very independent as a young child, less concerned with his parents input and oftentimes told them of his plans and the work he was sent to do, not typical of the average child. He disappears for days and not once is frightened or concerned in search of his parents. His teenage years are mysteriously absent from the Bible but according to some accounts he did extensive travel and was received in many countries.

He resurfaces in the Bible as a grown man, gets baptized by a reluctant prophet of God, accepts twelve disciples, challenges the status quo, preaches the gospel, heals the sick, feeds the hungry, associates with the lowest classes, breaks the religious rules of the day, gets betrayed by one closest to him and willingly gives up his life to "save the world" without ever resisting or even putting up a fight. Oh, and did I mention three days after he is confirmed dead and placed in a tomb, he is seen risen amongst many of his family and followers? If that's not a story for all time I don't know what is! As controversial as he was alive, he's even more controversial now that he's no longer here in the flesh.

Leading up to his crucifixion, it was dangerous to be associated with him. One of his own disciples betrayed him and even the ones who didn't betray him denied him. The following decades after his death laid the foundation for a new religion known as Christianity. However, it would be a liability to be considered a Christian, punishable by death. In time it would be acceptable to be a Christian but being the "wrong kind" of Christian would still be a liability, punishable by death. Approximately five hundred years following Jesus' death it would ultimately become a liability to *not* be a Christian; anything else could be punishable by death. With such controversy surrounding Jesus, the extreme mood swings of public opinion and the political ramifications associated with him, it is difficult to know what the truth is concerning him and what has been historical manipulation.

Obviously, there would be various figures over time that would have their own agendas concerning their beliefs related to Jesus as well as the public's belief concerning him. Although most religions are founded with good intentions, there are always those individuals within them who manipulate the religion for their own motives even to this day. This applies to not only Christianity but also all religions. Again, I think it's important to distinguish it's not necessarily the religions fault but rather those abusive individuals who were looking for a means to profit.

Chapter XX: The Lamb: Savior or Guru?

      With that said, we must acknowledge that anything in human hands is immediately subject to imperfection. There have been many bishops, preachers, pastors, Popes and Caesars along the way that would influence the course of Christianity to some greater or lesser degree for various reasons for all time to come. While I don't expect this dialogue to resolve any of the issues, I do think it can be beneficial and perhaps necessary to discuss some of these matters. We need to look at what the scriptures tell us, what other scriptures that are *not* included in the Bible suggest, what history shows us and most importantly what the words directly from Jesus state.

      Now this is not intended to be an extensive examination of Jesus' life but the first thing we should look at is the foretelling of his birth. While there are many prophecies in the Bible, his birth is particularly of importance because of his status as the one who would come to save the world from sin. There are quotes in the Old Testament related to "a child is born," "a son is given," and "the prince of peace." More importantly, in **Isaiah 7:14** it states **"Behold, a virgin shall conceive, and bear a son, and shall call his name Immanuel."** The name Immanuel means "God with us." Some would argue whether or not this was actually referring to Jesus but let's assume for purposes of this argument that it in deed represents Jesus.

      The next obvious question would be "was he born to a virgin." Now this concept of "immaculate conception" has actually been around even before Jesus' time. In fact, there are at least two other religions that I'm aware of, where the key figure was born immaculately. The spiritual figures Buddha and Krishna were both, according to their scriptural heritage, born without the act of sex. The main difference is that their births and stories were from hundreds to thousands of years before Jesus. But if we go back to the concepts discussed in the last chapter concerning the descending of the soul into flesh, we understand that the astral body is made up of twenty-four ideas that become electricities that lead to the gross body. It has been suggested that all liberated souls and heavenly bodies are able to produce life through sheer desire and will. Supposedly before the fall of Adam and Eve all beings were capable of creating "offspring" without the act of sex. Even today there are quite a few organisms and animals, including mammals, which are able to give birth without a partner to fertilize their egg. I'll let you weigh the evidence and decide for yourself.

Now as far as Jesus' ability to heal and perform miracles, I'm sure science would probably dispute all of it but if you believe in scripture then he was not unique in this aspect. The Old Testament, as well as other religious faiths, speaks of saints and prophets being able to perform miracles. In fact, there are people to this day who have been documented as being able to perform unexplainable feats. There are yogis who have been said to be able to heal others, "resurrect" their bodily forms even after death and bury themselves underground for months, while being monitored, only to be dug up later and resume activities as if nothing happened.

But more importantly than these minor details is the debate about whether or not Jesus was uniquely God, the only Son of God or perhaps just a divine being holding a spiritual status attainable by any person. Now a lot of people are fearful of discussing or, even worse, questioning Jesus' divinity as the Savior. Perhaps this is due to fear of retribution, punishment or just not wanting to show a lack of faith. I think this is a foolish approach for even Jesus encouraged dialogue. His own disciples constantly asked questions sought clarification and needed reassurance. Jesus never chastised anyone who sincerely desired to know him or the Father. Having faith doesn't have to be "blind" nor does it mean you have to stop using your intelligent discrimination.

Chapter XX: The Lamb: Savior or Guru?

Nothing examined here is an attempt to degrade Jesus but to better understand his nature so that man can better understand his relationship to Jesus as well as God.

Since his death, Jesus' status has been the cause of many debates. Religions always have the difficulty of trying to unify a spiritual figure's teaching with the intent of sending one consistent message to its followers. Unfortunately, it is always difficult to keep someone's teachings pure without tarnishing it with the day-to-day "business" dealings of trying to grow support and build a following. Keep in mind, around the time of Jesus' death, it wasn't exactly to your benefit to be associated with him. Those that were loyal followers would in time be the ones that would assist in laying the foundation for the Christian church.

One simple concept that we should be reminded of is the fact that the language of Jesus' time was Aramaic. However, there is argument about in what language were the earliest writings that led to the Bible written. Some say Aramaic, others Greek or perhaps Hebrew. I guess it will take a scientist to carbon date these writings, however, it can be a challenge at times to prove authenticity and to narrow a specific date to within a few decades if not centuries. Another issue concerning Jesus is a simple one surrounding his name. His actual Hebrew name is Yeshua although there is even debate about the true spelling. We today are customized as seeing his full name as Jesus Christ. However, this is just a shortening of a title. "Christ" is not actually his surname rather it was a title. So, it should be written as Jesus the Christ.

Now this may seem minor aside from the fact that no one has been associated with such a title since his death. But the actual title "the Christ" comes from the Greek term Khristos simply meaning "the anointed." As a translation of the Hebrew term it means "the Messiah" or "Anointed One." Now clearly, if it were simply a title, then in order for it to have existed prior to Jesus and to be applied to him, one would have to conclude that there must have been others who carried this title as well. If the word were meant to be a unique distinction, with only Jesus being worthy of carrying, then it wouldn't have even existed. They would have had to make up a new word to distinguish Jesus separately. The true word "the Christ" comes from Chrism, which today stands for oil used to anoint a Christian. However, originally this "anointing" was of a spiritual nature and meant one anointed by God. In other words, God anoints all. Those anointed have the power to anoint another. Hence, one who is anointed is blessed by God's "spiritual oil" being the Christ Consciousness or the Holy Spirit that permeates all of creation.

Of course, due to Jesus' popularity today we see all types of versions of his appearance. Although most people would have been trying to avoid him prior to his crucifixion, the masses now want to claim him as their savior. We see images of him with blonde hair and blue eyes all the way to yellow skin, possessing Latin features to Native American and of course with the dark skin and the wooly hair of an African. I don't have any idea of what his true appearance may have been but most likely he would have resembled the majority of the people still in that area of the Middle East today. During that time all of that area was considered the East or the Orient. Chances are he would've had somewhere between olive colored skin to bronze. His hair and eyes would've been most likely dark brown to black in color. Unfortunately, we are still a world consumed with physical appearances and less capable of recognizing the true nature of a person's character and spirit, which is invisible to the ignorant.

Now there are way too many details of the evolution of Christianity to cover them all here. But I will bullet point some of the important events and discuss some of their aspects. Most of these dates are approximations due to the changing of the calendars to A.D. short for "Anno Domini" meaning "in the year of our Lord." It was invented by Dionysius Exiguus to mark Easter but of course he wasn't even born until almost 500 years after Jesus the Christ. It was invented to replace the Caesar Diocletian's calendar because he was considered a tyrant who persecuted Christians.

- 6 – 4 BC: Jesus is born according to most historical scholars.
- 26 – 28 AD: John the Baptist begins his ministry, supposedly the "15th year of Caesar Tiberius."
- 28 AD: Jesus begins his gospel at the age of 30.
- 29 – 33 AD: Jesus is crucified.
- 33 AD: Shortly after Jesus' death his disciples begin spreading his teachings to various parts of the world.
- 34 – 37 AD: The Jerusalem church was founded as the first Christian church (following Jesus' teachings) made up of all Jews.
- 35 – 38 AD: The Antioch Church is founded and supposedly first place where the term "Christian" is used.
- 37 – 41 AD: Crisis under Caesar Caligula leads to public dissension between Rome and Jews and would influence Christian and Jewish relations.
- 47 AD: St Thomas creates Church of the East.
- Saul who was a leading persecutor of Christians is converted on his "Road to Damascus." He becomes Paul and one of leading advocates of Christianity.
- 50 AD: Incident at Antioch where Paul accuses Peter of "Judaizing" or making gentiles follow Jewish rites.
- 58 AD: Paul accused of being ringleader of Nazarenes – an ascetic sect of Jews that kept laws of Old Testament but also accepted Jesus as Messiah. Their practices were more similar to the Gnostics and sages of the far east.

- 68 AD: Great fire of Rome. Caesar Nero blames Christians and persecutes them viciously.
- 60-100 AD: Gospels of Mark, Matthew, Luke and John written.
- 210 – 276 AD: Mani founder of Manichaeism, now extinct, is a Persian prophet and preached a form of Gnosticism.
- 220 AD: Clement of Alexandria early church father and teacher of Origen cites Secret Book of Mark, values gnosis (knowledge through inner experience) and communion with God.
- 240 – 312: Saint Lucian of Antioch. Highly influential leader of Antioch Church known as a scholar and ascetic. Philosophy would influence Arianism.
- 244 – 311: Caesar Diocletian becomes renown for persecutions of Christians.
- 250 AD: Origen compiles Hexapla, which presented the Bible in six versions/ languages. Most controversially known for supporting Platonean concept of Ousia meaning "being" where God and Jesus were of one substance.
- 250 – 336 AD: Arian Controversy. Arian, a Christian Priest, raises question of Jesus' relationship with God. Are they of One substance?
- 272 AD: Constantine the Great becomes first Christian Roman Caesar.
- 325 AD: Constantine convenes First Council of Nicaea (First Ecumenical Council of Christian Church) to resolve Arian controversy, unite various sects of Christianity, and fix Easter date as well as other matters. Established the Nicene Creed.
- 381 AD: First Council of Constantinople – (2nd Ecumenical Council) Unresolved matters pertaining to Jesus' Divinity, repudiates Arianism and revises Nicene Creed to include Holy Spirit.

Chapter XX: The Lamb: Savior or Guru?

- 431 AD: Council of Ephesus proclaims Virgin Mary as Theotokos – "Mother of God." Reaffirms Nicene Creed. Assyrian Church of East separates itself.
- 451 AD: Council of Chalcedon adopts Chalcedonian Creed, which establishes "hypostatic union" meaning Christ had two natures – human and divine.
- 553 AD: Second Council of Constantinople – (Fifth Ecumenical Council) Emperor Justinian I brings final edict against Origenism.
- Emperor Justinian I attempts to unite Christian sects while being accused of persecuting as many as 100 million people as "heretics."

Now in summary, the highlights of these events that should be addressed are first that shortly after Jesus' death many people, Jewish and non-Jewish alike, believed in his teachings. Being a Jew had mostly a cultural meaning in terms of a nation of people as opposed to a religious faith. The Jews obviously had their scriptures and part of their ritual coincided with this practice of faith. Shortly after Jesus' death his disciples began spreading his gospel. As a consequence of their efforts many "gentiles" began to accept his teachings. It isn't until decades later that the term "Christian" evolves to identify those who follow his teachings. Early on, there were many people who supported his teachings that would've had many contrasting views on his essence or whether or not he was their Savior but would've considered themselves Christians meaning one who followed his gospel.

Again, this is just a human flaw, but the difficulty begins when we try to get a "consensus" on everyone's belief. Instead of allowing there to be diversity in faith, the leaders of any new faith feel they cannot survive unless they present a clear message to new converts about what it is that they should believe. Many early church leaders who were scholars and the most "qualified" to elaborate on the interpretations and translations of the scriptures of the time were initially appreciated and praised for their expertise. Of course, any "group of people" that becomes too large, even if under the name of a good cause such as the practice of faith, can be attractive to many but often goes hand-in-hand with becoming a "threat" to others. It is just the "human nature" of the ego to compete with one another. This can normally be constructive and innocent but quickly becomes corrupt when it falls into the hands of politicians, businessmen and those seeking to gain from what they see as an opportunity.

Thus, what starts out as a fair and necessary question to understand Jesus' essence evolves into an extremely problematic division between Christians. Whatever Jesus' essence is, by itself, isn't a major concern but it becomes major when the answer has the potential to influence that which we perceive ourselves to be. Because of the ego and our sense of guilt, we can't possibly imagine ourselves to be anywhere on the level of Jesus. While we are still under the influence of ego the simple answer is, we're not on his level. However, Jesus' essence and man's essence are one and the same because there is truly only one Essence which is God. The best way to examine this idea is to look at the words that came directly from Jesus' mouth.

First, it is important to distinguish the connotation that Jesus uses when referring to himself or to his fellow man. We see often in the Gospels the terms Son of Man and Son of God but what is the difference? When Jesus is talking about the son of man in reference to others he is talking about the body, the flesh, the ego or just the average man. When he uses the term son of man in reference to himself then he is talking about his own body or the persona known as Jesus. When he talks about the Son of God then he is referring to himself as the Christ Consciousness. However, he assures us that this is not a unique distinction for himself but rather we all

Chapter XX: The Lamb: Savior or Guru?

can become "Sons of God" when we overcome sin (the ego or sense of separation) as he did. Let's examine a few quotes to see the difference.

Here Jesus warns his betrayer with this quote. **"The Son of man indeed goeth, as it is written of him: but woe to that man by whom the Son of man is betrayed! good were it for that man if he had never been born." Mark 14:21 Clearly** Jesus knows that he shall be resurrected so he is referring to his body for he knows his true essence, the Christ Consciousness, cannot be killed or destroyed. Thus, when he refers to the "son of man" here he is referring to the body or persona of Jesus the man. But even when referring to every man and his behavior, he let's man know that rites and rituals were meant to serve man and not for man to serve them. Hence when a man, even though he may not yet be spiritually saved, does the bidding of the Father then religious rites are secondary to man. **"Therefore the Son of man is Lord also of the sabbath." Mark 2:28** Here he is saying that the "son of man" meaning every person is the "lord" of his own choices, actions, rites, rituals and institutions. Most importantly when a man is still under the dream spell of the ego then he is the son of man because he recognizes not his own divinity. **"The Son of man is come eating and drinking; and ye say, Behold a gluttonous man, and a winebibber, a friend of publicans and sinners!" Luke 7:34 In** this sense he is referring to the vast majority of man still ignorant of his spiritual nature and consumed with carnal desires.

But more important is how Jesus uses the term Son of God in reference to himself and to the individual that ascends his consciousness to know God. Jesus being one with God and the Christ Consciousness often spoke from this Universal Presence and not from identification with his little form of the body. Thus, he says, **"This sickness is not unto death, but for the glory of God, that the Son of God might be glorified thereby." John 11:4** It is his true oneness with the Creator and His will that he was able to identify with God's Consciousness and serve out God's will. His disciples in tune with his true nature spoke of him as such **"And we know that the Son of God is come, and hath given us an understanding, that we may know him that is true, and we are in him that is true, even in his Son Jesus Christ. This is the true God, and eternal life." 1 John 5:20** This clearly shows that it is the "Son of God" that is the true reflection of God Consciousness This consciousness that "brings understanding" exists within Jesus but also beyond him; most importantly it is present in all of creation and every man.

Now what becomes even more significant is how man is referred to repeatedly throughout the Bible. It is every man's potential to become the Son of God. Thus, we have quotes such as **"He that overcometh shall inherit all things; and I will be his God, and he shall be my son." Revelation 21:7** Also, we have **"For as many as are led by the Spirit of God, they are the sons of God." Romans 8:14** Repeatedly, we see scripture stating **"Behold, what manner of love the Father hath bestowed upon us, that we should be called the sons of God: therefore the world knoweth us not, because it knew him not." 1 John 3:1** Then there is **"Blessed are the peacemakers: for they shall be called the children of God". Matthew 5:9** For the faithful, we have **"But as many as received him, to them gave he power to become the sons of God, even to them that believe on his name:" John 1:12** When speaking of the "only begotten Christ Consciousness in creation" we understand **"He that hath the Son hath life; and he that hath not the Son of God hath not life." 1 John 5:12**

Lastly, we have the two quotes of scripture that most predominantly influenced the whole Arian controversy that began almost two thousand years ago. You can try to cover the truth but when Light is shed it expels all darkness. The first is stated by Jesus from **John 14:28 "Ye have heard how I said unto you, I go away,** *and come again unto you. If ye loved me, ye would rejoice, because I said, I go unto the Father: for my Father is greater than I."* For some reason this one creates turmoil when trying to reconcile Jesus with God. As stated previously, God in His Absolute state is the all in all. Every other aspect of God, as a Creator and Sustainer of all existence, cannot encompass His Perfect state of Unmanifested-ness. As we covered in Chapter I saying, "I am Love," "I am the Alpha and the Omega" and "I am that I am" may profess subtle greatness but words and personas in themselves are finite and limiting and thus cannot capture Infinity. God is indescribable and thus Jesus acknowledges that the Father is "greater." But it is important to remember terms like greater, better or worse only have relevance in the world of creation. Because man identifies with matter our consciousness cannot grasp with the mind how something can have distinction and yet be One. In Truth, God is the "hidden" essence within all things. All liberated souls know this but only in outward expression do things have any relative variation. But the Inner Essence is equally present in all *realized* Beings. Thus, Jesus can still profess, "I and my Father are one." There is no contradiction.

Secondly, there is *"Neither pray I for these alone, but for them also which shall believe on me through their word; That they all may be one; as thou, Father, art in me, and I in thee, that they also may be one in us: that the world may believe that thou hast sent me. And the glory which thou gavest me I have given them; that they may be one, even as we are one:" John 17:20-22* I don't really know what more can be said about this one. It is pretty self-explanatory. Jesus is praying for all of men that believe in his Oneness with the Father that through God's grace they can become one as well. This coincides not with the Orthodox Church's current views but most consistently with the mystic experience, the gnosis knowledge of self and the ascension of the consciousness expounded by the yogis of the East.

    The Church forefathers fell short because their minds couldn't grasp the concept of a hierarchy of Spirit and yet the oneness in the same. It would take them a couple hundred more years to finalize an answer for the church to uphold and even that was not without controversy. It took them many more councils to make the Nicene Creed make sense and to force its acceptance. Those "heretics" that refused to accept this notion became outcasts or worse were executed for not complying. Does this reflect the message of love and sacrifice that Jesus preached? **"But I say unto you, Love your enemies, bless them that curse you, do good to them that hate you, and pray for them which despitefully use you, and persecute you;" Matthew 5:44** These fellow Christians weren't even truly enemies; they just simply disagreed with the conclusion of a Council "dictated" by an Emperor.

    The shortcoming of the early Christian forefathers wasn't that they posed the question of the *Ousia* meaning "one being." The shortcoming was the frame and context in which they positioned it. The question shouldn't have been whether or not Jesus and God were of one being. Yes, they are *of* One Being. The true question is "what is *not* part of the One Being"? Because they couldn't imagine themselves to be a part of God, much less any other person who may have been of lower standing in society, they were stuck on how to connect Jesus with man and yet connect him with God such that his Divinity could not be questioned. They, under the influence of a Roman Empire, felt the need to make God's "kingdom of heaven" work like a man-made kingdom. Man attempts to project his limited logic onto God's Infinite Truth. This simply cannot be done except by one, such as Jesus, who knows the Father through inner realization. The church forefathers as well as all of mankind today should be asking the

Chapter XX: The Lamb: Savior or Guru?

question of "how do we fulfill Jesus' prayer" which is **that (we) all may be one**, for we all come from the Ousia – One Being. The man who has the answer to that question knows Jesus and God as no other does.

Fortunately, Jesus has already given us the answer to fulfill this prayer. **"Be ye therefore perfect, even as your Father which is in heaven is perfect." Matthew 5:48 The** church as a result of the Councils hindered the personal involvement, effort, understanding and spiritual growth needed by the individual in order to fulfill this declaration. What may have begun as a noble endeavor to establish clarity on the nature of Spirit instead created a "ceiling" for which the individual couldn't aspire beyond. In separating Jesus as being more divine than human, the forefathers limited man in striving for personal spiritual growth. This notion has caused idleness in the masses to simply sit back, indulge in the business of the world and hope that they may make it to heaven. By simply saying I accept Jesus as my Lord and Savior; they've removed the sense of "self responsibility." By suggesting that man is made of sin and incapable of becoming sinless, they've made it so that there is no point in even trying. All we have to do is continue to chase after our desires, sin and try to *time* our "repenting" perfectly before death and thus get a pass into heaven because Jesus has already done the hard work for us. It is this thinking that is detrimental to the soul. God created every child to be "made in his likeness." **"Jesus answered them, Is it not written in your law, I said, Ye are gods"? John 10:34**

If we look at Jesus' life, his teachings and practices, we see a lot of similarities with the teachings of the ancient sages of the East. The baptism rite with water actually comes from the cleansing practices of India. The Master and Disciple relationship Jesus had with his twelve disciples is more indicative of the relationship between a Guru and his disciple(s). If we first examine the idea of the Lamb, we understand it to represent innocence and purity. We can think of the liberated soul as the baby sheep and God as the Great Shepherd. The sacrifice of the "Lamb" is what allows one to be cleansed and freed from past sins and karma and thus becomes one's Savior. The West has mastered material and scientific comforts of life and yet the East has mastered the spiritual science of Life. Each has something of value to offer. The East has the longest traceable history relating to things of the spiritual nature. Hence, the Eastern Sages' definition of a guru is quite consistent with the concept of a Savior. Swami Sivananda defined the qualities of a guru rather eloquently. If we simply replace the word "guru" with "savior" it seems to fall exactly in line with what we think of pertaining to Jesus.

"You need a burning candle to light a candle. Equally so an illumined soul alone can enlighten another soul. A Guru (Savior) is necessary for aspirants. When difficulty arises even in the case of finding our way in the streets and road; to what does it speak of the difficulties along the razor-thin pathway of spirituality when one walks alone with closed eyes! In the case of the spiritual path, it is difficult to find your way. The help of the Guru (Savior) is necessary at every moment.

The mind will mislead you often. The Guru (Savior) will be able to remove pitfalls and obstacles and lead you along the right path. Association with the Guru (Savior) is an armor and fortress to guard you against all temptations and unfavorable forces of the material world. Every aspirant on the spiritual path must live under a Guru (Savior) for eradication of his evil qualities and defects. The nature of egoism is such that you will not be able to find out your own defects. It is only the Guru (Savior) who will find out your defects. He reveals the right path. A Guru (Savior) is absolutely necessary for every aspirant in the spiritual path. Grace of God takes the form of the Guru (Savior). The Guru (Savior) is God

Chapter XX: The Lamb: Savior or Guru?

himself manifesting in personal form to guide the aspirant. Man can learn from man only, and hence, God teaches through a human body. The Guru (Savior) is united with God. He has free and unhampered access into both the realms.

The Guru (Savior) is an eternal link between the individual and the Immortal. He purifies all. He tears your **veil of ignorance** (Apocalypse). To be a Guru (Savior) one must have a command from God. One who has direct knowledge of God (the Father) through experience only can be enrolled as a Guru (Savior). Mere study of books cannot make one a Guru (Savior). A Guru (Savior) is a knower of God. He is identical with the Supreme Self. The Guru (Savior) is God Himself. He is an ocean of bliss, knowledge and mercy. He shows you the right path. He tears your veil of ignorance. He transmutes your lower, diabolic nature. Gurus (Saviors) do not exhibit any miracles. (God is doer of all.) **"Seek and it shall be found, knock and it shall open unto you; ask and it shall be given."**

It is not as though there is any dearth of Divine Munificence or Divine Grace. But there is a law that we have to ask, we have to seek, we have to knock; and having done so, we must be ready to receive it. A Guru (Savior) is something spiritual, something mysterious that delivers the Highest Thing for why human life is here. Discipleship is in qualifying ourselves to attain that highest State. Gurus (Saviors) are guides of mankind. They show us the path, which takes us beyond all pain and sorrow; take us beyond this phenomenal existence, into a realm of Perennial Felicity, Infinite Bliss and Immortal Life. They are the people who awaken the dormant spiritual consciousness of the individual and take him up towards realization of his eternal union with Divinity, with the Universal Spirit."

Know Thyself: To Awaken Self-Realization

CHAPTER XXI

Beginning Your Journey

"The real meaning of religion is to know God, to see God and be one with God. Everything else about religion is an exercise in rites and rituals."
                                                                Meher Baba

    This brings us near our closure for this particular section of our journey. We've covered a lot of material thus far. It is important to give time to allow new ideas to "marinate" within our being. I'm sure you will have read things that may have been eye-opening for you and at the same time heard some ideas that you may not agree with. That is fine. My intent is not to tell you what to believe. You become a great thinker not by wholly swallowing someone else's truth. That practice has been one of the major problems with most religions – trying to force-feed you what is Truth. Everyone is at different points in their journey. What may be truth for one may not yet be truth for another. It doesn't mean the former was wrong it just means that for that moment in time two people may be witnessing the same truth from different perspectives.

    You should allow yourself time to not only ponder new ideas but to search within yourself for clarity to embrace new understanding. We all must humbly acknowledge that we have not yet reached our destination. If you have reached your destination, then there will be no mysteries in the universe that remain for you. You will know God as you know yourself. This will not be a hallucination, expression of imagination or an act of blind faith. To know the truth is to be one with the Truth. If your car isn't working properly and you already assume you know what the problem is without properly troubleshooting then you may not have identified the true problem. Not properly identifying the true error can mean the difference between getting an oil change and replacing an entire engine. You must thoroughly inspect the vehicle. If you focus all of your attention on the alternator thinking that it is broken, then you may not realize it was simply the battery that needed replacing. You must allow yourself to be open-minded enough to hear the news that may not coincide with your belief system or assessment. But if you can at least consider that the world may actually be round, even if just for a moment, then you will have opened up the doors to a new revelation. The entire world becomes yours.

It doesn't mean you have to throw away everything you've ever learned. You don't have to change your religion or your faith. But realize that there may be a new way of exercising your faith. There may be a new way to express and live within your faith. A Christian doesn't need to become a Muslim. A Hindu doesn't need to become a Jew. All paths of life lead to the same destination. God says He is the Alpha and the Omega. That means everything begins and will end with Him. You didn't have your beginning in hell and therefore your ending shall not be in hell. You will make it to heaven. This is truth!

Now this should not cause you to become complacent in your spiritual journey. What may be a blink of an eye for God may in fact feel like an eternity to you. You must practice self-control and raise your consciousness. Every moment your consciousness spends under the influence of ego is a temptation to sin. This sin is anything that pulls your understanding from truth in God to consumption in sense pleasures. The lust for sensuous fulfillments can drag your consciousness down to realms that can be downright "hellish." Although it is not meant for you to spend an eternity separate from God, an experience in evil surroundings

Chapter XXI: Beginning Your Journey

doesn't have to be on another plane, it can and often does take place right here on Earth. Feeling unable to change your experience and lift your spirits can be torture. Thus, take advantage of the opportunity you may presently have to sincerely and personally seek God.

Try not to get caught up in dogma, rather seek to understand the deeper underlying truths of God's creation. Go within yourself to find His divine purpose for you. It doesn't matter which faith you claim. They are all just many paths to the same Truth. I know this idea is still difficult for some of you to swallow. It is hard to imagine a possibility that goes against everything you may have believed your entire life! Can every religion, based in Love, lead to the same goal? Or is there a right religion? What if I were born in a different part of the world? Would I still be able to recognize the "right" religion and Savior? If I could recognize it, would I have the moral courage to go against my family, my religion, my country and my culture? I'm here to tell you your religion ultimately doesn't matter. It is your heart and consciousness that reflects who you are.

If Jesus is your Savior, then that is fine. But don't just claim him in words and not in deed. Jesus did not teach man to be idle. You should make every effort to know his teachings by heart. Ask yourself this: "If Jesus were to return today to this Earth, would I recognize him"? Many of you would say yes. But what if he didn't appear as you might have expected him? What if he doesn't descend in a cloud from out of the heavens? What if he, instead of in a Jewish body, appears with dark skin and dreadlocks? Would you still accept him as your Savior? What if he actually does come with blonde hair and blue eyes? Could you still accept him? Cannot an Asian person with yellow skin, dark hair and slanted eyes come back to save the world?

Instead of calling himself Jesus (Yeshua) this time, what if he referred to himself as Miguel or how about Pei or maybe Hans? What if instead of a male body "he" was to come back as a "she"? Would you still believe what she taught? Would this still be the Savior you envisioned? Or would she have to "prove" that she in fact is the Lord and Savior? Would the teachings and words that came from her mouth not suffice? Would she have to perform a miracle for you to believe? If she showed the ability to walk on water, would that be enough? Or would you insist on another miracle? Could her actions and expressions of Love be enough to assure you that she was sent by the Creator? If you cannot honestly say "yes" then how are you any different from the people of Jesus' day that didn't believe him to be the Son of God? You know the ones that mocked and spat on him...

It is easy to claim someone as your Lord and Savior after they've been crucified and resurrected. But what if all you had to go by was what he said and how he lived? What if you heard the rumors and the hearsay about his spiritual abilities but you never actually saw him raise someone from the dead, turn water into wine or heal the sick? Could you just be satisfied and happy to be in his presence? Would your consciousness, awareness and soul be in tune enough to know that you were in the presence of Divinity? Now if you think you could still see Jesus in spite of his outward form, ask yourself what if his name were Mohammed, Buddha or Krishna?

It shouldn't matter what the name, form or appearance Divinity takes, Spirit in truth is formless. If God wanted to appear as a talking turtle, he could do so! The question is will you accept Him? If not, then the spiritual figure isn't the problem it is *you* who must change. Love is the only power that transcends all forms and appearances. If you cannot give it to all forms and expressions, then you cannot receive it or recognize it. **"Behold, what manner of love the Father hath bestowed upon us, that we should be called the** *sons of God: therefore the world knoweth us not, because it knew him not." 1 John 3:1*

Will you know him by the truth he speaks? Let us remember the same Jesus that gave up his life as an expression of his love and sacrifice that said, **"For God sent not his Son into the world to condemn the world; but that the world through him might be saved." John 3:17** is the same Jesus that brought a radical spiritual approach to the masses to shake the ignorant out of their slumber. This is the same Jesus who went into the marketplace and overthrew tables in **Matthew 21:12**. Jesus stood for Love but also for Truth, which are synonymous. This is the Jesus, intolerant of ignorance, who spoke **"Think not that I am come to send peace on earth: I came not to send peace, but a sword. For I am come to set a man at variance against his father, and the daughter against her mother, and the daughter in law against her mother in law. And a man's foes shall be they of his own household. He that loveth father or mother more than me is not worthy of me: and he that loveth son or daughter more than me is not worthy of me. And he that taketh not his cross, and followeth after me, is not worthy of me. He that findeth his life shall lose it: and he that loseth his life for my sake shall find it." Matthew 10:34-39**

We started this "Know Thyself: Day One" exploring God as the Author of Life. We are likewise authors of our own lives. Our free will, bestowed by God, allows us to live as such. However, you should recognize the greatest story you can author is to coincide your story with the Bestower of all gifts. The fingers of your hand were created to work together to serve the body. Imagine if instead of working together they began to fight with each other. The thumb only wanted to be sucked all day. The middle finger only wanted to give people "the finger." The index only wanted to point. The ring finger wanted to learn how to snap and the pinky wanted to defect. The hand would develop ailments and the body would begin to suffer from the lack of being fed.

When man behaves selfishly and fails to work together for the greater good of the whole then the entire world suffers. It is for the greater good that the body parts work together to serve the entire body so every part flourishes. Likewise, every soul is at its greatest benefit when it strives to serve the whole community and thus finds its oneness in serving God.

The universe is God's story and yet He remains above this experience. Man should recognize as well that your job, spouse, family, dreams and aspirations may help to define your experience of life but ultimately your soul is "above" any of these temporary identifications. Your soul in and of itself is already complete in God. However, you are not your true self. The ego "sense of separation" has stolen your true identity. When you die you will be forced to shed your worldly attachments, but this does not destroy the ego.

The ego will seek to restore its identity, which will force your rebirth into another form, and you will find yourself in a new family with new attachments. Some things will be better, assuming you created some good karma, and yet some things may be "worse" for whatever bad karma you may have manifested. The only way to end this endless cycle is to transcend the ego and find your true immortality in Spirit, your True Reality. This will take conscious effort and Grace but once achieved, you will find the complete happiness you seek in life… Eternal Bliss.

As you work your way through this maze of life you will hit many "dead ends." All the adversity we experience is an opportunity to strengthen your awareness, your understanding and your resolve. Those who are fortunate enough to make it to the end of the maze will realize the Kingdom of Spirit is an island. God's kingdom is surrounded by a moat. This moat is not one of water but a bottomless moat of delusion. You alone don't have the power to cross this moat not by plane, boat or balloon. Only God can let down His drawbridge to allow one to cross. God may by His direction instruct one of His liberated souls to let down the bridge for you to cross.

Man, of his own will, can only do 25% to get to God's kingdom. God does another fifty percent, but it takes a Guru, Savior, and/or God's Angel to do the other 25% to help you cross the moat. Some would argue in truth God is the only doer whether it's through an unseen hand, the ego or a guru. It is difficult to find such a guru or savior to help us attain Salvation. If you envision Jesus as your Savior, then try to meditate on his form. Attempt to embody all that he stood for. When your devotion is strong then rest assured Jesus or the appropriate "messenger" will come to guide you across your moat of separation and remove your blindfold of ignorance in the Kingdom of Spirit.

The poem "If" represents man's potential. Man's greatest potential is God. There is no other function or purpose here on this Earth that satisfies this inseparable instinct in man. God made man in His image and it is our nature to realize, "make real," this Truth. At the end of the day it matters not whether you agree with me on reincarnation, evolution, involution, scientific data, scripture, religious beliefs etc. All you need to believe in is yourself. No one can deny that he seeks happiness for himself. Well, you can either keep chasing happiness in the ever-elusive objects of life or you can find the eternal happiness that satisfies all other desires.

Church membership and attendance has been declining for years now. It is not just because the world is somehow becoming more "sinful." It is because man internally is seeking more than just the outer worship and lethargic practices of listening to someone else tell you how to behave and live. Again, there is nothing wrong with religions, but they must begin to figure out how to satisfy the burning inner desire that every human being has to "know." This knowledge can only come from within. Anyone of any religion that knows how to show you the way to go within can help you find the spiritual answers you seek. **"But he spake of the temple of his body." John 2:21 Your** body is your temple and your soul is the sacred place for you to meet the Lord.

Now the good news is you don't have to worry about beginning your journey. Your soul began this journey long before your consciousness can even fathom. Your responsibility at this crossroads in your life is to consciously take control of the direction you're heading. Your journey can be scattered carelessly without direction just letting the circumstances of life dictate how you define yourself. Or you can reign in the wild horses of your thoughts and senses and direct them towards your way home. Your home is in the Infinite space of Spirit. Thus far, we have discussed the basic beginnings of creation, man's role and God's hand in all of it. We will dive deeper into these matters exploring in Day Two but for now if there is one thing you can take from this then let it be this: **"Neither shall they say, lo here! or, lo there! for, behold, the kingdom of God is within you." Luke 17:21**

These are not my words but rather the words of God brought to man through the messenger of Jesus. It should be pretty self-explanatory but what is says is that the kingdom of God will not be found above us or below us. It will not be found in our jobs, husbands or wives, nor our children or hobbies. It also means it will not be found in the future or the past. You can't wait for it to come and you can't get there by any outward means. There is only one way to find this kingdom that delivers us from evil, removes all sorrows and satisfies all hearts and that is to look within one's self. This "kingdom" is the inner place of all happiness, joy, bliss, wisdom and awareness. Now you just need to know how and where to look within.

Chapter XXI: Beginning Your Journey

    As already stated, your soul's journey began long before reading this book. The key difference at this juncture is for you to consciously take control of where you're heading. I would dare say perhaps nine out of ten people's journey begins from a negative motivation or consequence. For some they grow tired of their jobs, maybe they no longer want to chase money or find out their material possessions didn't bring them the satisfaction they sought. Perhaps a failed relationship causes one to start to self reflect. Those who may have spent time in prison or on drugs may simply say, "Enough is enough." For the vast majority of the population we are like hamsters on the wheel. We live life without passion or direction. Finally, we decide there must be another way! The first step is to put away the rules the world has set for us. Try something different. Be open to other possibilities or answers. You must take the initiative to change your life and take control. No one can stop the hamster wheel for you. You must decide to stop running and then step away. Allowing yourself to open up to the spiritual possibilities is your first real step! Step away and then you can ask, "Now what"?

    Regardless of your place in the world you should know this: All things begin with the Absolute; an Absolute Source, an Absolute Essence, an Absolute Consciousness, the Absolute Spirit. This Spirit is Unmanifest and yet gives rise to all things manifest. This Spirit is Omnipresent and there is no thing separate from Its Oneness. The soul is made in the image of this unmanifest Spirit and is one and the same with this Essence. It is Spirit that "dreams" itself to be the soul. The unmanifest soul identifies with the manifest, "becoming" man. Man becomes the prodigal son. The prodigal son is the "pseudo self" or the ego imagining itself lost and cannot find its way home. But no matter how lost one may imagine himself to be, you are never separate from your soul because it is you! It is your true consciousness and life! As you yearn to return home, Spirit begins to draw you back. As you return to your true Essence, you begin to realize the true Nature of yourself. This is Self-Realization! The soul realizes it was never "lost;" only dreaming it was. How can a soul be lost from Spirit when it is everywhere around and in us? Soul is Spirit; Spirit is Soul! This is God's Sole Revelation... **I AM!**

For now, let this be your guide. He who can light the torch of his Love shall find the way! Love all and most importantly love God. When you truly learn to love God then it is easy to love all, for God is in all. Until we cross paths again, God Bless you on your journey to... Know Thyself!

NAMASTE

YOGA CHITTA VRITTI NIRODHAH –
Mantra for Stillness

Repeat 108 times consecutively with reverence, preferably twice a day (morning and night), for 40 days and watch your life change!

Your thoughts, feedback and reviews are very important to the books we write and the work we do. Our goals are to help inspire others to live their lives to the fullest, educate the masses on holistic living in body, mind and spirit as well as encourage unity, love and tolerance. If you share our sentiment and enjoy what you've read, then please take a moment to leave a positive review on Amazon and/or other social media outlets! Thanks

INDEX

2012 – 51
Abraham – 75, 78, 79, 82, 83, 86, 178, 211
Absolute – 5-11, 22, 24-26, 28, 31, 35-37, 39, 40, 42-44, 46-48, 58, 64, 65, 83, 92, 93, 96, 97, 102, 110, 135, 168, 170, 185, 196, 219, 238
Angels – 8, 23, 42, 48, 66, 67, 72, 136, 190, 204, 208, 210
Apocalypse – 177, 178, 180, 185, 188, 242
Arjuna – 77, 191
Astral – 22, 28, 30, 31, 46, 47, 51, 52, 54, 64, 66, 70, 184, 185, 197-199, 202, 208, 217, 219, 222, 223, 229
Aum – 23, 24, 26, 31, 39, 71, 184, 202, 220, 226
Bhagavad-Gita – 77, 190
Book of Enoch – 5, 210
Buddha – *iii*, 3, 48, 77, 86, 124, 229, 248
Canon of Scripture – 5
Carnal – 145, 150, 171, 237
Causal – 22, 28, 46, 47, 56, 64, 67, 89, 142, 185, 198, 202, 222, 223
Chakras – 142, 170, 184, 185, 198-200, 203, 204, 208-215, 217, 218
Chart: Levels of Creation – 226
Christ Consciousness – *i*, 24, 25, 154, 195, 224, 232, 236-238
Christ/Christians – 24, 83, 155-157, 234

Devil – 29, 182
Dogma – 8, 75, 98, 132, 149, 247
Eastern – 13, 21, 28, 39, 53, 57, 68, 77, 86, 153, 157, 168, 184, 241
Egypt/ Egyptians 5, 13, 24, 53, 58, 66, 159, 184, 188, 200, 208, 209
Esoteric – 4, 39, 178
Ethiopian Orthodox Church – 5
Evolution – *iii*, 38, 44, 45, 63, 67, 70, 107, 149, 169, 180, 184, 199, 232, 251
Gandhi – *iii,* 124
Gnostics – 82, 84, 85, 147, 160, 233
Guru – 153, 157, 200, 224, 225, 227, 241-243, 250, 251
Hermes Trismegistus – 209, 210
Holy Ghost – *i*, 22, 23, 24-28, 30, 31, 39, 67, 71, 81, 82, 137, 155, 183, 184, 195, 197, 200, 201, 220, 232, 234
Illusion – 51, 66, 84, 94, 106, 220, 223
Involution – 38, 44, 63, 149, 219, 251
Islam – *iii*, 5, 66, 76, 79, 80, 82-85, 147, 168, 211
Jesus – *i, iv*, 3, 22, 24, 28, 29, 48, 56, 64, 65, 79, 81, 82, 86, 105, 123, 143, 144, 147-163, 177, 180, 182, 183, 187, 190, 192, 201, 224, 227-241, 247-249, 251, 252
Judaism – *iii*, 76, 78, 82-85, 99, 137, 147, 227

275

Karma – 11, 84, 94, 95, 106, 121, 125, 127, 128, 133, 134, 165, 241, 250
Koshas – 39, 40, 42-47
Krishna – *iii*, 48, 58, 77, 86, 191, 229, 248
Kundalini – 184, 185, 197, 198-200, 202, 204, 205, 209, 212-214
Law of Attraction – 3, 116
Lokas – 194, 195, 212, 217, 218, 223, 225
Liberation – 48, 72, 75, 84, 133, 153, 209
Mahabharata – 58, 190, 208
Maya – 29, 39, 42, 123, 191, 194, 221, 226
Mayans – 5, 53, 58, 200, 209
Meditation - 46, 47, 86, 87, 90, 131, 134, 148, 166, 169, 193-195, 205, 209, 212, 225
Metaphysics – 38, 57, 65, 68, 90, 160, 166, 185, 215
Mohammed's Night Journey – 211, 248
Mysticism – 3, 81, 83-85, 160, 161, 166, 200, 205, 209, 210-212, 215, 239
Nadis – 202-204, 212
New Age - 3
Nivritti – 142
Niyama – 214, 215
Poems "If" – 17
    "Love Is…" – 34
    "There is a God" - 106
Prana – 47, 71, 184, 197, 198, 200, 222
Pravritti – 142
Quantum Physics – 3, 20, 92
Realization – 3, 39, 47, 48, 85, 95, 102, 104, 105, 154, 169, 215, 240, 243

Reincarnation – 147-154, 156-162, 164-166, 251
Rishis – 53, 76
Samadhi – 3, 47, 85, 157, 166, 185, 195, 200
Satan – 29, 100, 183, 188, 210
Savior – 56, 66, 72, 75, 81, 95, 154, 155, 160, 163, 224, 225, 227, 230, 232, 235, 240-243, 247, 248, 250, 251
Sheaths – 39, 40, 42-48, 64, 175
Table of Yugas – 61
Vedas – 24, 76, 77, 83, 85, 191
Yama – 214, 215
Yoga – 13, 84, 86, 93, 166, 169, 183, 187, 199, 204, 205, 208, 212, 214
Yugas – 55-59, 61, 97

"The Golden Egg: Successful Behaviors, Financial Smarts & 10 Quantum Principles for Prosperity"
(ISBN: 1939199247)
by **Lateef Terrell Warnick**

We are not simply "attractors"... we are

"Creators!"

All ancient scripture tell us we are made in the image of an Intelligent Creator yet that Spirit doesn't need to attract anything... It merely creates what it chooses to experience; we likewise have the same ability!

Most are familiar with the concept of karma, you reap what you sow, what goes around comes around and so on. This isn't your "bubble gum" metaphysics.

This book was written for the sincere Truth Seeker that places Self-Realization first and foremost. Upon finding the Eternal treasure within, lasting prosperity is a natural result and not merely a measure of your material possessions.

P.R.O.S.P.E.R.I.T.Y. –

"POWERFUL REASONS OPTIMISTIC SERVICE PRODUCES EXPONENTIAL RICHNESS INEVITABLY THROUGH YOU!"

Published by **1 S.O.U.L. Publishing**. Purchase at all major retailers like Amazon, Barnes & Noble & Books-a-Million for just $11.95 or directly from our website at **www.onassiskrown.com** for just $9.95 plus shipping & handling.

www.ingramcontent.com/pod-product-compliance
Lightning Source LLC
Chambersburg PA
CBHW071303110426
42743CB00042B/1156